THE COMPLETE GUIDE TO

Preventing Foreclosure on Your Home:

Legal Secrets to Beat Foreclosure and Protect Your Home NOW

By Martha Maeda and Maurcia DeLean Houck

THE COMPLETE GUIDE TO PREVENTING FORECLOSURE ON YOUR HOME: LEGAL SECRETS TO BEAT FORECLOSURE AND PROTECT YOUR HOME NOW

Copyright © 2010 Atlantic Publishing Group, Inc.
1405 SW 6th Avenue • Ocala, Florida 34471 • Phone 800-814-1132 • Fax 352-622-1875
Web site: www.atlantic-pub.com • E-mail: sales@atlantic-pub.com
SAN Number: 268-1250

Library of Congress Cataloging-in-Publication Data

Maeda, Martha, 1953-
  The complete guide to preventing foreclosure on your home : legal secrets to beat foreclosure and protect your home now / by Martha Maeda and Maurcia DeLean Houck.
     p. cm.
  Includes bibliographical references and index.
  ISBN-13: 978-1-60138-230-6 (alk. paper)
  ISBN-10: 1-60138-230-8 (alk. paper)
  1. Foreclosure--United States--Popular works. I. Houck, Maurcia DeLean. II. Title.
  KF697.F6M325 2010
  346.7304'364--dc22
                                    2010009378

Printed in the United States

PROJECT MANAGER: Melissa Peterson • mpeterson@atlantic-pub.com
PEER REVIEWER: Marilee Griffin • mgriffin@atlantic-pub.com
ASSISTANT EDITOR: Angela Pham • apham@atlantic-pub.com
PRE-PRESS & PRODUCTION DESIGN: Holly Marie Gibbs • hgibbs@atlantic-pub.com
INTERIOR DESIGN: Samantha Martin • smartin@atlantic-pub.com
FRONT & BACK COVER DESIGN: Jackie Miller • millerjackiej@gmail.com

Printed on Recycled Paper

We recently lost our beloved pet "Bear," who was not only our best and dearest friend but also the "Vice President of Sunshine" here at Atlantic Publishing. He did not receive a salary but worked tirelessly 24 hours a day to please his parents. Bear was a rescue dog that turned around and showered myself, my wife, Sherri, his grandparents  Jean, Bob, and Nancy, and every person and animal he met (maybe not rabbits) with friendship and love. He made a lot of people smile every day.

We wanted you to know that a portion of the profits of this book will be donated to The Humane Society of the United States. *–Douglas & Sherri Brown*

The human-animal bond is as old as human history. We cherish our animal companions for their unconditional affection and acceptance. We feel a thrill when we glimpse wild creatures in their natural habitat or in our own backyard.

Unfortunately, the human-animal bond has at times been weakened. Humans have exploited some animal species to the point of extinction.

The Humane Society of the United States makes a difference in the lives of animals here at home and worldwide. The HSUS is dedicated to creating a world where our relationship with animals is guided by compassion. We seek a truly humane society in which animals are respected for their intrinsic value, and where the human-animal bond is strong.

Want to help animals? We have plenty of suggestions. Adopt a pet from a local shelter, join The Humane Society and be a part of our work to help companion animals and wildlife. You will be funding our educational, legislative, investigative and outreach projects in the U.S. and across the globe.

Or perhaps you'd like to make a memorial donation in honor of a pet, friend or relative? You can through our Kindred Spirits program. And if you'd like to contribute in a more structured way, our Planned Giving Office has suggestions about estate planning, annuities, and even gifts of stock that avoid capital gains taxes.

Maybe you have land that you would like to preserve as a lasting habitat for wildlife. Our Wildlife Land Trust can help you. Perhaps the land you want to share is a backyard— that's enough. Our Urban Wildlife Sanctuary Program will show you how to create a habitat for your wild neighbors.

So you see, it's easy to help animals. And The HSUS is here to help.

THE HUMANE SOCIETY OF THE UNITED STATES.

2100 L Street NW • Washington, DC 20037 • 202-452-1100
www.hsus.org

TABLE OF CONTENTS

Chapter 3: Steps to Avoiding Foreclosure   47

Chapter 4: Assessing Your Finances   63

Chapter 5: Reviewing Your Options   77

Chapter 6: Borrowing What You Owe: Refinancing 101

Chapter 7: Halting Foreclosure with a Legal Defense   119

Chapter 8: Selling Your House   161

Chapter 9: Deed in Lieu   181

Chapter 10: Filing for Bankruptcy   189

CHAPTER 1

What is Foreclosure?

Many people associate foreclosure with losing a home, but the actual repossession and sale of a home is only the final step of the entire foreclosure process. Foreclosure refers to the steps a lender takes to regain possession of a home or piece of property when the borrower either fails to make loan payments on time or does not make payments at all. It is not common for a bank or other lending institution to foreclose on a property because payments are a few days late, but they have the legal authority to do so. Miss a payment or two altogether, and you will find yourself in the beginning stages of foreclosure, although you still have time to make amends and save your home.

When you decided to buy your home, you probably did not have enough cash to pay for it outright, so you sought a mortgage loan from your local bank or credit agency. The lender gave you the money to buy your house and you agreed to put up the house as collateral and pay back a certain amount of money each month, with interest, for a specified period of time until the debt was paid in full. Your lender has every right to expect those monthly payments, no matter what else is going on in your life. If you fail to make them, the lender can — and probably will — recoup those losses by taking your house.

The foreclosure process begins with a call-in of your loan. The lender, fearing that you can no longer make your payments in full and on time, files a legal complaint asking for payment. Depending on the laws of your state, the court may require payment of the delinquent amount plus fees or payment of the entire outstanding loan amount. If you cannot come up with this large sum, the lender can sell your house to pay off the debt. The best way to avoid foreclosure is to never let the process get started. Once you receive an official notice of foreclosure on your property, you have only a few weeks in which to resolve the problem before you lose your home. The further the legal proceedings advance, the more difficult it becomes to halt or reverse the process. Many homes go into foreclosure because the homeowner did not understand the consequences of late or missed mortgage payments or did not know what to do when the first foreclosure notices started coming.

Tip: Know your legal obligations.

Foreclosure laws vary from state to state. It is important to understand the laws for the state you live in and to do everything possible to keep up with your payments. *See Appendix C for more information on the laws in each state and Web sites where you can find more information for your state.*

Foreclosure Myths

When the truth is likely to be unpleasant, a common response is to avoid it by remaining ignorant as long as possible. Several widespread misunderstandings about the foreclosure process contribute to homeowners' confusion and make it even more difficult to find an effective solution to the problem.

Myth: **The bank has the legal right to evict you after a single missed mortgage payment.**

Fact: While it is true that a bank or other lender can begin foreclosure proceedings after just one missed payment, it cannot force you to vacate your home until the process is complete and the title deed has been transferred to another owner. Even then, you may have anywhere from three days to six months to leave, depending on the foreclosure laws in your area.

 After foreclosure, my entire debt is forgiven.

Fact: In most cases, this is true, but not always. In the event that your home is sold for less than the amount you owe your lender, you may be liable for the difference. This is called a deficiency judgment. You continue to be responsible for paying off any home equity lines of credit (HELOCs) or other loans you took out using your home as collateral, even after it has been repossessed and sold.

 Bankruptcy is always better than foreclosure.

Fact: Not necessarily. Bankruptcy can do much more damage to your credit rating than foreclosure — and for a longer period of time. The average foreclosure remains on your credit report for seven years, while bankruptcy remains for ten. With so many people undergoing foreclosure, there is a good possibility that those who pay off their other debt and save money for a down payment in the next few years will be able to convince another lender to loan them money for their next house before the seven-year period is up. The same is not always so for those filing bankruptcy.

I have missed too many payments; I cannot refinance.

Fact: It will not be easy to get a new loan, but it is possible. As many as 70 percent of foreclosures are halted because of refinancing efforts.

Once my house is foreclosed on, it is gone forever.

Fact: In the vast majority of cases, a property foreclosure auction is the end of the line for the homeowner. Once the property is sold, it is gone forever. But in a few states, a redemption period is offered, giving homeowners a few more months to come up with the money to buy their house back from the new owners.

Myth: **There is no way to stop foreclosure once it has begun.**

Fact: Contrary to popular belief, the bank does not want your house. Foreclosure costs banks money, as much as $50,000 for a moderate-sized house, in addition to the lost revenue from the mortgage. Banks have difficulty selling homes in a tough market and are not set up to act as landlords. Landscaping and maintenance cost money, but if the home is allowed to deteriorate, it loses value. Every foreclosure represents a financial loss to the lender. Lenders are eager to find an equitable solution that will allow a distressed homeowner to keep the home and save money for the lender.

The Four Main Types of Foreclosure

Foreclosure can be a complicated endeavor. It begins with a few missed payments, and ends with your home being sold at auction, with a lot of steps in between. The laws and regulations governing the repossession and sale of your home depend a great deal on the type of mortgage you have and the foreclosure laws in the state in which the property is located.

Four main types of foreclosure are allowed in the United States, each with its own legal requirements, benefits, and timetables. The first step to finding a way to halt or delay foreclosure proceedings is understanding which type of foreclosure you face.

Strict foreclosure

In the past, a mortgage holder could repossess a property when a borrower fell behind on payments and sell it for a profit without ever reimbursing the borrower any of the extra funds generated by the sale. For instance, if a borrower who owned a piece of property worth $100,000 was two days late with a mortgage payment, the lender could foreclose even if the borrower only owed a minimal outstanding balance on the loan, sell it at a handsome profit, and keep all the money. This type of foreclosure is no longer allowed in most states, which is one reason why lenders are more willing to work with delinquent borrowers. Unfortunately, if you live in Connecticut, New Hampshire, or Vermont, you may still find yourself losing your home under strict foreclosure statutes.

Judicial foreclosure

The most common way to foreclose on a property, judicial foreclosure requires both lender and borrower to appear before a judge in order to determine the validity of the foreclosure and how to distribute the funds upon the sale of the property. It is a lengthy, time-consuming, expensive process. Judicial foreclosure is predominant in Colorado, Connecticut, Delaware, Florida, Illinois, Indiana, Iowa, Kansas, Kentucky, Louisiana, Maine, New Jersey, New York, North Dakota, Ohio, Pennsylvania, South Carolina, Vermont, and Wisconsin.

Non-judicial foreclosure

A faster way for a lender to unload a property, non-judicial foreclosure does not rely on the courts to oversee the proceedings, but instead allows the lender to handle it alone — under strict guidelines. One of the main benefits of a non-judicial foreclosure is that it often does not allow deficiency judgments. Should your home sell for less than the loan payoff amount at auction under a non-judicial foreclosure, the lender cannot require you to pay the difference. This is not the case in most judicial foreclosures. Non-judicial foreclosure is predominant in Alabama, Alaska, Arkansas, Arizona, California, District of Columbia, Georgia, Hawaii, Idaho, Michigan, Minnesota, Mississippi, Missouri, Montana, Nevada, New Hampshire, Oklahoma, Oregon, Rhode Island, South Dakota, Tennessee, Texas, Virginia, Washington, West Virginia, and Wyoming.

Oklahoma, North Carolina, and South Dakota combine elements of both non-judicial and judicial foreclosure.

TYPICAL FORECLOSURE TIMELINE

MONTH 1: Homeowner misses payment. Within two to three weeks, the lender sends a letter requesting the homeowner to pay.

MONTH 2: Homeowner misses a second payment. Within two to three weeks, the lender sends a letter and calls the homeowner requesting payment.

MONTH 3: Homeowner misses a third payment. Within two weeks, the lender files a notice to default, which is served by the sheriff's office to the homeowner. The homeowner has between 30 and 60 days to pay the loan in full, In some states, the court may order the homeowner to pay the delinquent amount plus fees to reinstate the loan.

MONTHS 4 TO 5: Homeowner has not been able to pay off the loan and has missed subsequent payments. The lender receives a judgment of foreclosure from the court and arranges an auction date for the property as soon as possible.

MONTH 6: The property has been sold at auction and the homeowner risks eviction from the new property owner.

Forfeiture

If you have signed a contract of deed or land contract with the seller instead of a mortgage, the foreclosure process can be quite different. When you buy your home with funds from a traditional mortgage, you become the legal owner and hold the property title deed. However, when you borrow the money for the home from the seller, as is the case in a contract of deed, the lender retains ownership and the deed until the loan is paid in full. If you fall behind in your payments, the lender can either foreclose on the property or request that you forfeit your rights to it, which does not require them to sell it. Either way, the courts are not involved unless you request a formal hearing in front of a judge.

If You Live in Connecticut, Illinois, Louisiana, Maine, Massachusetts, New Hampshire, Rhode Island, or Vermont...

Some states have alternative foreclosure approaches that fall under the judicial and non-judicial processes. If you live in one of the following states, be sure you are aware of these clauses.

ILLINOIS, VERMONT, AND CONNECTICUT

These three states have what is called "strict foreclosure" rules. In ordinary foreclosures, if a property is sold either by the homeowner or at auction to satisfy a loan, the monies gained first pay off any outstanding debts on the property. If there is money left over after all claims have been satisfied, the money belongs to the homeowner. This is often the case with older mortgages when default occurs after a significant portion of the debt has been paid down.

Illinois, Vermont, and Connecticut have legislation that gives all funds acquired through the sale of a property to the lender or lien holder. This means that even if your property sells for twice the amount owed, 100 percent of the proceeds of the auction sale go to whoever is foreclosing. Illinois also follows an "entry and possession" process.

LOUISIANA

Depending on the contract you signed, the foreclosure process may follow the steps described in the judicial method, or it may follow an "executory" process. In Louisiana, an executory foreclosure means the homeowner has essentially waived his or her right to the typical judicial process. After receiving the notice of default or complaint from the lender, the homeowner has three days to come up with the balance owed on the loan. If the homeowner fails to do this, the property is considered foreclosed and officially belongs to the lender.

If you live in Louisiana, you have very little time to resolve your missing payments with the bank before it can take your house. Many consider this method of foreclosure to be only barely constitutional, as it gives the homeowner little notice before his or her home is legally seized and put up for sale.

MAINE, MASSACHUSETTS, NEW HAMPSHIRE, RHODE ISLAND, AND ILLINOIS

Among the harshest states for foreclosures, these states can institute the "entry and possession" process when foreclosing. Like the strict foreclosure process, entry and possession takes full possession of the property and any money earned through its sale, but it does not require that the property be auctioned.

After payments have been missed for the amount of time specified in the mortgage agreement, the lender is allowed to take physical possession of the property. This form of foreclosure is rarely the first to be used in these states, but it does give the lender the right to physically evict a homeowner from the property in question. It also means that the lender can keep the property on the open market until a satisfactory offer is received.

The Steps of Foreclosure

Foreclosure does not happen overnight. The process can go on for months — sometimes for years — before you finally lose your home. The average foreclosure takes about six to nine months, but depending on the laws in your area, it can be as long as three years before your house is taken away. The backlog of foreclosure cases in America's court systems today is extending those estimated times considerably. With the possible delays due to the number of foreclosures in process, one to five years could pass before your house is sold at auction.

Foreclosure follows a specific legal process according to the type of loan you have.

Acceleration

Whether your lender pursues a judicial or non-judicial foreclosure to regain ownership of your property, the entire process begins with a step called acceleration. When it becomes obvious that the borrower can no longer keep up with their mortgage payments, and no other solution has been found by either the lender or the borrower, the lender will accelerate the foreclosure process by "calling in" the loan, or demanding that it be paid in full.

Every foreclosure is different, depending on the loan agreement and the laws of the area in which the home is located. Let us take a look at the procedures followed for both judicial and non-judicial foreclosures.

Judicial foreclosure

The most common type of proceeding, judicial foreclosures primarily take place when a mortgage agreement has been signed but does not include a "power of sale" clause, which gives the lender authority to sell the house if payments are not made in a timely manner. Because judicial foreclosures go through the court system, they take considerably longer to complete than non-judicial foreclosures. The following are the steps involved with a judicial foreclosure:

1. **Filing a complaint.** After 30 to 90 days of missed payments and notices from the bank, the lender files a formal complaint of non-payment with the circuit court, announcing its intention to foreclose. The lender or lien holder asks the court to grant a default judgment of foreclosure in its favor, allowing it to sell the property and recover its money.

2. **Recording a notice of pending action.** As soon as the complaint described above is filed, the lender must also record a notice of pending action, also called a *lis pendens*, in the recorder's office of the county in which the property is located. A notice of hearing is sent to all parties involved, appointing a date and time for a discussion of the matter and a decision on the foreclosure to be made by the judge.

3. **Answering the complaint.** Once a homeowner receives the formal complaint, he or she typically has 30 days to respond before foreclosure proceedings continue.

4. **Offering a reinstatement period.** According to state law, a lender must offer a homeowner one last chance to pay what is due before the house is repossessed. This is call the reinstatement period and varies from state to state. During this period, you can try to refinance or borrow money to pay what you owe.

5. **Discovery.** While waiting for a hearing date, you and your lender should take the time to gather the information you need to build

a case — either for foreclosure (done by the lender) or to stop it (done by you). This is called discovery.

6.   **Having a foreclosure trial.** The foreclosure hearing is held. Once in front of a foreclosure judge, the lender must prove that you signed the original mortgage papers and became delinquent on the loan, ask for approval to sell the property to recoup lost revenue, and decide whether a sale can legally take place. The homeowner is given an opportunity to prevent a summary judgment of foreclosure from being filed by mounting a legal defense. The homeowner can justify or explain why the debt has remained unpaid. For instance, there might be a discrepancy between the parties as to how much is actually owed on the property; or payments might have been made and not recorded by the lender. This is also an opportunity to show the court that the lender is not acting according to the mortgage contract, if that is the case. The homeowner can have the entire matter dropped if he or she can prove that the lender failed to follow any of the previous steps in accordance with state law. Otherwise, the lender is granted approval to place a lien on the home and move forward with the foreclosure.

7.   **Offering an equity of redemption period.** Between the time of the trial and the actual sale of the property sale, the homeowner is offered a redemption period in which he or she can pay off the loan in full and retain ownership of the property. This period is another opportunity to refinance and avoid foreclosure.

8.   **Writ of sale.** Once the court approves the sale of the property, the lender must submit a writ of sale to the county sheriff requesting a speedy sale.

9.   **Notice of sale.** Once a writ is submitted, the county sheriff must issue a notice of sale to the current homeowner, which gives the date of the auction. In most states, the sheriff must also post notice of the public sale at the property site itself, in the local newspaper, and at the courthouse. Announcements of the auction will be

posted in the newspapers for two to three consecutive weeks prior to the auction to attract as many potential buyers as possible.

10. **The foreclosure sale.** If the homeowner is unable to pay off the loan by the sale date, the property is sold under state foreclosure sale rules. When property is auctioned in a judicial foreclosure, it is done through a "sheriff's sale." A certificate of sale is issued by the court to the highest bidder at auction. The certificate officially transfers ownership of the property from the homeowner to the purchaser. If the property does not sell at auction, it becomes real estate owned by the lender.

11. **Deficiency judgments.** Some lenders seek deficiency judgments against delinquent homeowners. If the sale of the house does not bring in enough money to satisfy the debt, the lender can ask the court to issue a "delinquency judgment," a court order requiring the homeowner to pay any remaining debt.

12. **Post-sale redemption period.** Most states that use the judicial foreclosure process have a clause that gives the homeowner a period of time to buy back his or her property from the purchaser who bought it at auction. This is called a post-sale redemption period. To reclaim the house, the homeowner must be able to pay the mortgage off in full, plus pay the sheriff's fees, court fees, and any other fees associated with the foreclosure. Though few people have the means to buy their house back after a foreclosure sale, the option is available in many cases.

Non-judicial foreclosure

Non-judicial foreclosures take place when a deed of trust has been signed to secure the promissory note, rather than a mortgage. The title remains in the possession of a third party and remains in the name of the lender until the debt has been fulfilled, which means the lender is the actual owner of the property. Because the lender owns the property in question, it does not have to proceed through a court of law in order to foreclose. The non-judicial foreclosure process varies widely from state to state, with varying consequences.

In the deed of trust document, there is typically a "power of sale" clause that allows the lender to sell the property to satisfy the loan, should the borrower default. Mortgages that include this clause also allow a lender to foreclose outside the court system. Depending on the state you live in, a lender might be able to put a notice of sale in the newspapers after the first payment is missed and move the property to auction. Other states, however, require a few steps before the property is allowed to go to auction.

The following are the steps involved with a non-judicial foreclosure:

1. The borrower has missed payments, leaving the loan in default 30 to 90 days.

2. The trustee — an independent third party — files a notice of default. This notice is sent to anyone with an interest in the property — typically the borrower(s) and lender.

3. Some state laws require that the homeowner be granted a reinstatement period during which he or she can pay off the debt. During the reinstatement period, the homeowner has the right to pay the outstanding balance on his or her account — with penalties — and stop the foreclosure.

4. A notice of trustee sale is published in the newspapers to alert potential buyers of the property. No lender is allowed to hold a foreclosure sale without advertising the auction in the local newspaper or posting a notice at the courthouse, the property itself, or some other public place.

5. Once the reinstatement period ends, a redemption period begins that continues until the actual sale. During the redemption period, the only way the homeowner can stop the ultimate sale of his or her property is to pay the loan off in full.

6. If the homeowner fails to pay the money owed, a "trustee's sale," or public auction, is held to sell the property. The lender finishes the foreclosure by auctioning off the property to the highest bidder.

7. A trustee deed is issued within 30 days to the highest bidder on the property, transferring ownership. As in the judicial process, the original homeowner now becomes a tenant of the property subject to the new owner's discretion.

8. A redemption period may go into effect. As with judicial foreclosures, there may be a clause in the deed of trust that allows the original homeowner to buy back the property within a given amount of time.

Types of Foreclosure Notices and What They Mean

First, you receive a letter from your lender reminding you that your mortgage payment is late. Then, another notice comes, and another, until eventually, a court summons arrives. Now you know you are in trouble; the bank is about to take away your home. The foreclosure process takes months and even years, during which the delinquent homeowner receives numerous letters and notices from the lender. Understanding what documents you should receive from your lender, and when you can expect to receive them, can help you better determine whether your foreclosure is being handled legally.

State laws require a lender or lien holder to file certain documents to proceed with a foreclosure. The following sections detail the most common documents required in almost every state. *You will find samples of these documents in Appendix B at the end of this book.*

Notice of default

When a non-judicial foreclosure occurs, the lender is first required to file a notice of default with the county recorder's office stating that the borrower has failed to make one or more payments in a timely manner and that the lender intends to foreclose if payments are not brought current. This may or may not come after a series of letters have been sent, alerting the homeowner to missed payments. In some states, this document may be titled "notice of forfeiture." Anyone filing this notice must have it process served, or physically delivered, to all parties listed in the promissory note, in addition to having copies mailed.

Notice of complaint, or *lis pendens*

A notice of complaint, or *lis pendens* (Latin for "pending lawsuit"), is filed with the circuit court by a lender pursuing a judicial foreclosure. Like the notice of default, it makes public the fact that you have defaulted on a loan agreement and the lender intends to take legal action to redeem the property. Unlike the notice of default, homeowners have the opportunity to respond to this complaint by filing an answer, usually within 30 days. If an answer is not filed, it is assumed that you are not contesting the claims made by the lender, and a summary judgment of foreclosure is granted.

Summary judgment of foreclosure

After the lender has filed a complaint, you are given a certain amount of time to respond. The amount of time depends on the state in which you live. After this time has elapsed, the court decides whether there is enough evidence to bring the foreclosure to trial. If the evidence indicates that the foreclosure is legally justified and a trial is unnecessary, the court will grant a summary judgment of foreclosure in favor of the lender. A summary judgment avoids the need to go to trial and incur additional legal expenses. A homeowner who has a strong grounds for a legal defense against the foreclosure can also file a motion for a summary judgment, asking the court to dismiss the case. Sometimes, lenders file a motion for a summary judgment after the homeowner has responded to a notice of complaint, in an attempt to have the homeowner's defenses declared frivolous and avoid a trial hearing. As with most foreclosure documents, the summary judgment must be process served to each individual listed on the promissory note in order to be valid.

Notice of hearing

If the court decides to proceed with a foreclosure hearing, a date and time will be set. A notice of hearing announcing when and where a hearing will take place in court is required to be sent to all interested parties, including the IRS and any junior lien holders on the property. These are typically sent by certified mail, but can also be process served by the sheriff. Regulations regarding the delivery of notices of hearing vary from state to state.

Notice of sheriff's sale

Once a judicial hearing has been held and the court has decided in the lender's favor, a notice of sheriff's sale is sent to all interested parties, clearly outlining the day, time, and requirements of the sale as determined by the court. A notice may be posted on the front door of the property itself and will be printed in local newspapers for a given amount of time before the sale date. This document will list the property in detail, in addition to the date, time, and location of the sale. State law determines when and for how long a notice of sheriff's sale must be posted.

Notice of trustee's sale

The notice of trustee's sale is the same as the notice of sheriff's sale; the sole difference is that a notice of trustee's sale is used in non-judicial foreclosures. After the notice of default is served, the lender is required by the state to grant you a specific number of days to pay off the debt. If the debt has not been satisfied by the end of this period, the lender simply files a notice of trustee's sale specifying the date, time, and place of the sale with the county registrar; sends copies to all interested parties; and prints it in the local newspapers. Unlike in a judicial foreclosure, the lender can move quickly from notice of default to notice of sale without the courtroom visits.

Certificate of sale

After the sheriff's sale has taken place and an acceptable offer has been made, the courts will issue a certificate of sale that grants ownership of the property to the individual purchaser at auction. At that point, you become a tenant at will on the property and are subject to eviction by the new owner. State foreclosure laws determine the process for confirming that a sale complies with legal regulations; the process can take anywhere from a few days to several weeks. Some states mandate a redemption period after the sale to allow the homeowner the opportunity to buy back the home.

Once the sale is confirmed, the new owner demonstrates to the court a right of possession of the property, and the court then orders a sheriff to evict the tenants, usually within a short time.

Trustee deed

A trustee deed is issued to the new owner within 30 days after a trustee's sale has taken place. As with the certificate of sale, the trustee deed grants full ownership to the purchaser, and the previous homeowner becomes a tenant at will.

Deficiency judgment

If the sale of a property does not realize enough to pay off the mortgage, the lender can seek a deficiency judgment requiring the homeowner to repay any outstanding debt.

Property Documents

In addition to the security instrument you signed when you purchased your home and the paperwork involved in a foreclosure, you should also understand the documents that will be required during any legal proceeding concerning your property. *Samples of these documents are included in Appendix B at the end of this book.* If any legal notices related to your foreclosure do not list the same names, locations, and filing dates as these documents, you can ask the court to halt the foreclosure proceedings until all paperwork is in order. These documents establish who is the owner of your property.

Certificate of title

The certificate of title for real estate is essentially the same as the certificate of title for a vehicle. This document shows the legal owner of the property in question. If you used a mortgage as a security instrument to purchase your home, the title will remain with you, in your name, and a lien will be placed against the property to secure it. Any liens recorded against the property will be reflected in the title until you have satisfied the debt, at which time they will be removed. This is why a title search is performed when you attempt to purchase property. If a transfer is completed without the clearance of those debts, the debts transfer to the new owner.

Some states use a deed of trust instead of a mortgage to secure a home loan. If you used a deed of trust to secure the loan for a property, the title on the property remains in the lender's name and is held by an impartial third party — the trustee — until the day the loan has been paid in full. Deeds of trust are also used when the seller finances a home purchase.

General warranty deed

A warranty deed is a legal document guaranteeing that an individual owns the property, free and clear of any hidden debts. In it, an owner attests that there are no claims on the property other than those publicly listed — from a lender, for example. The owner affirms that he or she is the legal owner of the property and is allowed to sell it, and if the title should be contested or prove to have legal defects at any time, he or she will make compensation for any losses to the new owner.

Quitclaim deed

Quitclaim deeds are most commonly seen in divorce settlements, when one spouse signs over his or her share of a property to the other. A quitclaim deed comes with no guarantees — it simply transfers all interest an individual had in the property to another owner. In some "deed in lieu of foreclosure" arrangements, a lender will draw up a quitclaim deed instead of a deed in lieu. They serve the same function, but the deed in lieu of foreclosure draws attention to the reason for the transfer. *See Chapter 10 for more information on a deed in lieu of foreclosure arrangement.*

Grant deed

Some states and jurisdictions use grant deeds to transfer ownership of property. Grant deeds are essentially the same as warranty deeds. Unlike a warranty deed, though, a grant deed only implies that the property is free and clear of outstanding debts against it. It is a notarized statement that you are unaware of any claims existing on the property. A proper title search would be required to certify that information.

The Lasting Effects of Foreclosure

Foreclosure is an unpleasant experience. It affects more than your ability to keep your home; it can affect your relationships, your job, your family — even your health. The stress brought on by foreclosure has a lasting effect on the way you think and feel about yourself and those around you. A foreclosure impacts your credit rating and may make it difficult for you to maintain the lifestyle you are familiar with. If you have received a foreclosure notice, you must now devote considerable time and energy to working out the best possible solution to the problems that confront you — not only in the immediate future, but also for months and years ahead. In making decisions during the next weeks and months, you should be aware of the lasting consequences of foreclosure.

Foreclosure will change your life in both negative and positive ways. The key is to minimize the negative impact foreclosure can have on your lifestyle, relationships, and financial future by preparing ahead of time and doing what you can to mitigate the damage.

Loss of your home

The immediate result of foreclosure proceedings, if they run their full course, will be that you will have to move out of your home and find a new place to live. You may have to move your family from a large house to a small apartment or rental house, or seek temporary shelter with family or friends. Giving up your home can be a very emotional experience, because your house is an important part of your everyday life, representing security and comfort. Children suffer when they have to say goodbye to their friends, move into a smaller home, and adjust to new schools. It may be necessary to part with furniture and appliances, and even with pets, in some instances. Do not hesitate to ask for help from family, friends, churches, and government agencies who can provide counseling, housing assistance, and emotional and financial support while you are going through the foreclosure process.

The foreclosure becomes public knowledge

When a bank begins the foreclosure process, the bank posts public notices in newspapers to attract potential buyers. These notices might include your name, address, and the amount owed on your mortgage. Anyone reading the notice will learn that you are unable to pay your debts, and the effect on your social life can be devastating. People you considered friends might begin to distance themselves, or your own feelings of guilt and embarrassment might interfere with your relationships. Stress can put a strain on your marriage and home life. Depending on your reaction to the situation, financial problems can bring a family closer together, or they can tear it apart.

Your job could be in jeopardy

Just when you need your job — and your income — the most, it may be at risk. Some employers consider foreclosure grounds for termination. Many employers now require a credit report before hiring new employees, especially for higher-paying jobs that entail management or money-handling responsibilities. A foreclosure on your credit record will eliminate you from consideration for these types of jobs. If you already hold such a position, a foreclosure can be grounds for reassignment or termination. If you have a job that requires security clearance in the police, CIA, military, or private security, a foreclosure can rank just below a felony or a serious misdemeanor. A foreclosure can mean that your security clearance is revoked and you immediately lose your job.

Scammers are alerted to your predicament

Public foreclosure notices also alert scammers and mortgage assistance programs to your plight, so be wary of any fliers, letters, phone calls, or visitors offering to save your home by assuming the mortgage or offering you a new loan. *See Chapter 12 for more information on how to avoid scams and seek out genuine foreclosure assistance agencies.*

Your credit report is negatively affected

Foreclosure will negatively affect your credit score. Your first missed payment is recorded on your credit report. Each missed payment lowers your credit rating, and foreclosure can send it plummeting 200 to 300 points. Though it is factored in with the rest of your credit history, a foreclosure on top of other late or missed payments will make it almost impossible to qualify for loans or credit cards for at least seven years. Without these resources, you will have to pay for everything in cash, making large or unexpected expenses — such as car repairs or medical bills — a significant challenge. On loan applications, you will have to answer "yes" to the following questions under Declarations, Section VIII:

- Have you had property foreclosed upon or given title or deed in lieu thereof in the last 7 years?

- Have you directly or indirectly been obligated on any loan that resulted in foreclosure, transfer of title in lieu of foreclosure, or judgment?

Chapter 13 discusses steps you can take to rebuild your credit history.

Your attitude toward life changes

Dealing with a foreclosure can send you into a tailspin of negative thoughts, emotions, and actions. You might experience depression, sadness, anger, frustration, and physical symptoms of stress such as headaches, indigestion, loss of appetite, high blood pressure, sleeplessness, and back pain. You may find yourself in deep denial, or feel ashamed and embarrassed in front of your friends and family. It is important to recognize that such feelings are normal under the circumstances and to seek counseling and support if you need help. Foreclosure is a serious setback, but it is not the end of your world. It does not define you as a person, nor is it a reflection on your character and integrity. Many people have survived foreclosure and emerged happier and in better financial shape than when they were burdened with unsustainable mortgage payments.

CHAPTER 2

Understanding Your Loan

The first round of the current foreclosure crisis hit in late 2007 when thousands of subprime loans featuring extremely low teaser interest rates readjusted to much-higher — and more normal — rates, suddenly increasing monthly payments to amounts that homeowners were unable to pay. Many blamed unscrupulous lenders for not adequately explaining loan terms to borrowers, while others blamed the borrowers for rushing to accept loans that did not seem to "make sense" and were clearly beyond their means. Regardless of where the blame lies, the ultimate problem was that lenders eagerly granted loans even when the borrowers did not meet standard credit requirements, and few borrowers understood the terms they were agreeing to.

If you are one of the millions stuck with a mortgage you can no longer pay, you may think it is too late to "get to know your loan." Nothing could be further from the truth. Figuring out the ins and outs of your home loan may be one of your best defenses against foreclosure. You cannot fight what you do not understand, and understanding your mortgage loan is paramount to getting out from underneath a payment you can no longer handle.

Understanding your loan, and your ultimate foreclosure, begins with deciphering the paperwork. The day you closed on your house, you probably sat in the bank with your lawyer or your real estate agent at your side, signing paper after paper — and not feeling sure what all the legal jargon meant. Although the excitement of owning your own home may have eclipsed any uncertainty about the legal responsibilities you were agreeing to, those documents and the language they contain are exceptionally important and can determine the way your foreclosure process will transpire.

It is time to look at those documents again — with a clearer head this time. What started out as the American dream has turned into a nightmare, and you will not be able to fix this problem without understanding the paper you signed at closing. Let us look at the different documents you signed when you bought your house and how they can affect the way your house is foreclosed upon. This will help you understand what you agreed to at closing and ascertain whether the lender is acting within his or her legal rights. As you read through this chapter, have your own documents handy so you can check them against the information here.

Types of Mortgages

Aside from standard fixed-rate mortgages given to homebuyers with good credit who have saved up a down payment of 20 percent, there are several types of mortgages available to buyers in special circumstances such as veterans and low-income families. These may be subject to extra restrictions or be eligible for certain government assistance programs. The notorious "subprime mortgages" blamed for triggering the present banking crisis are designed for buyers with little or no down payment who are eager to enter the housing market. Many poorly informed buyers sign mortgage documents without a good understanding of the terms to which they are agreeing. The type of mortgage you hold will help to determine the best strategy to avoid foreclosure. For example, if yours is a fixed-rate mortgage, the solution may be as simple as reorganizing your finances so that you can make the regular monthly payments. If you have a variable-rate mortgage or an unfavorable interest rate, you might decide to refinance or try to renegotiate the terms with your lender. Some types of mortgage holders are eligible for government assistance.

Subprime mortgages

A "subprime" borrower is typically someone who is unable to obtain a conventional mortgage because of impaired or non-existent credit. The borrower has a low income or a poor debt-to-income ratio, maxed-out credit cards, bad credit or no credit history, or little or no down payment when purchasing the house. The person may have had financial problems in the past or a history of late payments on previous loans. Many subprime borrowers are first-time homebuyers, and many have not had previous access to credit. Subprime loans allow borrowers who otherwise might never be able to obtain a loan to get a mortgage. To compensate for the high risk that the borrower might not be able to pay back the loan, subprime loans have higher interest rates. Most offer low "teaser" interest rates or "interest-only" payments for the first few years; when this period ends, the amount of the monthly mortgage payment skyrockets.

Some subprime borrowers are unaware that once the teaser interest rate expires, their payments will escalate to unmanageable amounts. Most subprime borrowers accept the loans believing that as property values escalate and their incomes rise, they will be able to refinance with a more manageable loan. While this is sometimes true, often the household income does not increase as anticipated. A drop in housing prices that began late in 2006 triggered a banking crisis as subprime borrowers began to default on homes that were now worth less than they had paid for them.

Fixed-rate mortgages

The most common option for an average borrower, a fixed-rate mortgage, gives the safety of a fixed interest rate and the same monthly payment from the first day of the loan until it is paid in full. The only drawback to a fixed-rate loan is the possibility of a prepayment penalty, which may be charged if you pay off your loan early. Fixed-rate loans maintain high standards for income requirements and credit worthiness. The Federal Housing Administration (FHA) (**www.fha.com/fixed_rate.cfm**) makes it possible for many lower-income and first-time borrowers who do not qualify for conventional mortgages to get fixed-rate loans. Many state and local programs also help first-time buyers with home financing.

Adjustable-rate mortgages (ARMs)

A variety of these types of loans are available on the market, but all adjustable-rate mortgages (ARMs) start with a low interest rate for an initial period and then adjust or "reset" to a much higher interest rate. Some ARMs adjust yearly, quarterly, or as frequently as every month once the initial period has ended. A study released in March 2007 by a unit of real estate data company First American estimated that more than $2.28 trillion worth of ARMs originated in 2004, 2005, and 2006 — at the peak of the housing boom. When the subprime mortgage crisis broke, ARMs became much less common.

ARMs are appropriate for people who are assured that their income will rise before their loan resets. They can help borrowers buy a more expensive house while waiting for that new job or salary hike. Problems arise when the homeowner assumes he or she can refinance to a fixed rate later is not able to and is left with an unmanageable mortgage payment.

Interest-only loans

Interest-only loans allow borrowers to keep their initial payments low by paying only the interest on their home loan for a set period of time. Paying only the interest on your loan is a good way to keep payments down temporarily, but it is not a permanent solution. Many people who take this type of loan are shocked by the size of their "real" mortgage payments once they begin paying off the principal as well as the interest. Like the ARM, an interest-only loan makes it easier for buyers to purchase a home that they really cannot afford.

FHA/VA loans

FHA/VA loans are offered to veterans (VA) and low-to-middle-income families (FHA loans). Fixed rates, low down payments, and less stringent approval guidelines make these a good choice for first-time buyers.

The Federal Housing Authority (FHA) (**www.fha.com/fixed_rate.cfm**) has been making home loans available to those who might otherwise not be able to purchase a house for decades. The hallmark of the FHA loan is a low 3 percent down payment. VA loans are provided by the U.S. Department of Veterans Affairs and, like FHA loans, have more lenient requirements for borrowers. These loans are available only to veterans of the U.S. Armed Forces.

Jumbo loans

Loans that exceed the loan amount limits set forth by the Office of Federal Housing Enterprise Oversight (OFHEO) are called jumbo loans, or non-conforming loans. Because of their size, they are not eligible to be purchased, guaranteed, or securitized by Fannie Mae (Federal National Mortgage Association) or Freddie Mac (Federal Home Loan Mortgage Corporation). While most jumbo mortgages have fixed rates and can help people in high-priced areas get into a home of their own, their interest rates are typically a little higher than conventional mortgages to compensate for the increased risk.

Combo or 80/20 loan

A combo, or 80/20, loan is actually two loans comprising 100 to 110 percent of the home's equity. If the amount of a loan exceeds 80 percent of a home's purchase price, most lenders require the borrower to pay for private mortgage insurance (PMI) that will cover the costs of foreclosure if the borrower defaults. An 80/20 loan allows a homebuyer to borrow the entire cost of a home without paying for PMI by taking out one loan for 80 percent of the price and another for the remaining 20 percent. This type of loan is often sought by young professionals who earn a good income but have not had time to save up for a down payment and who are anxious to stop renting and start making payments on a home of their own. A combo loan is a good option for first-time buyers or those with less than a 20 percent down payment, but it leaves the borrower with no equity. Many people with this type of loan have now found themselves in an "upside-down mortgage," owing more than their house is now worth.

Second mortgage or home equity line of credit (HELOC)

A second mortgage or home equity line of credit is a cash loan using your home as collateral. HELOCs often operate like credit cards, allowing you to draw cash and repay it during a specified period of several years, with interest charged only on the amount you withdraw. The interest on a HELOC is treated as tax-free mortgage interest in most states. If your home is foreclosed on, the primary mortgage is paid off first, then the second mortgage. If your home goes into foreclosure, and the home equity loan is not paid through the foreclosure sale, the HELOC becomes an unsecured obligation. If you default on a HELOC, your home can be foreclosed on.

Private mortgage

A private mortgage is a mortgage contract in which the lender is not a registered financial institution. The loan might be from an individual investor, a family member, or an owner-financed arrangement. The lender can foreclose on the house if payments are missed according to the terms of the mortgage contract. Both the lender and the borrower are at a disadvantage in foreclosure: The borrower might not qualify for mortgage assistance programs because of the nature of the loan, and the lender does not have access to the same legal advice and financial resources as the loss mitigation department of an institutionalized lender.

Carry-back loan

A carry-back loan is a loan offered by the seller of a property to a buyer who is not able to borrow enough from the bank. For example, the bank might be willing to loan only 80 percent of the price of the home, but the prospective buyer does not have a 20 percent down payment. The seller lends the 20 percent to the buyer, and the bank lends the rest. The homebuyer then makes two monthly mortgage payments, one to the bank and one to the seller. Sellers give carry-back loans when the real estate market is slow and it is difficult to find qualified buyers, or when the price of the home is higher than the bank valuation. Carry-back loans are secondary to the primary mortgage. Proceeds from the sale of the home in foreclosure pay off the primary mortgage first, and there may not be enough left over to pay the carry-back loan.

Who Owns Your Mortgage

When your parents bought their home, they probably borrowed money from a local bank that held the mortgage for 20 or 30 years until it was paid off in full. Today, buying and selling debt is big business. Mortgages are securitized — bundled together with other mortgages — and sold to investment companies, sometimes only days after you sign the documents. Banks use the cash they receive from investment companies to make new loans. When your bank sells your mortgage to an investment company, it may continue to act as your loan servicer, receiving and forwarding your payments, or your loan may be serviced by its new owner. The investment company that bought your loan often resells it to yet another investment company and, after a decade, it may have changed hands many times. All of these transactions are tracked by Mortgage Electronic Registration Systems, Inc. (MERS). When you miss payments and the bank sends out a foreclosure notice, you might have to do some detective work to find out who your real lender is.

Second mortgages, or home equity loans, are typically owned by the bank that issues them and are not resold.

Types of Loan Documents

Three primary documents are involved in the buying of property: the promissory note, the deed of trust, and the mortgage. Each plays important roles in the ownership process, so you should be especially conscious of what each does.

The promissory note

When a lender agrees to lend someone money, it draws up a promissory note. Whether you are buying a home, a car, or paying for college, each loan comes with a promissory note, also referred to as a "note." A note is simply a document stating that you promise to pay back the amount of money loaned, according to the terms offered. Notes can be secured or unsecured, depending on the type. A secured note means that a physical item is used as collateral and can be sold to pay off the debt. When dealing with real estate, the property itself most often secures the note.

A standard note includes the specific details of the original amount of money borrowed, the repayment terms in time and interest, and often information on penalties and grace periods for defaulting on the loan. These terms establish exactly how much the lender is agreeing to loan, in addition to how you are agreeing to pay it back. Importantly, the promissory note specifies which type of security instrument is being used to secure the note — a deed of trust or a mortgage. The type of security instrument affects the way in which a lender is allowed to foreclose. A deed of trust does not require that the lender file a lawsuit before putting the property up for sale and, therefore, allows for a much faster foreclosure process than a mortgage — as little as three months total in some states.

Promissory notes are different from other debt acknowledgements, such as IOUs; an "I owe you" simply states that a debt is owed. A promissory note spells out exactly how that debt will be paid back and at what interest rate. It remains in the hand of the lender until the debt has been satisfied, at which point it is stamped "paid in full" and returned to the borrower.

When dealing with foreclosure proceedings, this document is central, as it is legally binding and enforceable by law. Make sure you know exactly how much was borrowed, what you have paid back to date, and how far behind you are in payments. Check the promissory note against the foreclosure documents to make sure the lender is acting according to the terms of the promissory note and has the correct information — even a bank can make a mistake.

The deed of trust

Depending on the state in which you purchased property, you also need to sign either a deed of trust or a mortgage agreement when you buy a house. A deed of trust is similar to a mortgage in that it is a legally binding document that establishes a real estate property as collateral for the promissory note. The deed of trust includes important information such as the amount of the original loan, the interest rate at which the loan will be paid back, and both the inception (start) and maturity (end) dates of the loan period.

Included in this document is also information on what will happen if payments are missed, what late fees may be charged, who is loaning and accepting the funds involved, and at what point the loan might be accelerated, or called in.

A certificate of title, or title, is a record of ownership. The title, a document stipulating who owns the property, is passed along each time a property is sold and recorded in the Registry of Deeds, a government office responsible for recording all land transactions for the district in which the property is located. When a deed of trust is signed to secure a promissory note, the title is kept by a third party, or trustee. The trustee will hold the title for the lender until the debt has been paid in full and then transfer it to the homeowner.

Tip : **A deed of trust differs from a mortgage.**

The main difference between a deed-of-trust document and a mortgage is that with a mortgage, the certificate of title remains with the homeowner rather than with a third party.

The mortgage

You do not actually "take out" a mortgage when you buy a home. You take out a loan, and the mortgage is the legally binding document that secures that loan. The mortgage stipulates that the property being purchased with the loan will serve as collateral until the debt has been cleared.

A mortgage document and a deed of trust contain the same basic information. The primary difference is that there is no third party, or trustee, in mortgage agreements. Depending on the state in which you live, the certificate of title may show the lender as the owner, with ownership reverting to the homeowner at the fulfillment of the debt, or it will list the homeowner as the owner, with a lien being placed on the property by the lender. Because the ownership arrangements in a mortgage involve two parties instead of the single trustee who holds the title in a deed of trust, foreclosure proceedings for a mortgage require more time and the participation of the court.

It is possible to both refinance a mortgage after a certain period of time and to arrange a second mortgage on the property. Because multiple liens can be attached to a piece of property, once the original mortgage loan has been paid down, it is possible to take a second loan, most often referred to as a home equity loan, with the property as collateral. This second mortgage is separate from the original and can fall into default even if the original loan is in good standing. It is essential to realize that either mortgage lender can begin foreclosure proceedings.

Understanding the deed of trust or mortgage

Now that you understand what these documents are in broad terms, let us break them down even further. There are many different parts to both deeds of trust and mortgages, and each part can have terms and conditions that affect whether the lender accelerates the loan. Some of the details contained in the fine print can become invaluable tools for negotiation when it comes to halting the foreclosure process. There might be clauses setting out exactly what the lender will do when a payments is late or missed. If there are errors or discrepancies in these documents, or if the lender does not follow the terms of the contract exactly, you might be able to delay the foreclosure proceedings or use a legal defense to halt foreclosure. For example, names and addresses should be correct, and there should be specific procedures for serving notices. Your signature at the bottom of the contract affirms that you can uphold all the requirements of the loan.

Parties involved

This is one of the simplest parts of a security instrument. The first few lines typically articulate who is involved in the arrangement, along with their addresses. In deed of trust documents, the homeowner or borrower is referred to as the trustor, the third party that holds the certificate of title is the trustee, and the lender is the beneficiary. Mortgage documents tend to refer to the homeowner as the borrower, grantor, or mortgagor; the lender is called the mortgagee.

Whoever's name is listed as trustor, borrower, grantor, or mortgagor is legally responsible for paying the debt back to the lender. This means that anyone who cosigns on the loan is equally responsible for the repayment. Missed payments and foreclosure proceedings will affect the credit of all individuals listed. The beneficiary or mortgagee is the party receiving loan payments.

Trustees listed in a deed of trust maintain a neutral stance. They are impartial and are only responsible for enforcing the terms of the security document. A trustee's sole job is to hold onto the title until you fulfill the terms of the promissory note — at which point the title is signed over to you — or you default on the loan and the lender requests a foreclosure.

Principal amount

Shortly after the parties involved in the mortgage are listed, the principal, or original amount of the loan, will be noted. This sum is the total amount borrowed from the lender, and it does not include arrangement fees, interest, or closing costs. This number is what the rest of the terms of the mortgage will refer to.

Amortization period

The term "amortization" means to kill off or terminate. In security instrument language, the amortization period, or term, is the amount of time you have to pay off the loan, with the accrued interest. This is the time between the inception of the loan and its maturity. Maturity dates can vary depending on the mortgage, but common amortization periods are 15-, 25-, and 30-year intervals.

Interest rates and contract type

The interest rate, type of loan, and structure of the contract are among the most important parts of a security document. This information may be placed directly into the document or attached as a rider; riders will be discussed in detail later in this chapter.

Just as many different amortization periods are available to a borrower, there are many different types of loans and interest agreements. Fixed-rate mortgages have fixed monthly payments. Graduated payment mortgages have fixed payments that increase or decrease according to a prearranged schedule. Variable interest rate mortgages adjust the monthly payments based on a number of indices such as the 1-year constant-maturity Treasury (CMT) securities, the cost of funds index (COFI), the London Interbank Offered Rate (LIBOR), or the bank's own cost of funds. Adjustable-rate mortgages (ARMs) start out with a lower interest rate for the first few years that later resets to a much higher rate. Interest-only mortgages allow the borrower to pay only the interest for the first five or ten years before beginning to pay off the principal. These loans are suitable for borrowers who expect their income to increase substantially in the future. No-down-payment loans charge higher interest rates, and many years pass before the borrower has substantial equity in the home. A balloon mortgage stipulates that the borrower will pay a small amount of money each month — often just the interest on the loan — for a specified period of time. At the end of that period, one large final payment is made that covers the balance of the loan. This type of arrangement is popular with people who "flip," or renovate to sell, property quickly. Check to see whether you have a fixed interest rate, a variable or adjustable rate, or a balloon payment, and how many years remain in your amortization period.

Payments

Each month, you make a payment to the lender on the loan, which may or may not cover interest and principal. This section will tell you exactly what date of the month payments are due and the amount. Keep in mind that if you have a variable interest rate, the interest is charged on the sum left to pay, not on a fixed monthly payment. For a loan that has a fixed monthly payment for three years before becoming variable, your monthly payment can easily go from $500 to $1,000 or more. Use online mortgage payment calculators such as the one on Interest.com (**www.interest.com/content/ calculators**) to determine exactly what your payments are, how much you will pay over time, and how the terms of your mortgage compare to other types of mortgages.

Conditions and consequences of default

Conditions are stipulated provisions that you agree to when you sign a deed of trust or mortgage. Lenders can include conditions such as the requirement of home and hazard insurance, payment of tax bills, preservation of the property to maintain value, and the acceptable use of the property according to law. Failure to adhere to the provisions in the agreement gives the lender probable cause to accelerate the loan and begin foreclosure.

For example, many cities and towns have legislation that states which buildings may or may not be used for business purposes. If the property you own is in a residential-only area, you are prohibited by law from running any business out of the home. If the lender discovers that you have been running even a small home business, it may decide to accelerate the loan because the contract has been breached. Although it is not a common reason for foreclosure, it is a legal one.

This area of the security instrument should spell out clearly the consequences of defaulting on the agreement. The most common reasons, after nonpayment or missed payments, are the borrower's failing to pay property taxes, letting property insurance lapse, and arranging a second mortgage on property that is not a primary residence, such as a vacation home. The consequences for default are likely to be either acceleration of the loan or additional fees and late charges. Look carefully at the document to see what the consequences are precisely. Look at the fine print in your monthly statement, also, for any notes about late payment charges. Confirm that your lender is adhering to the terms of the contract in seeking foreclosure, and determine what late fees, legal costs, and penalties you are liable for.

Clauses

Clauses are paragraphs or sections in the contract that relate to specific points. Most clauses articulate the lender's right to act should the homeowner not meet the provisions of the contract — such as paying home insurance or property taxes. Typical clauses found in the contract relate to acceleration and alienation.

An acceleration clause is a section that essentially allows the lender to call the loan in — demand payment in full immediately — should the homeowner default. Going into default is not simply missing payments on the loan; defaulting can refer to the homeowner's not meeting any given condition in the contract. An acceleration clause will specify the amount of time the homeowner has to come up with the money before the foreclosure process begins.

The other type of clause you are likely to find in your contract is an alienation clause. This ensures that the homeowner will not be able to sell or transfer the title on the property without satisfying the loan. If a homeowner sells or transfers the title, the loan is immediately called in. If you have violated any of the terms of an alienation clause, your lender is justified in accelerating the loan.

Depending on whether the mortgage is assumable (allows another buyer to take over the mortgage payments), there may also be a clause as to the requirements for a buyer who wishes to assume the mortgage, should the homeowner decide to "sell." Lenders may also include in this section of the contract the cost of late fees, as well as the procedure they will take should the homeowner default on any part of the loan.

Finally, almost all loan documents include a "negotiability" clause allowing the lender to sell your promissory note to a third party. Many investment companies, both private and institutional, "buy" outstanding debts from a lender. The lender often sells these debts for an amount lower than the total payments it would receive from the homeowners because it is clearing many debts in an immediate fashion. The investment company will assume ownership of the promissory note until the homeowner has fulfilled the debt. The top three mortgage investment companies in the United States are Fannie Mae (Federal National Mortgage Association), Freddie Mac (Federal Home Loan Mortgage Corporation), and Ginnie Mae (Government National Mortgage Association).

Make sure you know who legally owns your promissory note. You may not be notified if your promissory note has been sold. If you suspect it may have been, contact your bank to find out. Also, be certain you always notify your lender of any changes in address, marital status, employment, or the condition of the property, including the death of an individual listed in the security instrument or divorce between the two parties listed.

If you fail to notify your lender that a cosigner on the loan has passed away, for example, you can potentially be arrested for fraud and lose your home. A lender may have granted you the loan based on the security of the second individual. When they are no longer alive to guarantee payment on the debt, you become a much greater liability.

If you divorce and you or your partner grants the other a quitclaim deed, which basically gives you or your spouse the right to the entire property (and the mortgage) as part of the divorce settlement, a copy of the document should be sent to the lender and the appropriate name removed from the promissory note and mortgage. If you do not notify the lender, and the property goes into foreclosure, there is a good chance that the party who gave up his or her interest will have to fight legally to protect himself or herself from the responsibility of paying the debt. Check to be sure that the names on the promissory note and mortgage are correct.

Riders

Riders are attachments that can be added to the contract at any time during the amortization period. These include amendments to the agreement, schedule changes, modified conditions of the loan, or the assumption of the mortgage by a new company. These documents are called "riders" because they are physically attached to the original contract and considered to be legally part of the agreement without the entire document being rewritten. The rider cannot be attached, though, unless all interested parties have agreed to and signed it, which means that the interest agreement and amortization period cannot be changed unless you agree to the adjustment. If your contract has riders, read them carefully to see whether any of the details might affect your foreclosure proceedings.

Property description

Toward the end of the document, there is a legal description of the property being used as collateral to secure the loan. This will include deed and survey information, its address, and a physical description of the property at the time of sale — all of which helps to identify the property in question during any legal proceedings. If any of this information is not accurate, you can request that foreclosure proceedings be halted until corrections have been made.

Signatures

The last section in a deed of trust or mortgage agreement is the signature page. This is where all interested parties have committed themselves to the information contained within the contract. Without the signatures of all parties listed in the document, it is null and void. Make sure that all of the signatures are present, that the information is correct, and that there are no forgeries.

CHAPTER 3

Steps to Avoiding Foreclosure

hen you purchased your home, you spent days looking for a suitable property, making an offer, applying for loans, and going through inspections before signing the final documents at the closing appointment. All of this occupied your thoughts for weeks and took up considerable time and energy. Now you will have to make a similar effort to keep your home. You will need to determine whether you can meet your obligations under the mortgage contract and promissory note, seek out professionals who can assist you, negotiate with your lender's loss mitigation officer, possibly apply for a new loan, and make adjustments to your budget and lifestyle. Until you reach an acceptable solution, avoiding foreclosure will probably be your primary concern. If you ignore the situation, you will find yourself locked out of your home, with your personal belongings stacked at the curb.

The process of avoiding foreclosure starts long before the first foreclosure notice arrives from your lender, when your financial difficulties first become evident. The actions that you take, and the amount of time available to find a solution, will depend on when you first begin to face the challenge.

What to Do and When to Do It — Developing a Timeline for Success

Staving off a foreclosure is a race against time. In order to stop your lender from taking your home, you will need to reach a solution acceptable to both of you — a process that requires thought, patience, persistence, and considerable commitment on your part. Before you approach your lender, you must gather information and organize your financial affairs so you can negotiate effectively, all while deadlines and time limits are rapidly approaching. To be successful, you need to develop a schedule and follow it, step by step.

Step No. 1: Talk to your lender — now

The best time to talk with your lender is before you ever miss a payment, but few people call their lenders to tell them they anticipate missing payments in the next few months. Your lender might offer a solution that will help you avoid defaulting on your loan payments, such as granting forbearance for a few months until you find a new job or negotiating lower monthly payments.

CONTACT YOUR LENDER TO AVOID FORECLOSURE

Excerpt from the U.S. Department of Housing and Urban Development

www.hud.gov/offices/hsg/sfh/econ/contactyourlender.cfm

Many people avoid calling their lender when they have money troubles. Most of us are embarrassed to discuss our money problems with others or believe that if lenders know we are in trouble, they will rush to collection or foreclosure.

Foreclosure is expensive for lenders, mortgage insurers, and investors. HUD/FHA, as well as private mortgage insurance companies and investors like Freddie Mac and Fannie Mae, require lenders to work aggressively with borrowers who are facing money problems.

Lenders have workout options to help you keep your home. However, these options work best when your loan is only one or two payments behind. The farther behind you are on your payments, the fewer options are available.

Do not assume that your mortage problem will quickly correct itself. Do not lose valuable time by being overly optimistic. Contact your mortgage lender to discuss your circumstances as soon as you realize that you are unable to make your payments. While there is no guarantee that any particular relief will be given, most lenders are willing to explore every possible option.

FINDING YOUR LENDER

Check the following sources for lender contact information:

- Your monthly mortgage billing statement
- Your payment coupon book
- Online searching
- Directory assistance or phone book

INFORMATION TO HAVE READY WHEN YOU CALL

To help you, lenders typically need:

- Your loan account number

- A brief explanation of your circumstances

- Recent income documents such as pay stubs, social security benefits statements, disability, unemployment, retirement, or public assistance. If you are self-employed, have your tax returns or a year-to-date profit-and-loss statement from your business available for reference)

- List of household expenses

Expect to have more than one phone conversation with your lender. Typically, your lender will mail you a "loan workout" package. This package contains information, forms, and instructions. If you want to be considered for assistance, you must complete the forms and return them to your lender quickly. The completed package will be reviewed before the lender talks about a solution with you.

DO NOT IGNORE MAIL OR PHONE CALLS
FROM YOUR LENDER

Your lender will try to contact you by mail and phone soon after you stop making payments. It is important that you respond to the mail and the phone calls offering help. If your lender does not hear from you, they will be required to start legal action leading to foreclosure. This will substantially increase the cost of bringing your loan current, thus avoid ignoring your lender.

IF YOU HAVE AN FHA-INSURED LOAN

HUD's National Servicing Center works closely with customers who have FHA-insured loans. Check your mortgage document or ask your lender if your loan is FHA-insured. Do you feel your lender is not responding to your questions? Do you want assistance contacting your lender? HUD's National Servicing Center is ready to help you.

Step No. 2: Get organized

Fighting a foreclosure will entail filling out dozens of forms. Keep a copy of every notice, letter, and document pertaining to your loan. In front of a judge, these can serve as evidence of your good intent. Pull out old payment receipts and canceled checks to demonstrate your good standing, up until the point in which you found yourself in financial trouble. Keep a log of all phone calls and communications with your lender, including dates, times, and the names of the people you spoke with, as well as a detailed account of the conversations. Save a copy of every letter you write. Keep everything dated and organized in appropriate folders so you can retrieve it quickly and easily if needed.

Step No. 3: Get your finances in order

You will not be able to convince a lender to readjust your loan if you cannot prove that you will be able to make the new payment. Saying, "I'll do better now," is not going to suffice. Evaluate your finances, pay off or consolidate whatever debt you can, and devise a plan that will clearly show the lender how you plan to meet your obligations. *Chapter 4 guides you through the process of evaluating your finances and developing a plan for paying off your debts.*

Step No. 4: Look at your options

Many people do not realize how many options are available to homeowners threatened by foreclosure. Because of the mounting foreclosure crisis, lenders are more open than ever to loan modifications, refinancing, and even forgiveness of some of the principal. After careful consideration, you might find that selling your home, or even arranging a deed in lieu to hand it over to your lender, is the best solution for you and your family. *Chapter 5 explains the many possible solutions to a foreclosure.* Free foreclosure counseling is available through government agencies and non-profit organizations if you need help determining which option is best for you.

Step No. 5: Begin negotiations

Once you have let your lender know there is a problem, put your family on a budget, devised a solid financial plan, and chosen the loan option you feel most comfortable with, it is time to begin negotiating. Talking a lender into changing your loan terms or forgiving penalties and interest is not going to be easy — but it can be done. Thousands of homeowners have been successfully negotiating loan changes in recent months, and you can, too.

Step No. 6: Enlist help if you need it

While some homeowners are able to get back on track themselves and negotiate acceptable terms with their lender, others need professional help to stop a foreclosure from going into effect. Whether you need legal advice, credit counseling, or an advocate who can talk with your lender, seek out help when you need it. *See Chapter 11 for more information.*

Talk to Your Lender

Whether your financial woes have just begun or you are already in trouble, talk to your lender today. Ignoring late notices and collection calls will only make matters worse. After you miss a payment or two, your lender will initiate foreclosure proceedings and your credit score will drop, making it more difficult for you to refinance or negotiate a longer amortization period. Admitting to financial difficulties is never easy, but it is necessary if you want to save your home from foreclosure. The longer you wait to speak to your lender, the more difficult it will be to reach a settlement, and the more it will cost you in penalties, late fees, and legal expenses.

You should also contact your lender to make sure your mortgage file is up-to-date — and accurate. Confirm all mortgage information, including your account number, balance, pay-off amount, and late fees and penalties. There have been cases in which the lender's files contained inaccuracies, such as misreported payments that had a direct impact on foreclosure proceedings.

The first person you will talk with at your lender's office is a customer service representative who handles incoming calls and walk-in customers. A customer service representative cannot help you with finding out information regarding your mortgage; he or she is only authorized to answer phones and respond to basic questions. You need to speak with someone with authority. After listening to your initial explanation, the customer service representative will probably try to connect you with the collections department. Collections officers cannot help you, either; their job is to collect money owed, not to negotiate settlements. You need to talk to a representative in the lender's loss mitigation or workout department. Ask to speak with a contact person to whom you can write a formal request for help, asking for forbearance, modification, or forgiveness.

Write a letter to the loss mitigation officer explaining the reasons for your delinquency and the arrangement you hope to make with the lender. Your letter should:

- Be direct and simple
- Outline your situation
- Ask for a specific resolution
- Be directed to a specific person in a specific department
- Include your account number and the name on the account
- Be sent after initial contact has been made with that person

Sample letter to loan mitigation department:

January 10, 2010

Dear (insert name here),

Thank you for taking the time to speak with me on January 8 about my current financial situation and the possibility of reaching a resolution between your company and myself regarding my mortgage delinquency. Attached, you will find a letter from my state's unemployment office detailing my job search and the dates of my unemployment.

As we discussed during our conversation, I am seeking a six-month period of forbearance in my mortgage payments during which time I hope to gain employment. In the eight years since I have held a mortgage with your company, I had never been delinquent until I lost my job.

I will be following up with this letter next week. Thank you for your time.

Sincerely,
(Insert your name here)
Account number: 574269842

Negotiating With Your Lender

You might wonder why your lender would be willing to negotiate with you when you seem to be at such a disadvantage. If you and your lender can come to some type of agreement, you both win: You keep your home, and your lender avoids paying thousands in foreclosure fees and getting stuck with yet another house to unload in a stagnant real estate market. A national study of foreclosures during November 2008 revealed that lenders were averaging a loss of $124,000 on each foreclosure, approximately 57 percent of their investment. The average loss for foreclosures on second mortgages was almost 100 percent.

Your lender might not be eager to renegotiate your loan, but it will be motivated to consider your offer. You have shown courage and responsibility by admitting that you need help. Your lender knows that you are serious and are prepared to work hard to keep your home. If you can demonstrate that you have the means to make lower mortgage payments consistently, your lender knows it will benefit by modifying your loan.

Negotiation is a means of turning a conflict into an acceptable resolution for all parties involved. It requires certain skills, such as knowing what to say and what not to say when dealing with your lender. Do not be discouraged if you are not an experienced negotiator — you can succeed if you follow several simple principles:

- Think of negotiation as a *discussion* rather than as a *confrontation*. To be effective, you must find a way to work together so everyone is at least partially satisfied.

- Look for someone who is willing to listen to you and who has the authority to help you. A collections officer is not interested in hearing that you will be able to pay your debt next month because he or she has a quota to meet this month, and may give you an abrupt answer. Someone in the loss mitigation department, however, who is concerned with salvaging delinquent mortgages, will want to assist you in avoiding foreclosure.

- Stay calm and in control of yourself at all times. Allowing your emotions to take over will only thwart your efforts. In conversations with your lender, act and sound as professional and level-headed as possible. Try not to be overly emotional, no matter what the person on the other end of the phone says. Do not appear angry, judgmental, or even frustrated, because those attitudes will only antagonize the person you are speaking to, who is not responsible for your difficulties. Remember your goal, which is to achieve an equitable arrangement with your lender. Your lender is under no obligation to discuss alternative payment options. You are asking for special consideration. Be polite and seek the cooperation of the lender's representative.

- Consider your lender. You are reneging on your initial agreement and asking to change the terms of a business contract. The lender knows that whatever it does at this point, it will lose money.

- Ask your lender questions to demonstrate your willingness to work out a solution. Sample questions include:

– What do you need from me to make this happen?
– What are some of your concerns regarding my request?
– How can we make this happen?

- State your needs and be clear about what you want, whether that is an interest-rate reduction, forgiveness of penalties, a lower monthly payment, or another option.

- Offer your lender options. You can request a particular arrangement, but be open to alternatives. For example, you might want to renegotiate your loan to a 20-year fixed mortgage with a 3 percent interest rate, but you may have to settle for a higher fixed rate, a longer term, a refinance, a repayment plan, or some other option.

- Do not argue. Always voice your objections in a gentle but assertive way when negotiating new loan terms.

- Do not be intimidated by rules. Rules are made to be broken — especially during hard times. Your loan representative may tell you there is nothing he or she can do to help, but that is not true. Every lender has the ability to modify any loan it holds. The key is convincing the lender to do so.

- Do not leave your lender feeling cheated. Your lender is about to take a considerable loss on your loan, so be willing to give to make a deal. The best negotiators know the importance of making the other side feel as though it is walking away a winner.

Writing a hardship letter

It will take considerable patience and persistence to get your lender to change the terms of your loan. The first thing you will have to do to convince your bank to work with you on this matter is write a hardship letter. A hardship letter is a formal explanation of your inability to pay your loan, your request for a mortgage settlement to avoid foreclosure, and a plan of action to ensure you will not end up in the same situation again.

Contact your lender's loss mitigation department and get the name and address of a specific person to whom you can address a hardship letter. If possible, speak with that person about your situation before writing the letter.

A good hardship letter is short, succinct, and appealing. A bad one blames everyone else, including the lender, for the mess the homeowner is in and offers no real strategy for getting and staying out of trouble. Find a way to simply and honestly explain your situation and highlight what you are doing to rectify it. Try to keep the letter to no more than two typewritten pages. Be especially careful not to go into too much detail or ramble on about your personal problems.

Keep these basics in mind:

- Keep the letter brief and to-the-point.
- Do not be too vague or too technical.
- Identify the reasons for your failure to keep current with your monthly payments, including any dates that coincide with the delinquency period.
- State your offer to resolve your debt.
- Show a willingness to work out a solution and keep your house.
- Be polite. Thank the reader for his or her time and consideration.
- Include your current contact information.
- Enclose bank statements from the past two months, late notices on your car, last year's tax returns, and anything else you can find that can verify your financial state.

What not to include:

- Legal issues, such as details of your impending divorce.
- Educational issues.
- Any reasons you are overextended other than those that are out of your control, such as job loss, illness, death, or interest readjustment.

- The fact that you will claim bankruptcy if they do not approve your modification application.

- Any other threats of nonpayment.

Acceptable excuses for falling behind on your mortgage payments include:

- Adjustable rate mortgage reset
- Illness
- Job loss
- Reduced income
- Failed business
- Job relocation
- Death of spouse or co-borrower
- Incarceration
- Divorce
- Military duty
- Medical bills
- Damage to property — natural disaster or unnatural

After you have contacted your lender and sent the all-important hardship letter, your negotiation will begin in earnest. Stay calm, stay firm, and be flexible. The attitude and stance you take during your negotiations will have a big impact on the final agreement.

In November 2009, the Treasury Department released guidelines and forms for a new Home Affordable Foreclosure Alternatives Program (HAFA) that attempts to streamline negotiations between borrowers and lenders by standardizing processes, documents, and timeframes, and by providing financial incentives to those who participate.

If you encounter difficulty negotiating with your lender, seek the assistance of an experienced professional such as a foreclosure counselor or real estate attorney who can negotiate on your behalf.

AVOIDING FORECLOSURE: WHEN A LENDER WILL NOT WORK WITH YOU

Excerpt from the U.S. Department of Housing and Urban Development

http://portal.hud.gov/portal/page/portal/HUD/topics/avoiding_fore-closure/workingwithlenders

You have done all your homework, explored workout options, talked to a housing counselor, and tried to talk to your lender. But the lender still will not work with you. What do you do now?

FOR AN FHA-INSURED LOAN

Your lender has to follow FHA servicing guidelines and regulations for FHA-insured loans. If your lender is not cooperative, contact FHA's National Servicing Center toll-free at (888) 297-8685, or via e-mail. Whether by phone or e-mail, be prepared to provide the full name(s) of all persons listed on the mortgage loan and the full address of the property including city, state, and ZIP. We may be able to help you more quickly if you can also provide your 13-digit FHA case number from the loan settlement statement.

FOR A VA-INSURED LOAN

First, visit the VA Foreclosure Alternatives page. If you need assistance or have additional questions, talk to a loan service representative.

FOR CONVENTIONAL LOANS

If you have a conventional loan, first talk to a HUD-approved housing counselor at (800) 569-4287. They may be able to help you with your lender. You can also contact HOPE NOW or call the Homeowners Hope Hotline at (888) 995-HOPE to ask for assistance in working with your lender.

Know Your Rights

Knowing your rights as a homeowner can make the difference between losing your home and avoiding foreclosure altogether.

Your rights as a homeowner vary with the state you live in and the agreement you signed to secure the promissory note or mortgage loan on your property. Find your copy of that document, or get a copy from the lender if you do not have it. The terms stipulated in that agreement are crucial to what you do next.

As a homeowner with a mortgage, you have two basic rights. One is the right to communicate with your lender or lien holder. No one can demand a sum of money from you and be unwilling to discuss or explain it. You may not get the resolution or sensitivity you desire, but you have the right to explain your situation and seek out information. Speaking with the lender or lien holder to make arrangements before the lender initiates legal proceedings should be a priority.

You also have the right to be notified in writing of any hearings or judgments brought against you. No matter where you live, you have a right to be made aware of all complaints in a timely manner so that you can respond. This protects your right to representation in the courtroom — whether alone or with legal counsel. If you have not been made aware of any part of the foreclosure process, you may be able to bring the foreclosure process to a halt.

Your rights in foreclosure

When someone tries to foreclose on your property, he or she is required by law to follow a specific process — regardless of whether it is a judicial or non-judicial foreclosure. Because your rights are determined by the state in which you live, you need to fully understand what your lender can and cannot do regarding your foreclosure.

Ask yourself the following questions to determine your rights in a lender-initiated foreclosure:

- **How many missed payments are required before foreclosure can begin?** Look in your deed of trust or mortgage agreement to find the acceleration clause. Has the lender observed this stipulation? Check your promissory note to be certain the lender is acting according to the agreed-upon terms and not accelerating before it has a right to. Is the lender required, for example, to wait until the third nonpayment before filing? If you have only missed two payments and the lender initiates foreclosure, then this is grounds to stop the process.

- **How much notice are they required to give me?** Some lenders will contact you with a letter or phone call after the first or second missed payment. Others will wait until the third or fourth missed payment before filing their complaint or notice of default. They may or may not be legally required to let you know they are considering foreclosure.

- **Have I received a beneficiary statement?** You have a right to receive a beneficiary statement in non-judicial foreclosures, but you will probably need to request it in writing from your lender. This set of documents will include all the information about the original loan and where it stands at the present time. Check this against the information you have and the steps taken to date for foreclosure. If the amount listed as outstanding is incorrect, for example, the foreclosure process can be halted.

- **Do I have a "right-to-cure?"** In most states, there is a period of time between the foreclosure judgment and the sale of the property during which you can pay the outstanding payments, plus fees, and halt the foreclosure. The state you live in determines whether this period exists, how long it lasts, and what is owed.

- **Do I have a right to sell before foreclosure?** Again, your state laws will decide whether you have a right to sell the property to satisfy the loan after the judgment has been made, but before the property goes to auction.

- **Do I have a right to forbearance or hardship relief?** Some provisions are made by the federal, state, and local governments for veterans, the elderly, and holders of government loans. You may also have the right to request a short-term forbearance due to illness or unemployment. Talk to your lender and reread your mortgage contract to find out if you are eligible for forbearance or hardship relief.

- **Is there a redemption period?** Whether you have the right to a redemption period — a set amount of time after the property has been sold at auction to purchase back the property with additional fees and possibly interest — depends on your state, as does the length of the period. In some states, it does not exist, while in others, it ranges from less than a month to as long as one year. Nonjudicial foreclosures typically do not have redemption periods.

- **Do I have a right to surplus funds?** If your property went to auction and the sale price was higher than the debt owed, you may be able to claim that money. The funds will go first to the lender and then to any secondary lien holders. If any funds are left over, you may have a right to them. Strict foreclosure states, like Connecticut, do not return money to the homeowner, regardless of sale price.

Foreclosure initiated by a secondary lien

A secondary lien is a loan, in addition to the first mortgage, that is secured by your house, such as a second mortgage, a home equity loan, an unpaid tax obligation, or a lien placed on your house by an unpaid contractor or workman. These loans can also result in foreclosure. Though different from a foreclosure initiated by a lender, secondary lien foreclosures follow the same judicial route as the original lender would follow. They may use language such as "real property foreclosure" or "tax deed sale" instead of judicial foreclosure, but the procedure is the same. If you are facing a secondary lien foreclosure, get answers to the following questions:

- **Does the lien holder need to give notice?** Some states do not require that notice be given to a homeowner when a party other than the lender attaches a lien. This means that liens can be levied against a property without a homeowner's knowing it. It also means debts owed by one of the parties of ownership may incur a lien without the other owner knowing about it.

- **Does the lien holder have a signed contract with the property owner?** This is important and requires careful attention to the law. In Texas, for example, an individual cannot place a lien on a property unless he or she has a signed contract between themselves and all owners of the property in question. This means that if you are married, then unless both spouse's signatures are on the document, they cannot place a lien.

- **Does the lien holder have legitimate cause for the foreclosure?** Find out the minimum amount of outstanding debt required for a lien holder to pursue foreclosure. Some states regulate this amount, though others do not.

- **Is the lien currently in dispute?** There have been many claims in recent years of unjustifiable liens. If you have not paid a debt because the services outlined in a contract were not or were poorly rendered, protect your property by securing a bond to ensure foreclosure cannot move forward. A bond is a financial instrument that takes the place of your house as security for the debt owed to the contractor. While you are contesting the debt, funds are held by a third party. If the dispute is decided in the contractor's favor, it will make a claim against the bond rather than foreclosing on your house.

- **If the lien is related to non-payment of taxes, have I exhausted all my options?** As with many government-subsidized loans, you may have the right to arrange alternative payment plans rather than have your property seized. Find out what payment plans are offered by the IRS and state and local tax agencies. Installment agreements allow you to pay delinquent taxes in smaller, more manageable increments. You can find information on federal tax payment plans on the IRS Web site (**www.irs.gov/businesses/ small/article/0,,id=108347,00.html**).

- **Do I have a right to counter-sue?** This is particularly relevant if the lien you are contesting has been placed by a subcontractor or supply company whose debt was to be paid through a contractor. While you cannot stop the subcontractor, for example, from placing a lien on your property — after all, they were technically hired to do a job for you — you may be able to file a lawsuit against the contractor who was supposed to settle those debts out of the funds you paid.

CHAPTER 4

Assessing Your Finances

If you are facing the threat of foreclosure, your finances are clearly not under control. You may be asking yourself, "How did I get into this situation?" Many circumstances can throw you into financial turmoil, but regardless of how you got into your present dilemma, you cannot find a way out without clearly understanding the source of your problem and assessing the resources available to you. Getting out of this foreclosure mess means figuring out what you can — and cannot — afford, what debts you owe, and what — if any — funds you have available for a bailout.

Some cases of missed or late payments may be due to a lack of organization or poor planning, but the primary reason for becoming delinquent on a mortgage is that your monthly income is not enough to pay for your monthly expenses. According to a study by the Federal Reserve Bank, 40 percent of American families regularly spend more than they earn. Before you begin reviewing your options, establish a realistic picture of your financial circumstances. How much money is coming into your household every month and how much is going out? How is your money being spent? Could you afford your mortgage by eliminating unnecessary expenditures? Are you in a difficult situation because of a one-time event such as a serious illness or a family crisis, or are you trapped in an escalating cycle of debt that you cannot pay off? Until now, you may have avoided a close examination of your situation, hoping that everything would somehow work out. It is time to be honest with yourself and pinpoint the real source of your financial problems.

If you have missed a payment because of an isolated circumstance, but are able to afford future payments, you can get back on track with your lender by arranging to make up the missed payments. If you conclude that your mortgage payments have become unmanageable and your financial circumstances are not likely to improve, start making plans and reviewing your options for refinancing, negotiating lower payments, or selling the property before it goes into foreclosure. Clarifying your financial situation will help you decide which options are best for you.

Recognize Trouble When it Starts

A household rarely becomes unable to make mortgage payments overnight. The descent into unsustainable debt typically happens in stages, with plenty of danger signals along the way. Problems begin when changes in your life reduce your income or increase your expenses. You lose your job and begin using your savings to pay your bills. Someone in your family becomes seriously ill and unable to work, reducing household income while medical bills start to come in. Children grow older and their education expenses become a financial burden. Your mortgage payments increase as interest rates suddenly rise. You notice that you are using your credit cards more often to pay for everyday items like groceries and gas. Bills are being paid late — or not at all. These are all signs that your financial life is unraveling. Eventually, this will affect your ability to pay your mortgage, putting your house at risk.

It may seem as though foreclosure sneaks up on you, but in reality, it happens in full view. If only you had noticed and taken steps to avoid it — or at least delay it — in the first place. Little changes can make a big difference over time, even when it comes to saving your home from foreclosure. In the vast majority of cases, little changes over time caused the trouble in the first place, and it is going to take many little changes to fix the mess.

Financial danger signals

Here is a checklist of significant warnings that foreclosure could be on the horizon:

- **Your income level has remained the same or decreased, but your credit card debt has increased.** This is a sign that your finances are overextended and that your income is not sufficient to meet your expenses. You are unable to pay more than the minimum balance on your credit cards. This is definitely a sign of financial overextension and will likely end up costing you much more money than you originally spent. Paying off only the minimum balance each month means you are adding hundreds of dollars in interest to your annual budget — money that could have gone toward paying off your mortgage.

- **You have begun borrowing against one credit card to pay another.** Consolidating debt onto a card with a low interest rate is an effective way of minimizing debt. Borrowing to make minimum payments, on the other hand, adds extra fees and charges onto the interest you are already paying.

- **There are five or six credit cards in your wallet.** In 2009, one in ten American consumers had more than ten credit cards in his or her wallet, and the average number of cards per consumer was four. Having more than two credit cards is unnecessary and only encourages overspending.

- **You are using a credit card to pay for everyday expenses such as groceries.** Many people use their credit cards to pay monthly household bills, but if these debts cannot be paid off fully at the end of the month, it could be a message that you are living beyond your means.

- **You have to work hard to make credit card payments.** Do you look for overtime hours or part-time work on top of your regular job to help pay household bills? This is another sign that you have overextended yourself and could be on the road to foreclosure.

- **There is no room left on your credit cards for emergencies — your credit cards have all been maxed out.** Points are deducted from your credit score when you use more than 50 percent of the credit limit on any type of credit card. Moreover, what will you do in an emergency?

- **You have no savings.** If you have been using savings to pay monthly household bills, or your income does not allow for savings, you could be in trouble. A healthy budget allows for a minimum monthly savings of around 10 percent. Every homeowner should have a savings account to cover unexpected costs, such as a leaky roof or a car repair.

- **In the last six months, at least one bill was paid late each cycle.** Are you deciding who should get paid each month instead of paying everyone you owe?

- **You are receiving this month's bills while last month's are still unopened.** Sometimes, trouble results from a lack of organization, rather than from financial hardship. Open every bill as it comes through the door. Know what you owe to whom so that you can arrange payments in a timely manner.

- **Creditors are calling.** Has the gas company called to request payment? Has the phone company turned off your telephone? Is your car subject to repossession? Do not ignore these warning signs. They can damage your credit just as badly as missing a loan payment.

- **You have received notice of foreclosure.** If your bank has sent letters, or you have been formally served with a notice of default, foreclosure is looming.

If even one of these warning signs applies to you, it is time to take action. There is a good possibility that other warning signs will soon appear.

Identify Your Income and Your Expenses

Before attempting to negotiate a settlement with your lender, you must identify your net income — the amount of money you take home after taxes, health and dental insurance, 401(k) contributions, and any other deductions are taken out by your employer. Add up the income contributed by all members of the household. Include income from self-employment, alimony and child support, insurance settlements, disability payments, investments, and social security.

Next, make a detailed list of your monthly expenses, including those of anyone living in your household. If your property taxes are not included in the mortgage, calculate how much you pay in taxes each month by dividing the annual amount by 12. Remember to include your homeowner's and automobile insurance, and homeowner's association or condominium fees, if applicable.

If you use a debit card to pay for most purchases, you can use your bank statements to calculate your expenses. Most banks now offer free money management applications on their Web sites that will automatically categorize your expenses using the names of the businesses where you made purchases and show you where your money is being spent.

Each month is different. Make sure to account in some way for months when you have extra expenses because of birthdays, Christmas, back-to-school, or summer camp for children. *Appendix D contains a worksheet that you can use to keep track of your income and expenses.* Below are important items that might belong on your list:

- Cable or satellite service (including specialty channels)
- Cell phone
- Children's tuition
- Church
- Club memberships
- Credit card payments
- Dining out
- Extracurricular activities
- Gas for your car
- Gifts
- Groceries

- Gym memberships
- Haircuts
- Health expenses (including insurance, co-pays, medication)
- Hobbies
- Holidays
- Landline house phone
- Laundry services
- Lawn care
- Mortgage payments
- Personal care items
- Recreation
- Residual divorce costs/fees
- School, supplies
- Student loans
- Utility bills (including gas, water, electric, sewage, garbage)
- Vacations
- Vehicle costs (including inspections, maintenance, licenses, parking fees, tolls, gas, insurance)

Are You Overextended?

Add up your list of monthly expenses and subtract that amount from your monthly income. How much, if any, is left over? Be realistic. Is your monthly income enough to make your mortgage payments and cover your monthly expenses? What percentage of your monthly income is going toward your mortgage payment? According to financial experts, housing costs, including insurance and taxes, should take up no more than 31 percent of your monthly income.

If your housing expenses are greater than that, your financial stability is in jeopardy. You may be able to manage the payments for a time, but you will sacrifice other areas of your life and might not be able to build up savings to carry you through emergencies or pay for a family vacation, a child's education, or your retirement. It might be in your best interest to sell your house.

If you are behind on mortgage payments because your monthly income is not sufficient for your expenses, and you want to keep your house, there are only two possible courses of action: increase your income or reduce your expenses.

Do you expect a raise in your salary in the near future? There might be something you can do on the side to earn extra money or someone in the household who can get a second job. Perhaps your income will increase when you receive an inheritance, an insurance settlement, or a pension.

Until late 2007, job prospects were optimistic, and mostly anyone with marketable skills and experience could hope to find a well-paid position within a few months. But in 2008, 2.6 million Americans lost their jobs. According to the U.S. Department of Labor, during the 24 months from December 2007 through November 2009, more than 5 million people filed for unemployment as a result of mass layoffs. In an effort to cut costs, many companies replaced employees in well-compensated management positions with younger, lower-paid workers.

Most of these people have little hope of finding another job with the same level of compensation and have been forced to accept lower salaries. If you are in this position, you may no longer be able to sustain high mortgage payments. Unemployment benefits provide only half of the recipient's previous income. Part-time jobs are scarce. Many families face a double blow: One or more members of their household have lost a job, while their houses have lost value because of a falling real estate market.

Help with your budget

Office supply stores sell home budget books and ledgers that help you record your spending and your target goals for each month. There are also many good books and workbooks that take you step-by-step through the process of creating a budget and offer helpful suggestions along the way.

Many banks now offer personal budget applications as part of their online banking systems, which automate many of the processes of tracking your expenses and incorporate guidelines and financial advice. Data can be imported directly from all your online accounts, including investment accounts, 401(k)s, and credit cards with other providers. Your spending patterns are illustrated on graphs and pie charts. Some programs track your spending and show how well you are conforming to your budget. They might even send you alerts when you are close to exceeding your targets. Personal finance software automatically categorizes many of your expenses by using the names of the businesses where you made purchases. You will still need to review the entries and break down purchases that include multiple categories.

Some personal budget software programs allow you to maintain your budget on your computer instead of on the Internet, or keep you up-to-date with the latest financial news. More than 60 budget applications are available for the iPhone.

YNAB

You Need a Budget (YNAB) at **www.youneedabudget.com** is an affordable personal finance software program incorporating a methodology of four simple rules to help you work toward living on your previous month's income and getting out of debt. It can be used in conjunction with a spreadsheet program or as a stand-alone Windows application. You can export information from your online accounts and then import it into YNAB so the information is housed on your computer and not online.

Mint.com

Mint.com (**www.mint.com**) is a free online budget management tool. It allows you to set up an anonymous account online and automatically imports data from your bank, credit card, home loan, and finance accounts, and it categorizes your expenses. The information is updated automatically through secure connections to 7,000 banks and financial institutions. Mint's budgeting tools show your average expenditure in each category and help you set goals and track your spending. You can view your balances using your iPhone and set up text message or e-mail messages to alert you when you exceed your budget. Mint.com is funded through targeted advertising; the site identifies credit card offers and other products appropriate for each user.

Quicken

Quicken offers a variety of money management products. Quicken Online (**http://quicken.intuit.com/online-banking-finances.jsp**) is a free money management tool that gathers information from all your online accounts and organizes it into an overview of your finances. It helps you set budget goals and tracks your spending to help you meet those goals.

TOOLSFORMONEY

ToolsforMoney.com (**www.toolsformoney.com/personal_budget_software.htm**) sells an inexpensive budgeting tool that utilizes Excel spreadsheets. It includes a financial planning tool that projects your family finances far into the future and shows how various circumstances, such as a disability or loss of income, might impact your finances.

Reduce Your Expenses

Review your list of expenses for items that are not necessities, such as dining out, cable TV, or club memberships. By eliminating unnecessary expenses, you may be able to come up with extra money for your monthly mortgage payment. If you have not used a budget to control your expenditures in the past, create a budget now and follow it. When you know where your money is going, it is easier to control your spending.

Write down a list of your debts with a detailed description of each. What is your mortgage payment? Look at your mortgage or deed of trust to see if you are paying a fixed or a variable interest rate. If it is variable, when does it change over, and what is the highest amount the lender can charge you? Use the mortgage calculators on the Interest.com Web site at **www.interest.com/content/calculators** for additional help. You need to have a solid sense of how much a monthly mortgage *potentially* can become. What are your monthly car payments and credit card payments, and when are they due?

Consider lifestyle changes that could reduce your expenses, such as sending your children to public rather than private school, or driving one car instead of two or three. Selling off a motorcycle or a second car can save you hundreds of dollars a year in insurance, gas, and maintenance. The adjustment may be painful at first, but it is may be necessary if you want to keep your house.

Try to reduce your existing bills. Shop around for cheaper auto and home insurance, and take advantage of any insurance discounts. You can lower your insurance premiums by raising your deductible — the amount you will be required to pay before the insurance takes over. Check to be sure that you are getting all available discounts on your auto insurance premiums, including multi-line discounts and "good student" discounts for young drivers. If you are driving an older car, consider removing collision damage from your policy; if your car is totaled in an accident, you will only be reimbursed for its current market value, which is likely to only be a few thousand dollars at most.

Pay down high-interest debt. If you are in financial turmoil, you probably have been using credit cards to manage your bills. Look at the interest rate on each card and the amount you are paying each month in "finance charges." If you can manage to pay down some of the balance, you will free up extra dollars for your monthly expenses.

Know What You Owe

Look at your loan agreement and determine exactly how much you owe each month. From the bank's point of view, an incomplete mortgage payment is just as bad as a missed payment. You could go into default by mistakenly paying the wrong amount one month. When you make a late payment, the next month's payment typically includes a late payment fee. If you do not include that extra amount in your next payment, your lender could treat it as a partial payment.

If you have an adjustable-rate mortgage (ARM), your monthly payments can vary from month to month as interest rates fluctuate. You could be paying the incorrect amount unless you know exactly what you owe. If your monthly payment is made by an automatic debit from your bank account, make sure the payment is adjusted to the amount due each month and is not a fixed payment.

What are You Worth?

Your net worth is the amount you hold in equity and savings. The equity in your home is equal to the amount you have already paid off on the mortgage, plus the down payment you made. Another way to calculate equity is to subtract the amount outstanding on the mortgage from the market price of your house. A homeowner who has only been making mortgage payments for a year or two does not have a large amount of equity; someone who has made payments for 20 years, while the value of the house was increasing, could have a substantial amount of equity.

Tip : Are you "upside down" or "underwater?"

In 2008, the U.S. housing bubble burst with a loud pop, and home prices began to plummet. People who had purchased homes from 2005 to 2007 suddenly found that their houses were now worth considerably less than the original purchase price. They owe more on their mortgages than the houses are worth. This is called negative equity, or being "upside down" or "underwater." When you are upside down, you do not have the option of selling your home to pay off the mortgage because there will still be an outstanding balance.

Total the value of all your assets, including cash, retirement accounts, college funds, investments, cars, boats, jewelry, antiques, musical instruments, equipment, and anything else of value, plus your equity in your home. Next, total your current debts and compare the two numbers. The difference between the amount of assets and amount of debt is your "net worth." Your net worth determines the strength of your position negotiating with your lender for mortgage refinance or a loan modification with a lower monthly payment. If your net worth is:

- **Negative:** The more your debt exceeds your assets, the less likely the possibility that you will be able to negotiate a new loan with your lender.

- **Positive:** You have some worth. The bank will expect you to cash in some of these assets in order to lower your mortgage balance before it will consider negotiating a new deal.

Check Your Credit Report

Before confronting your lender, obtain copies of your credit report and check them over for any mistakes. You can obtain a free copy of your credit report once a year from any of the following reporting agencies:

- Equifax: 800-685-1111 (**www.equifax.com**)
- Experian: 888-397-3742 (**www.experian.com**)
- TransUnion: 800-916-8800 (**www.transunion.com**)

Look over your credit report for discrepancies or late payments you can have corrected or removed. Dispute any erroneous credit card claims, and clear up problems right away. Your credit rating has suffered enough without being lowered because of inaccurate information.

Get Through the Crisis

You have reviewed your income, monthly expenses, and debts, and you have determined that you can maintain regular monthly mortgage payments and stay in your house, especially if you are able to negotiate a lower monthly payment. In order to get back on track, you still need to tackle a major obstacle — the missed payments, penalties, and fees that initiated that first foreclosure notice. You will need to find the money for those delinquent payments by selling something of value, cashing out a retirement account, or borrowing from someone. It is not easy to ask your friends and family for help, especially if you must acknowledge that you have made mistakes, but it may be necessary in order to save your home from foreclosure.

Though it should be a last resort, borrowing money from a family member or friend for a short time might be the most practical way to keep your home out of foreclosure. When you borrow money from a friend or relative, create a written agreement listing the interest rate at which you will pay back any money borrowed and a timeline for repaying the loan. This will serve as an assurance that you intend to pay the loan back and are not simply taking advantage of your relationship.

> $\mathcal{T}\!\!\!\!/p$: Keep property taxes and property insurance up-to-date.

In the midst of a financial crisis, you may be tempted to defer some expenses with every intention of paying them later on. But do not defer payment of property taxes or property insurance. The tax collector can put a tax lien on your property, meaning that an investor takes over your tax payments for a period of time, with an option to take possession of your house in the future if you do not pay. The obligation to insure your home against damage is probably a clause in your mortgage agreement, and failing to do so could jeopardize negotiations with your lender. Home insurance exists for a reason. If your home is destroyed in a fire and you do not have insurance, you will be left to pay off a mortgage on an empty lot.

Credit Counselors

A credit counselor is a professional who evaluates your expenses and income and then helps you establish a new spending plan and negotiate with credit card companies and other lenders for lower payments. If you discover during your financial evaluation that your debt is outstripping your ability to pay it off, your next step should be a consultation with a credit counselor.

Talk to a housing counselor

Excerpt from the U.S. Department of Housing and Urban Development
http://portal.hud.gov/portal/page/portal/HUD/i_want_to/talk_to_a_ housing_counselor

Want advice on buying a home, renting, default, foreclosure avoidance, credit issues, or reverse mortgages? HUD sponsors housing counseling agencies throughout the country to provide free or low-cost advice. Search online for a housing counseling agency near you (**www.hud.gov/offices/hsg/sfh/hcc/ hcs.cfm**), or call HUD's interactive voice system at (800) 569-4287. If you are facing foreclosure and want the assistance of a housing counselor, search the list of Foreclosure Avoidance Counselors (**www.hud.gov/offices/hsg/ sfh/hcc/fc/**) or visit the Making Home Affordable program Q&A for Borrowers (**www.financialstability.gov/docs/borrower_qa.pdf**).

CONSUMER FEES FOR HOUSING COUNSELING

Foreclosure prevention counseling and homeless counseling services are available free of charge through HUD's Housing Counseling Program. Housing Counseling agencies participating in HUD's Housing Counseling Program are not permitted to charge consumers for these specific housing counseling services. Counseling recipients should not pay for these services. However, housing counseling agencies are permitted to charge reasonable and customary fees for other forms of housing counseling and education services, including pre-purchase, reverse mortgage, rental, and non-delinquency post-purchase counseling services, provided certain conditions are met:

- Agencies must provide counseling without charge to persons who demonstrate they cannot afford the fees.

- Agencies must inform clients of the fee structure in advance of providing services.

- Fees must be commensurate with the level of services provided.

- You should contact your local HUD office if you encounter housing counseling agencies that you believe are not complying with these requirements.

You should contact your local HUD office (**http://portal.hud.gov/portal/ page/portal/HUD/localoffices**) if you encounter housing counseling agencies that you believe are not complying with these requirements.

Protect yourself

When you have established a plan for managing your finances so that you can keep your house, create a back-up plan to keep yourself on track if something goes wrong. Create an action plan for eventualities such as a job loss, an illness, or a sudden increase in your monthly ARM payments.

Begin putting money aside in a savings account for an emergency fund, even if it is only a small amount. Identify a friend or family member who would be willing to loan you money in a crisis. Consider purchasing a term life insurance policy that would allow your family to continue making mortgage payments if something happens to you.

CHAPTER 5

Reviewing Your Options

After evaluating your finances, determining the causes of your current financial crisis, and establishing a realistic picture of your current and future financial status, you are ready to decide on a course of action for avoiding foreclosure. Avoiding foreclosure does not necessarily mean staying in your home; it means avoiding an expensive and stressful legal process in which your lender repossesses and sells your home at auction, and not having a foreclosure listed on your credit report for the next seven years. If you can continue to make monthly mortgage payments and you want to stay in your home, avoiding foreclosure means negotiating affordable payments and paying off fees and delinquent amounts. If you cannot afford to continue paying for your home, avoiding foreclosure means finding another way out of your mortgage, such as selling your home or forming a voluntary transfer of ownership to your lender.

Your first foreclosure notice is only the beginning of a long process that could lead to several outcomes. Your situation is unique, and the choices you make depend on many variables:

- Are you behind on your mortgage payments because of a one-time crisis — such as a temporary job loss — that is not likely to be repeated, or because your circumstances have changed permanently?

- Do you have other financial resources, such as investments or an IRA?

- Is your mortgage payment more than 50 percent of your monthly income?

- How long have you had this mortgage? How much equity do you have in your home?

- What other debt obligations, such as credit card debt, student loans, or car payments, do you have?

- Can you borrow money from friends or family and pay it back later?

- How much does this home mean to your family? What sacrifices are they willing to make to continue living there?

This is an emotional time, and you are under a great deal of stress, but the decisions you must make are business decisions. It is important to stand back from your emotions and think clearly and rationally. The choices you make now will affect your family's future. This chapter reviews many of the options available when you are faced with foreclosure.

Halt the Process Before it Starts

The fastest way to halt a foreclosure is to pay your outstanding payments and any fees or penalties before you receive a foreclosure notice or during the reinstatement period. It is not easy to find the money to do this when you are already having financial difficulties, but if you are confident that you can continue to make your mortgage payments after the crisis is resolved, it is a good solution.

Aside from borrowing funds from family or friends, there are other ways to find money to make up the missing payments.

School loan forbearance

If part of your financial crisis involves college loan payments, speak with the lender to request either a deferment or forbearance, and explain the reason for your difficulty. You can defer payment of student loans if you go back to school or serve in the military. Most lenders will grant you forbearance — the suspension of loan payments for a specified number of months — during a period of unemployment or economic hardship. Interest continues to accrue on your loan during this period and could result in your ultimately paying more for your loan, but by eliminating a student loan payment from your monthly expenses for a period of time, you could gather the funds necessary to catch up on back payments.

State mortgage assistance programs

During 2008, several states initiated programs that give loans or grants to eligible homeowners who risk foreclosure because of temporary financial problems. Check to see if your state has a program that could help in your particular case. *Appendix C has a list of state government Web sites where you can look for information on foreclosure assistance programs.*

If your home is in Pennsylvania, you may qualify for the Homeowner's Emergency Mortgage Assistance Program (HEMAP). This program is not a grant of funds, but a loan that must be paid back. HEMAP offers continuing and non-continuing loan assistance, depending on the financial situation of the borrower. It is important to note, though, that FHA Title II loans are not eligible for this program. Participating counseling agencies can be found at **www.phfa.org/consumers/homeowners/hemap.aspx.**

New Jersey's Mortgage Assistance Pilot (MAP) program (**www.state.nj.us/dca/hmfa/consu/owners/map**) provides temporary financial assistance to income-eligible homeowners who wish to remain in their homes but are in imminent danger of foreclosure due to short-term financial problems beyond their control.

Liquidate nonessential assets

Can you sell something that you own to come up with the money for the delinquent payments? What are you willing to sacrifice in order to save your home? It may seem radical, but sometimes it is the fastest way — short of borrowing from others — to come up with the money needed to stop the foreclosure. If you have a car, valuable jewelry, or expensive electronics that could bring in a large sum, sell them. These items can always be replaced.

Reinstatement

Reinstatement is simply the term lenders use for making your delinquent account current once again. If you are expecting some sort of income, such as a large bonus, retirement payoff, or inheritance that can be used to bring your account up-to-date, reinstatement may be an option. Some lenders will hold off foreclosure if you can prove that you can pay all those missed payments, penalties, and interest by a certain date. Total reinstatement means paying the full outstanding amount in a single payment with a certified check.

Tip : **To reinstate, you must pay fees as well as the outstanding loan payments.**

You must pay late fees, penalties, and legal costs in addition to outstanding loan payments in order to reinstate your loan. If you pay only the outstanding monthly payments, or if you fail to pay even a few cents of the costs and penalties, your lender may continue the foreclosure process. Call your lender or the foreclosing attorney to ask for "reinstatement figures" — the exact amount necessary to reinstate the mortgage.

Reinstatement timelines vary by state. Most states require lenders to offer reinstatement before initiating foreclosure and at various periods during the process. This is the most common method of preventing foreclosure and the most popular with lenders because they get all their money. Contact your lender to ask how to reinstate your loan.

Homeowners with an FHA mortgage who are four to 12 months behind on their payments can apply for a partial claim, an interest-free loan available through HUD that provides funds to reinstate a mortgage.

Tip : **Be sure you can afford reinstatement.**

Reinstatement is the most expensive way to keep your home. You must pay fees and costs in addition to the outstanding loan payments. If you have to borrow money from somewhere else to reinstate your loan, you are taking on an additional debt burden and will be paying interest on that loan too. Reinstatement allows you to keep your home for the time being, but if you really cannot afford the mortgage, you will ultimately face foreclosure again.

Commercial Mortgage Assistance Programs

Many commercial mortgage assistance programs offer to help you evaluate your finances, negotiate with your lender, and reach an equitable solution to your problem, for a fee or commission. These programs are businesses that make a profit from assisting homeowners faced with foreclosure. Under normal circumstances, you should be able to negotiate with your bank yourself. If you are having difficulty getting your bank to agree to a repayment plan, or the bank's terms seem unreasonable, a professional foreclosure negotiator might be helpful.

Tip : **Watch out for foreclosure assistance scams.**

- Be wary of any company that offers to take over your mortgage during the pre-foreclosure period.
- Even when you are dealing with a reputable mortgage assistance program, make sure they do not ask for more than you are willing to pay.
- Be wary of anyone who tells you not to speak to your lender or its attorneys. There is no legitimate reason to avoid these individuals; often, regular communication with the lender and its attorneys can bring a satisfactory resolution.

- Always consult your own lawyer before committing to an assistance program, particularly if you have been asked to sign a quitclaim deed, which involves signing away the ownership of your home to another party.

- You should never have to rent your house from a program in return for their assistance, or pay exorbitant fees.

- Never make mortgage payments to anyone other than your lender — even if they promise to pass the funds along.

- If you are already in the foreclosure process, no amount of money other than the full amount of payments plus fees will stop the foreclosure. Partial payments will not be accepted toward making good on the debt, so do not send anything but the full amount requested.

- Report suspicious activity to relevant federal agencies, such as the Federal Trade Commission, and to your state and local consumer protection agencies. Reporting con artists and suspicious schemes helps prevent others from becoming victims. If you cannot resolve your problem directly with your bank, contact the Office of the Comptroller of the Currency (OCC) Customer Assistance Group by calling (800) 613-6743, by e-mailing customer. assistance@occ.treas.gov, or by visiting **www.helpwithmybank.gov.**

Consult the Better Business Bureau (BBB) in your county or state to find out the reputation of any agency that contacts you or that you are considering using. Assistance programs can be a solution, but an unscrupulous company can embroil you in unexpected charges and legal difficulties. Be careful about what compensation you give in return for assistance by any program. Never sign over your property with a quitclaim deed or other document, even if the program promises to pay you money. You should never have to rent your house from a program in return for their assistance, or pay exorbitant fees. Get references and check with the BBB and an attorney before agreeing to anything.

Foreclosure rescue scams

Excerpt from "Money Matters," an educational Web site of the Federal Trade Commission

www.ftc.gov/bcp/edu/microsites/moneymatters/your-home-foreclosure-rescue-scams.shtml

The possibility of losing your home to foreclosure can be terrifying. The reality that scam artists are preying on the vulnerability of desperate homeowners is equally frightening. Many so-called foreclosure rescue companies or foreclosure assistance firms claim they can help you save your home. Some are brazen enough to offer a money-back guarantee. Unfortunately, once most of these foreclosure fraudsters take your money, you lose your home, too.

You can save yourself money and heartache by avoiding any business that:

- Guarantees to stop the foreclosure process — no matter what your circumstances

- Advises you not to contact your lender, lawyer, or credit or housing counselor

- Collects a fee before providing any services

- Accepts payment only by cashier's check or wire transfer

- Encourages you to lease your home so you can buy it back over time

- Tells you to make your mortgage payments directly to it, rather than to your lender

- Advises you to transfer your property deed or title to it

- Offers to buy your house for cash at a fixed price that is not set by the housing market at the time of sale

- Offers to fill out paperwork for you

- Pressures you to sign papers you have not had a chance to read thoroughly or that you do not understand

To do:

- Contact your lender or servicer immediately if you are having trouble paying your mortgage or have received a foreclosure notice. You may be able to negotiate a new repayment schedule. Lenders generally do not want to foreclose; it costs them money.

- Contact a credit counselor through the Homeownership Preservation Foundation (HPF), a nonprofit organization that operates a national 24/7 toll-free hotline (1.888.995.HOPE) with free, bilingual, personalized assistance to help homeowners avoid foreclosure. HPF is a member of the HOPE NOW Alliance of mortgage servicers, mortgage market participants, and counselors. More information about HOPE NOW is available at **www.995hope.org**.

Refinance

Refinancing your home can be a viable option if you are having trouble paying because of interest rate changes. Refinancing involves obtaining a new mortgage with affordable monthly payments and using it to pay off the old mortgage. Not all homes or borrowers will be eligible for refinancing. During 2009, many lenders tightened their credit requirements, making it more difficult for applicants to qualify for refinancing. If you live in an area where property values have declined significantly over the last few years, your equity will have decreased, and you may not be able to borrow enough to pay off the old mortgage. You may be denied a new loan because:

- The payment is too high.
- Your home is no longer worth enough to cover the new loan.
- Your credit rating has suffered.
- You do not have the funds available to cover the associated fees and closing costs.

Most refinancing options require you to own more then 20 percent of the equity in your home, but the Homeowner Affordability and Stability Plan introduced by the federal government in 2009 is intended to help homeowners who otherwise would not qualify for refinancing obtain a more favorable 30- or 15-year mortgage with a fixed interest rate. Homeowners whose homes are now worth less than they owe on them will be eligible for these loans if the new mortgage (including any refinancing costs) will not exceed 105 percent of the current market value of the property. This plan is available to homeowners whose mortgages are financed by Freddie Mac or Fannie Mae.

To refinance, you can apply for a new mortgage from your existing lender or from another bank or lender. Refinancing can incur closing fees and other costs of between 3 and 6 percent of the loan principal. The rule of thumb in the past was that refinancing is worthwhile if you can lower your interest rate by 2 percent, but even a decrease of 1 percent can significantly lower your monthly payment.

If you believe refinancing is the best option for you, it is best to begin applying before you miss any monthly payments. Missed payments lower your credit score, and that will make it more difficult for you to qualify.

Sell or Offer a "Deed in Lieu"

Is the house you are trying to save truly the best one for you and your situation? If not, consider selling it before the foreclosure process begins. You can move to more affordable housing, avoid the negative effect on your credit score, and maybe even come out ahead financially. However, during 2008 and 2009, the supply of houses greatly exceeded the demand, and unless your home is in a very desirable area, you might not be able to sell it quickly enough to avoid foreclosure. After your lender initiates foreclosure proceedings, you will have only a few weeks or months in which to sell your home, so if you anticipate having to sell, it is best to put your house on the market as soon as possible.

If you have decided that it is not in your best interests to keep the property, but you do not want it to be foreclosed on and you cannot sell your home in a timely manner, a deed in lieu (DIL) is also an option. The DIL transfers the ownership of the property to the lender without going to court or auction — and avoids foreclosure being listed on your credit report. The Home Affordable Foreclosure Alternatives Program (HAFA), part of the Making Home Affordable initiative, is intended to facilitate deeds in lieu. A lender who accepts a deed in lieu can avoid the costly court proceedings associated with foreclosure by directly taking over ownership of the home. *See Chapter 10 for more information on utilizing DILs to avoid foreclosure.*

Declare Bankruptcy

Bankruptcy, a legal appeal to have your debts discharged because you cannot pay them, may be a blow to the ego, but it might save your home and leave you more financially stable than foreclosure. Four different types of bankruptcy are available, depending on your situation, and each of them provides different options. Once it has become apparent that you will lose your home, filing Chapter 13 bankruptcy will legally halt the foreclosure process until the court can establish a new repayment schedule for your mortgage and other debt. *See Chapter 7 for more information on filing for bankruptcy.*

Options for Those in Military Service

If you are a veteran or serving in the military, the Service Members Civil Relief Act, previously known as The Soldiers' and Sailors' Civil Relief Act of 1940, contains measures that can enable you to stop the foreclosure process and keep you in your home. The Act limits the interest that can be charged on mortgages incurred by a service member (including debts incurred jointly with a spouse) before he or she entered into active military service to 6 percent during periods of active military service, and monthly payments must be recalculated to reflect the lower rate. To get the interest rate reduction, you must submit a written request to your lender, accompanied by a copy of your orders, no later than 180 days after you are released from active duty. Many lenders allow service members to suspend payments on the loan principal while they are on active duty, though they are not required to do this.

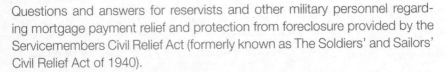

Details of relief available to military personnel

Questions and answers for reservists and other military personnel regarding mortgage payment relief and protection from foreclosure provided by the Servicemembers Civil Relief Act (formerly known as The Soldiers' and Sailors' Civil Relief Act of 1940).

Excerpt from the U.S. Department of Housing and Urban Development

www.hud.gov/offices/hsg/sfh/nsc/qasscra1.cfm

WHO IS ELIGIBLE?

The provisions of the act apply to active duty military personnel who had a mortgage obligation prior to enlistment or prior to being ordered to active duty. This includes members of the Army, Navy, Marine Corps, Air Force, and Coast Guard; commissioned officers of the Public Health Service and the

National Oceanic and Atmospheric Administration who are engaged in active service; reservists ordered to report for military service; persons ordered to report for induction under the Military Selective Service Act; and guardsmen called to active service for more than 30 consecutive days. In limited situations, dependents of servicemembers are also entitled to protections.

AM I ENTITLED TO DEBT PAYMENT RELIEF?

The act limits the interest that may be charged on mortgages incurred by a service member (including debts incurred jointly with a spouse) before he or she entered into active military service. Mortgage lenders must, at your request, reduce the interest rate to no more than 6 percent per year during the period of active military service and recalculate your payments to reflect the lower rate. This provision applies to both conventional and government-insured mortgages.

IS THE INTEREST RATE LIMITATION AUTOMATIC?

No. To request this temporary interest rate reduction, you must submit a written request to your mortgage lender and include a copy of your military orders. The request may be submitted as soon as the orders are issued but must be provided to a mortgage lender no later than 180 days after the date of your release from active duty military service.

AM I ELIGIBLE EVEN IF I CAN AFFORD TO PAY MY MORTGAGE AT A HIGHER INTEREST RATE?

If a mortgage lender believes that military service has not affected your ability to repay your mortgage, they have the right to ask a court to grant relief from the interest rate reduction. This is not very common.

WHAT IF I CANNOT AFFORD TO PAY MY MORTGAGE EVEN AT THE LOWER RATE?

Your mortgage lender may allow you to stop paying the principal amount due on your loan during the period of active duty service. Lenders are not required to do this, but they generally try to work with service members to keep them in their homes. You will still owe this amount but will not have to repay it until after your complete your active duty service.

Additionally, most lenders have other programs to assist borrowers who cannot make their mortgage payments. If you or your spouse find yourself in this position at any time before or after active duty service, contact your lender immediately and ask about loss mitigation options. Borrowers with FHA-insured loans who are having difficulty making mortgage payments may also be eligible for special forbearance and other loss mitigation options. More information about help for homeowners who are unable to make payments on a mortgage is available on the HUD Web site at **www.hud.gov/foreclosure/index.cfm**.

AM I PROTECTED AGAINST FORECLOSURE?

Mortgage lenders may not foreclose, or seize property for a failure to pay a mortgage debt, while a service member is on active duty or within 90 days after the period of military service unless they have the approval of a court. In a court proceeding, the lender would be required to show that the service member's ability to repay the debt was not affected by his or her military service.

WHAT INFORMATION DO I NEED TO PROVIDE TO MY LENDER?

When you or your representative contact your mortgage lender, you should provide the following information:

- Notice that you have been called to active duty
- A copy of the orders from the military notifying you of your activation
- Your FHA case number
- Evidence that the debt precedes your activation date

HUD has reminded FHA lenders of their obligation to follow the act. If notified that a borrower is on active military duty, the lender must advise the borrower or representative of the adjusted amount due, provide adjusted coupons or billings, and ensure that the adjusted payments are not returned as insufficient payments.

Will my payments change later? Will I need to pay back the interest rate "subsidy" at a later date?

The change in interest rate is not a subsidy. Interest in excess of 6 percent per year that would otherwise have been charged is forgiven. However, the reduction in the interest rate and monthly payment amount only applies during the period of active duty. Once the period of active military service ends, the interest rate will revert back to the original interest rate, and the payment will be recalculated accordingly.

How long does the benefit last? Does the period begin and end with my tour of duty?

Interest rate reductions are only for the period of active military service. Other benefits, such as postponement of monthly principal payments on the loan and restrictions on foreclosure may begin immediately upon assignment to active military service and end on the third month following the term of active duty assignment.

How can I learn more about relief available to personnel?

Read more information about the Servicemembers Civil Relief Act, sponsored by the Legal Assistance Policy Division, Office of The Judge Advocate General, U.S. Army.

Servicemembers who have questions about the SCRA or the protections that they may be entitled to may contact their unit judge advocate or installation legal assistance officer. Dependents of servicemembers can also contact or visit local military legal assistance offices where they reside. A military legal assistance office locator for each branch of the armed forces is available at **http://legalassistance.law.af.mil/content/locator.php**.

File a Lawsuit to Enjoin

A lawsuit to enjoin is a legal proceeding to obtain a court order requiring the lender to halt foreclosure. You must file a petition with the court, serve it on your lender, wait for a written response, then attend a court hearing in which you present your argument for why the foreclosure should be stopped. If your lender is pursuing a non-judicial foreclosure, you may be able to halt the process based on errors made by the trustee or lender. These errors often involve administrative acts, such as the filing of paperwork and giving of notice. *You can learn more about possible errors in Chapter 8.*

Forbearance

A special forbearance (SFB) is a written repayment agreement between a mortgagee and mortgagor, which contains a plan to reinstate an asset that is minimum three mortgage payments due and unpaid. You can request this type of payment plan from your lender's Loss Mitigation Department or Mortgage Forbearance Agreement Department. There is no limit on the number of months allowed for paying back the delinquent amount, but that amount can never exceed the equivalent of 12 monthly payments.

Special mortgage forbearance agreements are designed for borrowers experiencing a temporary financial hardship due to unexpected circumstances such as an illness or sudden job loss. If you qualify, you may be allowed to postpone mortgage payments for four months. Most lenders will require that the deferred amount be paid back later in one large sum, extend the loan to accommodate an easier payoff, or require the deferred amount to be paid back in increments over a six- to 24-month period, similar to a repayment plan. Interest will continue to accrue on the loan during the forbearance period, adding to the time it will take to pay off the mortgage.

Forbearance is only an option when the homeowner is in excellent credit standing with the lender, has asked for help before any payments are missed, and can prove that the financial difficulties are temporary.

Repayment Plans

If you can prove you are now able to repay what you owe, your lender may be willing to set up a repayment plan in which you make your regular monthly payment plus a partial repayment of the past due amount over a period of several months until the entire delinquent balance is paid in full. These plans do not permanently halt foreclosure until the overdue amount has been paid off. If you fail to complete the repayment plan, the lender will go ahead with foreclosure.

Contact your lender's loss mitigation department to negotiate a repayment plan. You will need to produce evidence that you will be able to make the payments. Lenders are likely to be willing to consider a repayment plan because they will not lose any money.

Loan Modification

The amount of a monthly loan payment can be reduced through loan modification — the renegotiation of the terms of a loan to lower the interest rate or extend the payment period. Most homeowners also ask for some sort of forgiveness on accruing penalties and interest. In rare cases, a portion of the loan's original principle amount may also be forgiven in order to make the new payment manageable. It is best to seek loan modifications before you start missing mortgage payments.

Loan modification is now regarded as the most practical way out of the current foreclosure crisis, and both federal and state governments offer incentives to lenders that modify loans for qualified borrowers. Look at your state and local government Web sites for information on loan modification programs or visit MakingHomeAffordable.gov (**www.makinghomeaffordable.gov**). Many banks post information about their loan modification programs on their Web sites. Almost 75 percent of U.S. home loans are eligible for the Making Home Affordable program, which reduces loan payments to 31 percent of a homeowner's monthly income.

Assumption

Instead of selling your home outright, you might be able to find someone to assume, or take over, your mortgage. Your deed of trust, or mortgage, will state whether mortgage assumption is an option. Many lenders do not allow it, but if it is permitted, assumption could be an excellent alternative to foreclosure. Mortgage assumption involves selling your home to a buyer who takes over the payment of your mortgage. Together, you and the buyer agree to a purchase price, as with a traditional offer. The buyer compensates you directly for the amount of equity you hold — the difference between the original purchase price or the current market value of the home and the amount outstanding on your mortgage — and then simply takes over the loan payments on the original terms agreed to by you and your lender.

Assumption is a good option for buyers who may not want or be able to arrange a mortgage of their own, especially if the terms of your mortgage are better than what is available in the current market. Loans through the FHA and VA are assumable, provided the buyer qualifies with the lender. Other mortgages may only be assumable if the interest rate is renegotiated.

Even if the interest rate has to be renegotiated, a buyer can benefit by assuming a mortgage because the amortization period does not renew. If you have paid 13 years on a 30-year mortgage, the buyer assuming your mortgage will have 17 years to pay the loan back, rather than starting a new 15-, 25-, or 30-year term.

Many lenders have no-assumption provisions in mortgage agreements because the lender is the only one who does not directly benefit from the arrangement. A new borrower takes over the old loan, with all its provisions, and the old borrower walks away having recovered his or her equity in the property.

Tip : You will have to pay capital gains tax on the down payment you receive when a buyer assumes your mortgage.

The payment you receive from the buyer who assumes your mortgage is subject to capital gains tax on the portion that represents a profit over the original price for which you bought the house. Consult a tax advisor for help calculating the taxable portion and for advice on possible exceptions to the tax.

Short Sale

In today's depressed real estate market, an increasing number of lenders are agreeing to a short sale — the sale of a home for less than the loan amount — in order to avoid the high cost of foreclosing. Short sales are especially popular in areas where property values have plummeted and sales are sparse. Short sales are also known as "pre-foreclosure sales" because they take place before the lender forecloses on the house and allow both the lender and the borrower to avoid lengthy and costly legal proceedings. A short sale requires the consent of the lender. The lender might agree to accept the sale price as payment in full of the debt, or it might seek to make the borrower liable for the difference between the sale price and the amount owed (known as the "deficiency"). Some states require the lender to accept a short sale as payment in full.

If you carry private mortgage insurance (PMI), your lender will probably agree to a short sale because it can recoup that lost revenue through the mortgage insurance. *For more information on short sales, see Chapter 9.*

Tip : **A short sale has a negative effect on your credit report.**

Though you have officially "paid off" your mortgage, a short sale listed on your credit report can affect your credit score negatively for at least seven years.

FHA-/VA-Backed Loans

When you take out a loan backed by the FHA or VA, the federal government guarantees that the lender will be paid in full, even if you become delinquent in your payments. This payment guarantee gives the homeowner additional safeguards in response to possible foreclosure.

To find out what type of help the FHA can give you, call the FHA National Servicing Center at 1-888-297-8685 and ask to be assigned a loss mitigator. He or she will help you evaluate your financial situation, determine the best course of action, and negotiate new terms with your lender. Keep in mind that to qualify for any special options offered by FHA, you must request mitigation within six months of becoming delinquent, and the process must be complete before the thirteenth late payment is due. Exceptions to this rule apply if:

- The loan is reinstated.
- You agree to special forbearance.
- The loan is modified.
- The loan is reinstated by a partial claim.
- You sell your property.
- You deed your property back to FHA.
- The lender has already initiated foreclosure.

FHA and VA loans may also qualify for the following solutions:

Partial claim

A partial claim is a special interest-free loan given by HUD in the amount of the delinquent payments, interest, and fees so that your loan can be reinstated. It is a one-time-only loan that requires a lien be placed on your property until the monies are paid back. A partial claim can halt foreclosure when you are confident that you will be able to make your future mortgage payments. To qualify for a partial claim, you must:

- Demonstrate your ability to repay the loan and make normal payments over the term of the mortgage.

- Show that you are unable to qualify for a forbearance agreement or workout plan.

- Prove that the financial hardship that caused you to become delinquent is over.

- Continue to live in the property and keep it in good condition.

- Have missed payments for at least four months, but not more than 12 months.

If you think you qualify for a partial claim (see **www.hud.gov/offices/hsg/sfh/nsc/rep/pcfact.pdf**), contact your lender immediately. If your lender is uncooperative, you may need to seek professional assistance to apply for a partial claim. Some lenders automatically dismiss such requests because they are unfamiliar with the program.

Non-retention options

Although non-retention options — such as selling your home and transferring the deed back to the lender or FHA — are not designed to keep you in your home, they can be used as a way to transition you into more affordable housing and may help get you into government sponsored, low-income housing when necessary. Information on non-retention options is available on the HUD Web site at **http://portal.hud.gov/portal/page/portal/HUD/topics/avoiding_foreclosure.**

Disaster-area relief

If you face foreclosure because of a natural disaster, you may qualify for special mortgage relief, including:

- The suspension of payments for one to six months.

- A reduction in payments for up to two years.

- A longer payback period — essentially an extension of your loan terms.

- Having any late fees waived for a set period of time.

- Having negative credit reporting waived immediately following a disaster.

Those carrying FHA mortgages automatically qualify for a 90-day foreclosure moratorium, or freeze, following a natural disaster if:

- They live within a presidential-declared disaster area, in which case they are automatically granted a 90-day foreclosure moratorium without even requesting it.

- Someone in their household was killed, missing, or injured due to the disaster.

- Their financial ability to pay their mortgage was affected by the disaster.

Contact your lender to discuss your situation and determine whether you are eligible for disaster relief. More information on disaster relief is available on the HUD Web site (**www.hud.gov/offices/hsg/sfh/nsc/qaho0121.cfm**).

Strategic Default

At the beginning of 2010, one in four U.S. homeowners, or almost 11 million people, owed more on their mortgages than their homes were worth. In some areas, including Florida, Nevada, Michigan, California, and Arizona, more than 40 percent of homeowners were "underwater." In Nevada, the number was 63 percent. Economists calculate that it will be 60 years before the market value of some homes will again equal what they sold for in 2005 to 2007. Even if you can afford your monthly mortgage payment, it might be a sound financial decision to let the bank take your house if the balance you owe is far greater than the market value of your home. The rental market is flooded with affordable housing. Why continue to shoulder a heavy financial burden when you can rent a house for less and have money left over for living expenses and retirement savings?

Defaulting on your loan will seriously damage your credit score for the next seven years, but if it frees up more cash for your living expenses, you might not need to use credit. You can find a calculator to compare the financial consequences of renting with maintaining mortgage payments at YouWalkAway.com (**www.youwalkaway.com/output24/Interective-FlashCalculator.html**).

Strategic default: A "moral dilemma"

In 2009, national credit bureau Experian and consulting company Oliver Wyman analyzed a sample of 24 million individual credit files in an attempt to better understand the behavior of homeowners who suddenly default on their mortgages without exhibiting other signs of financial difficulty, such as late payment or nonpayment of credit card debt. They identified a "strategic defaulter" as someone who deliberately stops making mortgage payments even though he or she can afford them. They counted 588,000 strategic defaulters in 2008 — more than double the 2007 number. The study found that the relative numbers of strategic defaults were highest in areas where home prices had soared and then crashed, like California and Florida. Two-thirds of strategic defaulters had only one mortgage and were abandoning a home that they lived in. People with high mortgage balances were more likely to be in this category than people with low balances, and borrowers with the highest credit scores were far more likely to deliberately default than those with low credit scores. Experian and Oliver Wyman interpreted these statistics to mean that strategic defaulters are treating the default as a business decision — why keep paying off a $500,000 mortgage when the house is only worth $250,000? They also concluded that strategic defaulters are financially sophisticated and are fully aware that they are seriously damaging their credit ratings when they default.

Other experts argue that the number of strategic defaulters in the study — 588,000 in 2008 — is exaggerated. Experian and Oliver Wyman followed a time-honored assumption that consumers pay their mortgages first and use remaining funds to pay other debt, such as credit card bills. If a consumer suddenly stops paying his or her mortgage but the other payments are up-to-date, the study assumes that he or she can afford to pay the mortgage but is deliberately choosing not to. In fact, many consumers faced with unmanageable debt stop paying their mortgages, even at the risk of foreclosure, so they can use that money for other obligations, such as car insurance and credit card payments.

Critics claim that lenders are trying to shift the blame for the high foreclosure rate to borrowers by making it appear as though large numbers of defaults are deliberate and by accusing consumers of irresponsibly borrowing more than they can afford.

Advocates of strategic default argue that a mortgage is a business contract in which the lender retained the right to seize your house and sell it if you did not meet the terms of your mortgage, and that you have the right to stop making payments if doing so is no longer in your best interests. They point to a recent decision by Morgan Stanley to stop making payments on five office buildings in San Francisco and to an announcement by Tishman Speyer Properties in January 2010 that it had decided to walk away from a 56-building apartment complex in Manhattan, which it bought for $5.4 billion in late 2006 and which is now valued at $1.8 billion. If corporations can make "business decisions" to deliberately default on huge mortgages, why are individual homeowners any different?

There is a lively media debate about whether it is "moral" to walk away from a mortgage when you can still afford to pay it. Former Treasury Secretary Henry M. Paulson, Jr. said, "Any homeowner who can afford his mortgage payment but chooses to walk away from an underwater property is simply a speculator — and one who is not honoring his obligation." The Wall Street Journal recently quoted John Courson, president and CEO of the Mortgage Bankers Association, as saying that homeowners who default on their mortgages should think about the "message" they will send to "their family and their kids and their friends." Brent T. White, a professor at the James E. Rogers College of Law, University of Arizona, asserts that many homeowners who are "underwater" continue to pay their mortgages even when a strategic default would be the wisest financial decision because they are "encouraged to behave in accordance with social norms of 'personal responsibility' and 'promise-keeping.'" He contends that emotions of fear, shame, and guilt are "actively cultivated by the government, the financial industry, and other social control agents in order to induce individual homeowners to act in ways that are against their own self interest, but which are ... argued to be socially beneficial."

The long-term effect of strategic defaults will be, of course, that lenders will tighten their criteria for giving mortgage loans and increase requirements for down payments. Some economists believe that strategic defaults might have a beneficial effect on the crisis by clarifying the situation for lenders, clearing away unrealistic expectations that homeowners will pay off inflated mortgages, and opening the way for more flexibility in modifying loans.

Walk Away

If your monthly mortgage payments are unmanageable, and you have been unsuccessful in negotiating another solution with your lender, your best option may be to let the foreclosure proceed. Depending on the state you live in, if the house sells for a reasonable price, you might get some of your equity back. Moving to more affordable housing will liberate you from a heavy financial burden and free up cash for your other expenses and financial priorities, such as saving for retirement or a child's education. Foreclosure is an unpleasant experience, but you must go beyond it and plan for the future.

A foreclosure will impact your credit score for the next seven years, and you will probably not be able to get car loans, open credit card accounts, or qualify for another mortgage during that period. Foreclosure is preferable to bankruptcy, which will remain on your credit report for ten years.

However, walking away should remain a last resort, after all other possibilities have been exhausted. If you can successfully transfer ownership back to your lender without going through foreclosure, or find a buyer for your home, you will be able to move on more quickly and with fewer negative financial consequences.

Tip: Let things take their course.

You may have heard stories of people who mailed their house keys back to their lenders with a note telling them they could have their house — and their house payments. Do not act in haste; you will cheat yourself out of a place to live while you figure out your next move. Foreclosure can take many months. The time between your decision to give up the fight to keep your home and the date you have to move out of the house can be an opportunity to save money and make important plans for your family.

FORECLOSURE
NOTICE
THE CIRCUIT COURT OF TH
GEN
was tried before the court. On
JDGED that:
, is due $ as prin
for title search expense, $
s' fees with $ court costs
for unearned insurance premium
$
FEDERAL RESERVE NOTE
AG 78178755 A
G7

CHAPTER 6

Borrowing What You Owe: Refinancing

Refinancing your mortgage is a good option when you are concerned that foreclosure is on the horizon, but your credit rating has not yet been lowered because of missed payments or action by the bank. You will be able to qualify for a new loan more easily while your credit is still in good standing. If you are already in the first stages of foreclosure, though, keep reading — this could still be a good route for you.

If you have had your mortgage for fewer than ten years, and if your financial difficulties are likely to persist in the future, refinancing is an effective way to lower your monthly payment. It is also a good choice if you have an ever-rising variable interest rate.

When you refinance your home, you are simply taking out a new mortgage with new terms, such as a lower interest rate, a longer amortization period and, consequently, lower monthly payments. A new mortgage is created for the outstanding balance, and the original loan is paid off with the funds from the new loan. Refinancing your mortgage should not be confused with acquiring a second mortgage on your home. The latter is simply a second lien on the property to acquire cash. If you cannot pay your current monthly mortgage, having a second mortgage could bring you closer to foreclosure.

If you have been making payments on a 30-year mortgage for ten to 20 years, refinancing may not be best for you. By refinancing, you are creating a new loan agreement that restarts an amortization period. Consider a shorter-term loan to reduce the amount of interest you pay on the property over the length of the loan. If the interest on the shorter-term loan is higher than the interest on your mortgage, refinancing is not a good idea because you will pay more in interest.

It is best to refinance before your lender sends any notice of foreclosure because you will still have time to shop around for a new loan before your credit score is affected. If you are trying to refinance *after* being given notice, pay close attention to both the interest rates offered and the amount of time you have before the property goes to auction. If the rates are acceptable, and you can pay the original loan off before the auction, great — but if the funds will not be available to pay off your current lender before the foreclosure sale, refinancing is not going to help. It does you no good if your home will be put up for auction next week, but the funds will not be available until next month.

A mortgage broker is a professional who negotiates with lenders to find the best possible terms for your loan. Mortgage brokers charge fees that are usually paid at closing. The primary purpose for refinancing your mortgage is to reduce the monthly payments and interest. If a mortgage broker cannot do both of those for you, look for another. The interest rate and terms offered you by a lender are based on a number of factors, including your credit history, the nature of your employment, your assets, the appraised value of your home, and the real estate market in the area where you live. If you have consulted several mortgage brokers and none of them are able to get your payments and interest down, it means that you do not qualify for refinancing on better terms than your existing mortgage, and you should look for another solution.

Your Existing Mortgage

If you have not done so already, look closely at your security instrument — your mortgage agreement or deed of trust. What are the terms listed? Do you have a fixed-rate interest agreement or an ARM? What is the interest rate currently being charged, and how might it change? How does the interest rate on your loan compare to the current interest rates on the market?

If you have a fixed-rate mortgage, look in the conditions area to see whether there is a prepayment penalty. A prepayment penalty is often used to dissuade homeowners from refinancing a fixed-rate mortgage when the interest rates go down. If there is a penalty, what is the cost? Does the clause allow for a certain percentage of the principal to be paid without penalty? Some lenders allow up to 20 percent to be paid early before a penalty is imposed. You will need to determine whether paying this fee to get a smaller mortgage payment and lower interest rate is worth it.

If you have an ARM, be sure you know how high the interest rate, and your monthly payment, could potentially become. Compare this with the current market interest rate for fixed-rate mortgages. ARMs can be good in times of national economic stability. When the economy is unstable, however, interest rates can fluctuate like a roller coaster. While they cannot increase or decrease more than 2 percent in a given year, this small percentage can spell big costs or savings to homeowners. With a $100,000 loan on a 30-year term, for example, that could mean the difference between 4 percent ($4,000) and 6 percent ($6,000) in a 12-month period — a monthly difference of $122.13.

Interest-only mortgages are the only type of loans where the monthly payments can be reduced without refinancing. If you make a prepayment of a portion of the loan but do not refinance, it reduces the amount of the principal on which interest is charged. In this case, assuming a second mortgage (or home equity loan) at a lower interest rate for the portion of the original loan you wish to pay could *potentially* save you money. The math is tricky, though; work through the figures carefully before acting.

Because the point of taking out a new loan is to reduce your monthly payments, do not assume another loan that pays off only a portion of the original debt. Paying down the principal of your loan does not reduce the monthly payments, but shortens the amortization period. Instead of making your life easier, you will put yourself at far greater risk of losing your home by taking on two loan payments every month and reducing the amount of time you have left to repay the debt. If you cannot refinance the *entire* sum owed, consider alternatives.

Is Refinancing the Best Choice for Me?

Before approaching a lenders or broker about refinancing, you should take into consideration the following points:

- **Decide how long you intend to stay in the home.** If you are planning to move within a few years, entering into a new mortgage agreement might not be practical because you will have to pay additional expenses, closing fees, and other costs associated with taking out a new loan. If you plan to stay in the house for more than four years, negotiating a lower monthly payment makes sense.

- **Look at your credit score.** Have you struggled to make mortgage payments? Do you have a high amount of credit card debt? Are you currently overextended? You can still refinance if your credit score is less than "good" or "excellent" on the rating scale, but the interest rates and points (broker fees) associated with a new mortgage may be higher than the interest on your existing mortgage. It does not make sense to refinance into a mortgage payment that is higher than the one you currently struggle to pay. If you are able to take a few months to pay down the credit card debt so that your score rises, do this before trying to refinance.

- **Consider how much equity you have in the property.** Did you originally take out a mortgage for more than 80 percent of the value of your house? How much of that loan have you paid down? What is the property worth in today's market? If you were to refinance, would the amount mortgaged be 80 percent or less of the current market value? If your house has depreciated in value due to changes in the real estate market, or if you have not made much of a dent in the original mortgage, it is unlikely that you will find good interest rates through refinancing because you are in no position to bargain. The point of purchasing property is to build equity. Interest-only mortgages require only payments of interest for the first years of a mortgage and are used by homebuyers who expect their incomes to increase or who have fluctuating incomes. At any time, holders of interest-only mortgages can pay off principal in addition to the interest and start building equity in their homes. If you have held a mortgage for more than three years without building equity, it could be a signal that your finances are overextended, and you cannot really afford your house.

- **You must have a steady income.** If you are facing foreclosure because of a job loss, refinancing will not work. You cannot get a loan to buy property if you do not have an income, and you cannot refinance for the same reason. Lenders want to be sure that the person to whom they loan money has a means of paying it back now, not at some indefinite time in the future. Even if you have to take a lower-level position to keep an income, do it. You can always try to get another job when one becomes available.

- **Understand why you are in your current situation.** Do you have a spending problem that has caused you to be overextended? Are you considering refinancing to consolidate your debts? Using your home equity to pay off luxury debts is not a good long-term solution, especially if you are struggling to avoid foreclosure, because you could end up in the same circumstances again. Carrying a large amount of debt will probably push interest rates up on any new mortgage.

Know How Much You Owe

Assuming that you have not been served with a foreclosure notice and are pursuing preventative measures, find out exactly how much money you owe on the first loan before consulting any new lenders about refinancing. Ask your lender for the up-to-date balance of your account. You need to be certain of the exact amount you owe on the original debt.

Have a title search performed to find out whether there are secondary (junior) liens against your property. Are back taxes owed? Has a lien been recorded against your property for work done by a contractor, but left unpaid? Remember that the initial lender is not the only one who can fore-close on your property. If you cannot pay off all these debts by refinancing, it is not a viable option. Having a title search done yourself will also save you the embarrassment of finding out during refinance negotiations that there is a lien on your property of which you were not aware.

Keep a list of all liens against your property. Organize them according to the date they were recorded and the amount owed. When it comes to fore-closure — and bankruptcy — the debts against the property will be paid off in order of their recording date rather than the amount owed.

Get a Valuation

In order to understand what your equity in the home is, you need to have a current assessment of your property made. Contact three different real estate agents and ask for a consultation. Tell them that you are considering putting your home on the market and would like an estimate of its value. Assessing the market value of your home is one step in deciding whether to refinance or sell.

At this stage, you do not need to hire an appraiser and spend more money. When you actually enter into a refinancing agreement with a lender, it will select an accredited appraiser to assess the fair market value of the home. Unfortunately, the lender's appraisal will not always give you an exact valu-ation on the property; the lender will simply agree or disagree that the property is worth the amount you want to borrow. Getting an estimate of the value of your home lets you know where you stand before you enter into refinancing negotiations.

$\mathcal{T}ip$: Do not hire your own appraiser.

Most lenders will not accept an appraisal done by someone whom you have personally hired, because the appraiser might favor you by valuing the house at more than it is worth. If you have funds available and want to get an official appraisal, have a third party do the hiring to give the numbers more credibility. A separate valuation will still be performed by someone the lender selects, but the lender will be more likely to consider your appraisal in the comparison.

Do your own research into the market in your area. Visit homes that are currently on the market and are similar to your own so that you know how your property compares. What are they selling for? How does the physical condition of your home compare? How many similar homes are currently on the market? Read newspapers and housing circulars. This will not only help you understanding the value of your property, but the likelihood that it will sell if you decide to put it on the market.

Many factors affect the value of your home. If you have owned it for some time, property values in your area may have gone up or come down. Improvements to the landscaping or interior of the home increase its value, while neglect and structural damage bring its value down. By knowing how much money you owe on the property and what its fair market value is, you can establish the amount of equity you have.

If you originally purchased the home with a mortgage that covered 90 percent or more of the price and you are required to pay private mortgage insurance (PMI), this valuation could work in your favor. Depending on the terms of your security instrument, you may now have paid enough of the principal that PMI is no longer mandatory. This is important because PMI rates are most often 0.25 to 0.50 percent higher than other insurances.

Will I Qualify?

Whether you qualify for refinancing on your home will depend on a variety of factors. The primary factors are your current credit rating, the amount of equity you have in the property, and the loan-to-value ratio required by the lender. If you have this information on hand, you will already know what response to expect from a broker or lender.

Understanding your credit score

Somewhere along the line, a group of mathematicians and statisticians came up with a formula for calculating how likely you are to pay back a debt. Using information gathered in your credit report, such as the number of missed and late payments in a given period of time and how much you currently owe, a computer compares you to everyone else in the United States with a credit history. This comparison generates a score representing how likely you are to return borrowed money.

Lenders use this score to determine what interest rate you will be offered. The higher the score, the more likely you will get low rates. According to the Fair Isaac Corporation (FICO), the company that developed the formula, you will get the best interest rates if your score is 760 or greater. As scores decrease, interest rates increases proportionately. On a 30-year fixed mortgage, for example, there is a difference of 3.784 percent between the interest rates charged to someone who has a FICO score of 619 and someone who has a score of 760.

There are three major credit reporting agencies in the United States: Equifax, TransUnion, and Experian. When a lender requests a credit report, it receives reports from all three. Every individual is allowed one free copy of his or her credit report each year, and one within 30 days of being rejected for a loan. If you have not seen a recent copy of your credit report, request a copy online at **www.annualcreditreport.com**, the only Web site officially authorized by the Federal Trade Commission. Other Web sites offer "free credit reports" to lure potential customers for various financial services.

How is your credit score calculated?

An individual's credit score is based on five elements. The regularity with which you pay your current debts — including utilities, car loans, and insurance — makes up about 35 percent of the number. Paying on time is good for your score, while being late occasionally will bring it down.

Outstanding debt that has gone to collection has a strong negative effect, as does bankruptcy and foreclosure. Reviewing a copy of your credit report is important because you may have forgotten about an outstanding debt (such as a clothing store credit card) that can bring your score down.

Approximately 30 percent of the score reflects the amount of money you have at your disposal. How many credit cards do you have? What percentage of the credit limit have you used on each one? What do you owe on car loans, your mortgage, and school loans? How much debt do you carry? Owing a substantial amount of money is not necessarily bad if you are paying regularly each month. Try to avoid carrying high balances because it suggests that you do not have the funds to pay the debts off.

The duration of your credit makes up about 15 percent of your score. The longer your credit history, the more information is available to make an accurate assessment. Try to keep credit cards for long periods of time, paying them off regularly, rather than opening and closing accounts.

Types of credit make up about 10 percent of your score. People with a mix of credit cards, school loans, mortgages, and car loans will have a better score than those with only school or credit card debt. Keep in mind, though, that suddenly applying for new types of loans will not help if you do it all at once. Opening too many new accounts in a short period of time negatively affects your score.

The final 10 percent of your score is decided by the number of inquiries made about your credit history in a given period of time. Lenders assume that these queries are made because you are seeking additional loans or lines of credit, suggesting that your finances are overextended.

These are the only five factors considered in your credit score. Your age, employment, marital status, and education are irrelevant. Lenders might use this information when considering your refinancing options, but it will not have any influence on your FICO score.

What should you do with your credit report?

Your credit report tells you much more than your chances of securing a good interest rate and new mortgage. Not all creditors are efficient at reporting changes to your credit status with them. For example, you might have contested a charge on a department store credit card. The debt went to collection before you were aware it was owed and could contact the department store to resolve the problem. Even if the debt has been cleared, the department store or collections agency might not have fixed it on your credit report, which means that your score could be unfairly affected.

Often when people get their credit reports, they find that they have outstanding debts they were unaware of. Did you think your college roommate paid the final utility bill when you both graduated and left town? If that bill was in your name and it was not paid, it is on your record. Did you lose a credit card years ago and fail to report it? If someone else used the card to make purchases, the debt is yours. If you have moved many times over the years, bills may not have been forwarded and could remain outstanding. Worst of all, someone may have stolen your identity and taken out loans in your name without your knowing it. Review your credit report for errors and have them corrected before you approach a lender.

Improve your credit score

You can improve your credit score by reporting or contesting any inaccuracies. Speak with the creditors immediately; explain that you have just found out about the debt and want it investigated. Find solutions to get the negative aspects removed from your credit report as soon as possible. File a "challenge to incorrect credit report entry" with the credit bureau, sending the form by certified mail with a return receipt for your records. These forms are available directly from the credit agencies. You can also file a challenge online through the credit bureau Web sites.

You can also raise your score by reducing your outstanding debts, such as credit cards. You will be surprised how quickly your score will improve after even one or two months.

Determining Equity

To determine the equity in your home, deduct the amount you have left to pay on your mortgage from the current market value of your home. Also, subtract any second mortgages or liens against the property. The amount left over after all the debts against the property are paid is your equity.

Equity becomes important in the refinancing if your original loan was for more than 80 percent of the purchase price. Those types of mortgages have high interest rates and often require homeowners to carry PMI. If your equity has increased to 20 percent or more, PMI is no longer required, and you can probably refinance at a lower interest rate.

Loan-to-value

Loan-to-value (LTV) is a percentage used by lenders to assess the risk of a loan. When you applied for your original loan, the lender divided the amount of money you needed to borrow by the cost of the house you were purchasing to get your LTV. For example, if you purchased a home for $150,000 with a $20,000 down payment, then your LTV was 87 percent — or $130,000 divided by $150,000.

This percentage is important because the higher the LTV, the greater the risk for the lender. A homeowner with little equity in the property is not losing as much as the lender if it is foreclosed on. Every lender has an LTV cap that they will not exceed, based on the other factors involved in determining loan eligibility. If the LTV is over 80 percent, PMI will be probably be required to cover the lender in case of default.

In a refinance, the equity you have in the home takes the place of a down payment. To calculate the LTV for your property, divide the amount you owe on your current loan by the fair market value of your home. This ratio is expressed as a percentage; the lower the percentage, the greater your chances of getting a great refinancing deal.

Being Prepared

Before you arrange to talk with a broker, you need to be prepared and organized. Advance preparation will speed up the process of refinancing — and time is a precious commodity at this point. Gather the following items in a folder to take to the broker:

- **Information on your current loan.** In order to know whether a new arrangement will work in your favor, you need to know what you already have. The broker should be able to look at the details of your current agreement and know whether he or she can get you a better deal in the current market.

- **Information on what you want from a new loan.** Do you want a lower interest rate? Longer repayment terms? Write your wish list, and let your broker determine what is reasonable under the circumstances.

- **A list of any claims on the property.** Has the IRS attached a tax lien to your home? Is there a mechanic's lien for the remodeled kitchen? List every claim that exists on the property so your broker does not waste time trying to get you a loan that you do not qualify for. Document the amounts, and let the broker know if your new loan will pay off these old debts.

- **Personal details of anyone on the loan.** Make sure that all addresses and names are correctly listed. Has anyone who cosigned the original mortgage moved? Has anyone gotten married or divorced? Include social security numbers and current employers.

- **Copies of tax returns for the past two to three years, paycheck stubs, and evidence of any other income.** Your new lender will want proof of employment. If you work for yourself, a profit-and-loss statement for the last six months might be requested in addition to tax returns.

- **A list of all other debts and liabilities, such as credit cards and vehicle loans.** Account for all expenses so the broker can see what your monthly cash flow looks like.

- **Documentation of all assets.** Bring bank account statements, information about any other property you own, and documentation of anything else that can be considered an asset, including stocks and bonds, life insurance, retirement funds, automobiles, and anything else that could build your value as an individual.

By having this information clearly organized from the beginning, your broker will be able to work more quickly and easily to find a new loan to save your property. All the information you submit must be verified, so double check that the details are correct — including employer addresses and phone numbers.

Talk with a Broker

When you have gathered information about your credit history, equity, and debts owed, discuss your options with a qualified mortgage adviser or broker. Find out what terms and interests rates you will be able to get. Remember to include accrued fees and interest in the amount that must be paid off.

A mortgage broker can help you to find the best deals in a short time. Make sure that the broker is credible, has good references, and is willing to be flexible. Try to find a broker who does not charge you a fee, but takes a commission from the lender instead. Brokers who receive commissions from lenders do not get paid unless they find you a loan. Do not feel obligated to accept a loan that is not working in your favor.

A good broker works with many different lenders, not just one or two, and with various types of lenders. If you have bad credit or are self-employed, for example, there may be alternatives to conventional lenders that could serve your needs.

You do not have to speak with your lender about refinancing unless you wish to refinance through your original lender. Consider the relationship you have with your current lender and whether refinancing was suggested as an option to solve your financial difficulties when you met with them originally. You already have a long-term relationship with your original lender that could work to your advantage, particularly if your current difficulties are temporary or you had a good payment record until recently.

Do not settle for just any deal. If you feel a broker is being too aggressive in trying to get you to commit yourself to a particular loan, find another broker. Do not enter into an agreement if you are uncomfortable with the terms. Refinancing should be a positive solution to keeping your home, not another obstacle for you to deal with later on.

Where to Find Money

You do not have go to a mortgage broker to secure refinancing. You can look for money on your own, using the information you have gathered about your current loan arrangement and your income. Refinancing is simply taking out a new loan with better terms so that you can pay off the old one. Possible sources of loans are:

- **Your regular bank.** If you have a strong, established history with a bank, they are likely to offer you good terms when it comes to refinancing — assuming your first loan is not through them. Do not stop with your personal bank; visit its competitors in the area to see what they might be willing to offer.

- **Credit unions.** These non-profit, cooperative groups often loan money if the loan can be secured by real property, such as a home. You must be a member of the credit union, however, in order to borrow. If you are not a member of a credit union but think you have enough time to join and inquire about a loan, do so.

- **Mortgage companies.** You may or may not be able to gain access to a mortgage company without a broker. Look them up in the phonebook or on the Internet to see what their requirements are.

- **Life insurance companies.** Many lenders require that you buy life insurance when you agree to a loan. The irony is that this life insurance policy may be borrowed against in order to protect the loan from going into default. Check with your representative to find out if, and how much, you can borrow against your current policy.

- **Brokerage firms.** It may seem odd to go to a stockbroker for a home loan, but some larger firms will offer refinancing to individuals. Look up the larger firms in your area and call them to find out what they might offer.

- **Hard money lenders.** Many individuals and small investment companies will loan homeowners money for a short period of time at higher interest rates than those charged by banks. These loans are backed by the value of the property and not by the credit rating of the borrower. Hard money lenders typically advertise with slogans such as "no money down" or "easy credit" to catch your eye. You can find directories of hard money lenders online at Web sites such as Moolah.com (**http://moolahlist.com**) and REIClub.com (**http://reiclub.com/hard-money-lenders.php**).

- **Private individuals.** Family, friends, and private investors may be willing to offer you a loan for a short amount of time. These agreements should be treated professionally, regardless of who loans you the funds.

Compare Your Refinance Options

Your broker should help you to narrow down your refinancing options to the best three. If you have chosen to look for refinancing on your own, create a chart similar to the following chart. Compare the interest rates, fees, and other costs involved in each arrangement. Include the cost of any penalties for prepayment on the old loan in your assessment.

Will the monthly payments be less than you are paying now? Is the difference enough to help you keep the property from going into foreclosure? Has the length of time to pay the mortgage increased? Will you pay additional interest over the term of the loan?

Also, consider whether a reduction in interest on the loan will affect your taxes. Because interest on mortgages is tax-deductible, a decrease in the amount you pay could result in an increase in your taxable income and the taxes you pay. If you save money in one area but lose it in another, the losses may outweigh the benefits of refinancing.

Mr. Joe Anybody (current fair market value = $250,000)

	CURRENT LOAN	OPTION #1	OPTION #2	OPTION #3
PRINCIPAL	$136,000	$90,000	$90,000	$90,000
AMOUNT OWED	$90,000	n/a	n/a	n/a
INTEREST RATE	6.5 percent	6.5 percent	6.0 percent	6.25 percent
TYPE OF LOAN	Adjustable rate	Fixed rate	Fixed rate	Fixed rate
LTV	89 percent	36 percent	36 percent	36 percent
MAX. TERM	30-year	15-year	25-year	25-year
TITLE INSURANCE	$170	$230	$210	$200
VALUATION FEE	$200	$300	$350	$300
ORIGINATION FEE	$300	$650	$400	n/a
BROKER FEE	$1,360	$2,200	$2,500	$2,500
CREDIT REPORT	n/a	n/a	$20	n/a
GOV'T FEES	n/a	n/a	n/a	n/a
PREPAY PENALTY	n/a	$2,700	$2,700	$2,700
LATE FEE	5 percent	5 percent	5 percent	5 percent
ESCROW FEE	$250	$300	$300	$300
PROPERTY TAXES (YEARLY)	$2,500	$2,500	$2,500	$2,500
PROPERTY INSURANCE	$500	$500	$500	$500
MO. PAYMENT	$1,198	$839.57	$621.62	$633.28
TOTAL COST	$115,860.94	$144,743.19	$180,006.60	$183,984.78
TOTAL INTEREST	$25,860.94	$54,743.19	$90,006.60	$93,984.78

Calculations were made using the refinance calculator at www.mortgage-calc.com.

In the example chart above, Joe Anybody is interested in refinancing his property. In his new mortgage, he is including all the fees and penalties incurred by refinancing, but opting to pay his home insurance and taxes separately each month. The "current loan" column shows the costs of Joe's original loan and the amount of his monthly payment. The "total cost" and "total interest" rows show the total amount that will be paid to the lender from the refinance date onward during the term of the loan.

When Joe looks at the numbers, he wonders whether refinancing is really a better option than continuing with his current loan. Securing a new fixed-rate loan with a smaller monthly payment will make a big difference for him and his family immediately by freeing up more of his monthly income for daily expenses. When he looks at the amount of interest he will pay over the life of the loan, though, he realizes that he will pay an extra $28,882 to $68,124 for this benefit — an amount that could make a significant difference to his and his wife's retirement account. Though options No. 2 or No. 3 would give Joe an extra $500 to spend each month, Joe decides that refinancing to Option 1 is in his best interest. The interest rate on the new loan will not go down, but it cannot go above 6.5 percent. Joe will fix his interest rate at 6.5 percent, while reducing his monthly payment by $358.49. Though he will end up paying $28,882 more on the loan in interest if he pays it off in 15 years, Joe has determined that it is worth it to keep his home secure.

Making an Educated Decision

When you have determined the real value of your home and compared refinancing options with your current arrangement, you will be able to see whether refinancing is the best long-term solution. Is the difference in the new monthly payments worth the price? How much will you have paid for your home over the life of your loan? Is there another way to resolve your financial difficulties and make the monthly payments on your current loan?

Refinancing is not the best choice for everyone. There are costs associated with refinancing, just as there were with the original mortgage, including title search fees, closing costs, and settlement fees. It is almost as if you are buying your home from yourself. Most of the time, the equity you have in your home is enough to cover these expenses, but if it is not, you will have to come up with those funds initially.

Before committing to refinancing, you should be confident that the new terms and payments are going to be manageable for years to come. It is not wise to use your home to secure a loan for much less than the house is worth and lose it to foreclosure down the road. Remember that in states with strict foreclosure laws, you will not receive any of the proceeds when your home is sold in foreclosure, even if it sells for far more than the amount of the loan. You could lose all the equity in your home.

Nothing prevents you from refinancing now and doing it again in a few years with better terms. If your credit score is low and your LTV is high right now, but you know that a new arrangement will enable you to pay off debt and build up savings, consider refinancing with the mental note that you can refinance again in a few years.

CHAPTER 7

Halting Foreclosure with a Legal Defense

Facing a possible foreclosure can be one of the most frightening and stressful experiences in your life. Once you have achieved the American Dream of owning your own home, it may seem inconceivable that it can be taken away from you. If you are one of the millions of people threatened with a foreclosure today, the explanations of economists and financial experts will be little consolation for you. You need a solution right now that will help you keep your home or at least protect your credit rating so you will be able to purchase another home in the near future.

You can halt a foreclosure by paying what you owe, refinancing your loan, selling your house, or handing it over to the lender. You may also be able to defend yourself against a possible foreclosure in a court of law. When a bank files foreclosure proceedings, it is essentially suing you for breach of a contract — your mortgage. Your mortgage, like any other business contract, may contain errors, miscalculations, or stipulations that can get you out of the foreclosure proceedings — legally.

Mortgages and, in turn, foreclosure proceedings, are grounded in details. Many of the legal defenses below are based on loopholes created by the law.

There are ways to get even the slightest infraction by the lender to work for you. Each strategy offers a way for you to use the law to your advantage. Some strategies could succeed in getting foreclosure proceedings dismissed forever, while others will only buy time to make other arrangements, and some strengthen other legal defenses.

The home-buying process and legal defenses

The purchase of a home is the most complicated and largest transaction that many people will ever make. If mortgages were simple, there would be no need for bank representatives, title insurers, closing specialists, realtors, or real estate attorneys to be involved in the process. Few homebuyers think about the possibility of foreclosure while they are signing the endless documents that go along with purchasing a home. In the current climate of economic instability, however, reading and understanding the fine print in those documents is more important than ever. Every legal defense to foreclosure is based on the legal documents that the homebuyer signed at the closing. These defenses are all based on understanding the language of the mortgage and the laws that govern its use.

To successfully meet the commitment of paying a loan back, a home purchaser needs to be familiar with every aspect of it. Millions of Americans are learning the hard way that they did not really understand the terms of the loan they were signing or that they should not have trusted their mortgage broker or lender with their home purchase. Being informed and asking questions whenever you are confused can help you avoid foreclosure in the end.

Some homeowners are in trouble because they overestimated what they could afford or because they jumped at the chance to buy a home without reading the fine print in their loan documents. There are also trustworthy, creditworthy people who have been forced into foreclosure by the sloppy and even negligent lending practices of a bank.

It is your legal right and your obligation to understand everything you are signing before you actually complete the paperwork to buy a home. As a home-buyer or a homeowner seeking to refinance, it is your responsibility to be aware of the structure of a mortgage and of the laws that protect both lenders and borrowers.

How a Legal Defense Works

A mortgage is a legal, binding contract signed by both parties when a property is purchased. It lays out, in detail, how the money will be paid back, by whom, and over what period of time. Each part of the mortgage is governed by state and federal laws and must conform exactly to these laws. The basis for a legal defense to foreclosure proceedings is that the borrower finds some item in the original mortgage document that did not follow the letter of the law. If the borrower can prove that the lender made an error, through either negligence or a simple mistake, the lender might not be able to follow through with the foreclosure, or at least the foreclosure must be delayed until the error is corrected.

The foreclosure process is a lawsuit by the lender against the borrower, which makes you, the borrower, the defendant. Many people feel completely helpless when they are up against a bank, but the law works for everyone — if you understand how to use it to your advantage.

This chapter outlines 23 legal defenses that can be used to combat foreclosure proceedings. One of them might help you stay in your home longer, end the foreclosure proceedings altogether, or even get money back from your lender.

Tip: Be aware of the statute of limitations.

Many legal defenses to foreclosure are subject to a statute of limitations — a time period after which the defense is no longer valid. Understand the statute of limitations of the defense you are going to pursue and the possibility that your lender is going to respond with its own strategy.

The world of mortgages and foreclosure can be confusing and difficult for an ordinary consumer to navigate. Banks assume that you will go along with their foreclosure proceedings and be so intimidated or ashamed about losing your home that you will simply accept it as your fate. But bank employees and mortgage brokers make mistakes just like anyone else. It is time to get out all the documents associated with your mortgage and go over them carefully, looking for lapses or errors that might give you a legal foothold.

You can legally use the defenses in this chapter to challenge your lender and ensure that you do not become a victim of negligence or predatory lending. If you examine your mortgage documents and think you may have grounds for one of these defenses, consult a lawyer or a mortgage assistance counselor.

Defense #1: Violations of the Truth in Lending Act (TILA) that will result in rescission

The Truth in Lending Act (TILA) was enacted in 1968 to help consumers understand the terms of their credit. As consumers, we are accustomed to seeing the TILA sections in car loans, credit card applications, and mortgages. Before the TILA, lenders were not required to disclose the amount consumers would pay or how the interest on that loan would accrue. Some lenders even compounded interest weekly, making it difficult to determine the actual amount of interest paid in a year. The TILA requires the disclosure of annual percentage rates (APR), the amount of interest charged on a loan, in the loan documents.

In a few cases, a violation of the TILA can result in rescission, or a complete refund of all monies paid by the borrower to the lender over the course of the loan. This type of restitution is available only for refinances, not original purchases, and is subject to a three-year statute of limitations.

What is it?

A violation of the TILA is an error, either by mistake or through negligence on the part of the lender, in calculating the actual interest paid over the life of the loan. There need only be an error of more than $35 in calculating the finance charge for it to be a violation of these regulations. Figuring out how the finance charge is calculated might take some detective work.

How do I find it?

A section in your settlement documents outlines your APR, the finance charge (which is the amount you will pay over the entire life of the loan), the amount financed, and the total of all payments. When you signed your mortgage, this was probably one section you did not really want to look at closely because it shows exactly how much you are paying over the entire period of the loan — a staggering figure when interest is calculated.

How do I use it?

Pursuing a violation of the TILA for rescission is a painstaking process that will require you to go through every line of your mortgage documents carefully. You must also have every piece of paperwork you received at settlement so that you can compare the amounts on the closing paperwork to the amounts listed on each individual document, such as the insurance policies or title fees. For each fee you are required to pay, there will be a statement to either include or exclude these charges from your total finance charge.

The following items are included in the finance charge:

- Title insurance premiums
- Yield spread premiums
- Credit report fees
- Notary fees
- Appraisals

When you are looking over your mortgage documents, list all the fees included in your finance charge, and then all the fees that should have been excluded from the finance charge total. These two categories will be essential in determining whether an error has occurred in the tabulation of finance charges.

Compare the amounts on the settlement documents with other documents from your closing. If the credit report fee is listed on your mortgage paperwork as $65, but you have other paperwork proving that the credit report cost $20, you have found an error that could possibly result in rescission of your mortgage. Lenders often inflate charges or simply use an average cost — a bad business practice that may be the key for you to avoid foreclosure.

Defense #2: Violations of TILA that will result in damages

Rescission is not the only option when pursuing a violation of the TILA defense against foreclosure. Any time the lender violates the TILA, there is a penalty — the amount depends on the terms of the loan and the circumstances of the residence. When the violation does not meet the guidelines for rescission, it can still result in damages being paid to the borrower.

What is it?

When the lender overstates finance charges by any amount or neglects to provide certain disclosures, the borrower may be entitled to damages. Countersuing your foreclosure with a TILA defense for damages is appropriate if the loan in question was used to purchase the property, because a rescission is only possible with refinances of the property.

How do I find it?

The same procedure outlined defense number one for finding a TILA violation can uncover this type of violation. Verify every charge that went into calculating your overall finance charge as stated in your settlement paperwork. Any discrepancy may be cause for a suit alleging violation of the TILA for the purpose of obtaining monetary damages.

How do I use it?

Contact an experienced real estate attorney to see if you can collect monetary damages because of errors in your mortgage documents.

Defense #3: Home Ownership and Equity Protection Act (HOEPA) violations

The Home Ownership and Equity Protection Act of 1994 amended TILA and addressed certain unfair and deceptive practices in home equity lending. It establishes requirements for certain loans with high rates or high fees, also know as "Section 32 loans."

What is it?

A violation of the HOEPA is typically an omission of the necessary disclosures required by HOEPA in your loan documentation. The HOEPA covers refinance loans that are taken on homes whose original loans were less than $120,000 or that had an interest rate of more than 10 percent at closing.

If a mortgage has violated the HOEPA, the borrower may be entitled to a rescission of the loan as well as statutory damages in an amount that would be equal to all the fees and finance charges associated with the loan. A successful HOEPA defense could halt foreclosure and return to the borrower all the money he or she has paid to the lender, plus damages. If the bank does not take possession of the house within a specified period of time, the borrower could retain it, but this rarely happens.

How do I find it?

Begin with your settlement documents. You will find a list of fees associated with your loan; check these against the government's standard for maximum fees allowed under HOEPA. More information about HOEPA can be found on the Federal Trade Commission Web site (**www.ftc.gov/ bcp/edu/pubs/consumer/homes/rea19.shtm**).

The following disclosures must be included with loan documents that fall under HOEPA, and they must be provided to the homebuyer three days before the loan closes so that the guidelines of this type of loan are understood:

> "You are not required to complete this agreement merely because you have received these disclosures or have signed a loan application."

> "If you obtain this loan, the lender will have a mortgage on your home. You could lose your home, and any money you have put into it, if you do not meet your obligations under the loan."

These additional safeguards were added under HOEPA because of the prevalence of subprime loans and the government's desire to reign in predatory lending practices.

Your loan must also list all the amounts correctly. Additionally, your HOEPA loan may not include any of the following terms:

- Negative amortization
- Balloon payments (except in the event of construction bridge loans)
- Rebates
- A rate increase after default
- Advance payments
- Prepayment penalties

How do I use it?

If the interest on your loan was more than 10 percent at closing, and your original mortgage was less than $120,000, it is worth your while to investigate a HOEPA defense against foreclosure. A HOEPA defense will result in rescission if completed within three years of the loan origination.

Defense #4: Failure to provide a correct notice of the right to rescind

A mortgage, like any other contract, must give a notice of the right to rescind, meaning that changing your mind about the contract within a specified time period will make it null and void. The TILA requires that, with a refinance, the lender give accurate notice to the borrower of his or her right to rescind the contract within three days of the closing.

How do I find it?

The right-to-rescind document may be titled "Notice of Right to Cancel" or something similar and will be a part of the documents you received at settlement, but it will not be a part of the closing documents where you found the interest rates and finance charges. It may not even be something that was signed at closing, but may be among other paperwork that is covered under a general acceptance form that you signed at the closing, which would have stated that you received several types of documents.

The property in question must be your residence, and in general, the refinance must be with a company other than the original provider of the purchase loan. In certain cases, this defense may still be used with cash-out mortgages, but it is most often applicable to second mortgages or refinances on a primary residence with a secondary lender.

How do I use it?

If you discover that you were never notified that you had a right to re-scind the contract within three days of closing, you can sue to have your foreclosure halted. The statute of limitations on this defense is three years from closing. If you discover that a "right to rescind notice" was never given to you, it is essential to notify the lender immediately of your intention to sue using this defense so that they cannot remedy the situation by providing you with a corrected right-to-rescind notice. If the lender sends or delivers a corrected right-to-rescind notice to you, and you have not already mailed your signed notice of rescission, you have lost your grounds for suing. When three days have elapsed after you receive such a notice, it is as though the lender had notified you of your right to cancel as originally required.

Because the notice of rescission is effective when mailed, use registered or certified mail to notify the lender of your intent to pursue rescission due to a failure to provide a correct notice of the right to rescind the mortgage contract.

Once the defense is complete, the following will occur:

- The transaction will be rescinded.
- All principal and interest paid will be refunded to the borrower.
- All closing costs will be refunded.
- Down payment monies will be refunded.
- The mortgage will be terminated.
- The borrower will keep the property if no further monies are owed.
- Damages may be sought if there are other TILA violations.

Defense #5: Breach of contract

A mortgage, refinance, or home equity line of credit is a contract. The lender agrees to provide the money for you to purchase or refinance a home or is giving you cash with your home as collateral, based on the current value of the home and your credit score. You agree to pay back that loan in a specified amount of time, at regular intervals and at a rate of interest that is mutually agreed upon in the terms of the contract.

What is it?

Because you made a commitment to timely payments in the original loan contract, the lender has the right to sue for the property when you have breached the terms of that contract. Once you have missed payments, you have essentially broken the terms of your contract, and your lender will begin the foreclosure proceeding according to the laws of your state and the terms of your mortgage.

Occasionally, a lender breaches the contract by violating one of the terms set forth in the loan contract, making it your primary defense against a foreclosure. If the lender has force-placed insurance — taken out an insurance policy on your behalf and required you to pay the premiums — on your property or on your refinanced loan, which was not included in the original terms of the loan and has consequently caused you to be unable to make your monthly payments, you have grounds for a breach-of-contract suit. You can allege that the cause of your breach of contract was the primary breach of contract on the part of the lender.

How do I use it?

A breach-of-contract defense is frequently used against foreclosure in addition to one of the other defenses outlined here. Once you have begun the process of a legal defense to foreclosure, a breach of contract claim could be included along with TILA or HOEPA violations because the omission of information or misrepresentation of a portion of the fees and charges also constitutes a breach of contract. Contract law is complicated and encompasses many aspects of the mortgage writing process, so it is wise to include this type of claim with the main defense you are using.

A breach-of-contract defense can result in an award of damages paid to the borrower by the bank. In some cases, it can result in rescission — the lender returns all money paid by the borrower, and the original loan contract is canceled. You will have avoided foreclosure and might have enough money for a down payment on a new home.

Defense #6: Real Estate Settlement Procedures Act (RESPA)

When you purchased your home, you probably used the services of a real estate agent, a title insurance company, and even a mortgage broker. The Real Estate Settlement Procedures Act (RESPA) was passed in the 1970s to ensure that no inappropriate relationships between these service providers would harm the borrower. Although your real estate agent may suggest a title insurance company or a mortgage broker, you are not required to use those companies, nor are those companies allowed to pay your real estate agent for any kind of a referral. Many provisions of this act can be used as a defense to foreclosure using federal laws, though other infractions carry no civil penalties.

What is it?

The following items are subject to the provisions of RESPA:

- The information booklet
- Good faith estimate (GFE)
- HUD-1 statement
- Notice on servicing
- Qualified written request

- Unearned fees and kickbacks
- Yield spread premium (YSP) exception
- Forced title insurance
- Escrow accounts

Of these items, the information booklet, the GFE, escrow accounts, and the HUD-1 settlement breaches do not carry a civil liability, but they may become part of a TILA defense, as discussed in earlier sections. The information booklet must be mailed to the borrower within three days of completion of the loan application and contains the following information:

- A breakdown of the purpose of each cost of the loan.

- An explanation of escrow accounts and what their purpose will be in the case of the particular loan.

- Details about the choices available to the borrower with respect to services needed to make settlement on a property.

- A warning about what practices may be unfair and what charges would be unreasonable with regard to a real estate transaction and eventual settlement.

The GFE, a detailed estimate of fees and charges for the planned settlement, is also mailed within three days of the acceptance of the loan application by the lender. At settlement, the HUD-1 (HUD standing for Housing and Urban Development) statement takes the place of the GFE and shows the exact breakdown of fees and charges. Additionally, the borrower cannot be charged for the preparation of these documents.

How do I find it?

Many borrowers find it hard to negotiate a defense based on RESPA because the majority of this paperwork is given to the borrower before closing, and many people do not keep all the documents they received prior to settlement. Gather all the documents related to your loan and look through them carefully.

How do I use it?

If you find errors or omissions in your loan documents, you may be able to halt or delay foreclosure, or at least collect monetary damages.

The following are items that carry civil liability under federal law:

Notice on servicing

The notice on servicing is a disclosure telling the loan applicant whether their loan may be sold or transferred at any time during the life of the loan. If this disclosure was not included in the pre-settlement paperwork or if it did not provide the borrower with all the necessary information, the borrower may be entitled to damages. These could include any actual damages incurred by the borrower and an additional penalty of up to $1,000.

Qualified written request

If there are any errors in the loan documents or any questions from the borrower during the loan process, the borrower sends a qualified written request (QWR) to the lender. Once the borrower has requested a change or asked a question, the lender must acknowledge the receipt of the letter and respond within a specific amount of time. Failure to comply with this part of RESPA can result in an award of actual damages to the borrower, as well as up to $1,000 in additional damages.

Failure to respond to a QWR does not halt foreclosure proceedings, but it can be incorporated as part of a legal defense alleging that the lender has been negligent or failed to comply with government regulations.

Kickbacks and unearned fees

No payments may change hands between mortgage brokers and real estate agents, or between title insurance companies and agents or brokers, for either purchase of the home or the loan to complete that purchase. All the services can coexist, but they cannot employ a system of payments for services between the different providers. If such behavior is discovered and proved, damages can include a penalty in an amount three times whatever was paid for the services, as well as all court costs accrued by the borrower. You would have to find evidence of kickbacks such as receipts, documents, or other court cases brought against the same individuals and companies for similar offenses in order to prove your case.

Yield spread premium exception

The yield spread premium (YSP) is a bonus paid by the lender to the mortgage broker when he or she writes a loan that has an interest rate higher than the minimum approved by the lender. That may sound like a sure defense in many cases, because the predatory lending and subprime markets have expanded during the last few years, but a YSP exception is highly subjective and difficult to take to court. The Department of Housing and Urban Development has guidelines for testing the validity of a YSP claim.

Forced title insurance

Related to the kickbacks provision of RESPA, a seller cannot require that the prospective buyer of their property purchase title insurance from a particular company as a condition of that purchase. In case of violation, the borrower is entitled to damages of three times the total charges for all title insurance.

Defense #7: Fair Debt Collection Practices Act (FDCPA)

Many people, especially those in dire financial circumstances, do not realize that they have rights even when they have fallen behind in payments to a mortgage lender. The Fair Debt Collection Practices Act (FDCPA) was developed to protect borrowers from abusive debt collection tactics. The act allows the borrower, even when he or she has defaulted on a debt, to demand that the lender cease communication with them.

What is it?

There are several stipulations that affect how the FDCPA can be used to a borrower's benefit in the event of a foreclosure. The law requires specific disclosures to be given to the borrower, and then the borrower can contact the lender in writing to request that the collection stop.

- The lender must notify the borrower of the debt and its intention to proceed with collecting the debt.

- The borrower has a period of 30 days to refute the debt, or it is considered valid.

- Once collections have begun, the borrower may notify the lender in writing that they are refusing to pay the debt or demanding that they cease communication.

If the lender violates the terms of this act, it can be held liable for damages related to the debt as well as additional penalties of up to $1,000 and attorney's fees incurred by the borrower.

How do I use it?

The best way to implement this defense is to know your rights under the act and keep careful records of all communications between yourself and the lender. The act also protects against harassment or abuse of the borrower by debt collectors or their agents.

Defense #8: Fair Credit Reporting Act

The Fair Credit Reporting Act (FCRA) regulates how the three major credit bureaus collect and distribute information regarding your credit. Credit bureaus are subject to laws that govern how they disclose information and to whom.

What is it?

Credit bureaus are required to provide correct information to your lender from the origination of your loan throughout any further process with your lender, such as a refinance or loan modification. Your credit score affects the lender's decision to accept your loan application and the interest rate you are charged. As the consumer, it is your responsibility to ensure that the information credit bureaus have about you is correct. Once you have been notified that a refinance or modification has been declined, you are entitled to view your credit report, possibly along with an explanation of why you were denied.

How do I use it?

If you find a discrepancy in your credit report, you must verify or dispute the information with the credit bureau. Once the credit bureau has been notified of the mistake, it cannot continue to knowingly report inaccurate information about your credit.

When you applied for your loan, you received a notice regarding the FCRA, which detailed how your credit score figures into the loan process and your responsibilities to maintain good credit and make sure that your credit report is accurate. If errors in your credit report have caused a lender to be unwilling to negotiate or have impeded your efforts to refinance with a new loan, you can challenge these decisions using the newly corrected credit report.

Defense #9: Real party in interest

So far, we have explored defenses that relied on technical errors: an omission of disclosures, a miscalculation of fees and interest, and even mistakes made by an outside party. This defense requires detective work, and if you succeed, it could keep you in your home for good.

What is it?

Mortgages are bought and sold frequently by banks and investors. A few years after you begin paying your mortgage, it is rare to have the same lender as you did on the day you closed on your home or when you refinanced. You have probably received notices when the lien holder has changed, and you may even have had to change where and how you send your payments. The terms of your loan remain constant throughout the changes in ownership of your mortgage.

You may not know that every time your mortgage changes hands, the lender is required to generate a written statement that ownership of the mortgage and promissory note has been transferred to the new lender. There is only one mortgage and one promissory note for your loan, signed by you. This defense alleges that the company who is suing you for foreclosure does not own your mortgage because it does not have the documents to prove that it owns the promissory note and, therefore, cannot sue you for defaulting on the loan.

How do I use it?

Your mortgage company may not actually own your mortgage. This happens frequently, especially with large lenders who become careless with their documentation and rely on electronic transfers to move loans from one owner to another. It is only when that loan is in default that the "chain of title" becomes essential. If the lender cannot produce written documents detailing each transfer of your mortgage, from the original to the current owner, it has no legal ground to stand on. In fact, "standing" is the legal term used in this type of lawsuit. Your defense is that the lender does not have the legal standing to sue you and cannot prove that it owns the mortgage. If any link in the chain is broken — that is, cannot be proved with written and signed documents — the entire foreclosure lawsuit can be dismissed. Even though your mortgage may have been sold to just one new lender, it probably went through a corporation or a bank on its way from one owner to the next — and the bank must show all that in its documentation.

If the lender is not able to produce adequate documentation to prove it has the legal standing to bring a foreclosure suit against you, the foreclosure may be dismissed. It will certainly be delayed while the lender attempts to find the ownership documents. Even when the foreclosure suit is not dismissed, a lender in this position is more likely to be willing to negotiate a loan modification. In some cases, the property may be secured with no mortgage or lien through a quiet title action — a lawsuit seeking a court order to prevent any further claims on the property by the lender.

Defense #10: Unconscionability

Unconscionability in defense against foreclosure is almost like an insanity defense in a criminal case — it is hard to prove and only used when there is dire need.

What is it?

Unconscionability means that one party — in the case of a mortgage, the borrower — did not have the ability to make a meaningful choice when he or she agreed to the terms of the loan. In addition, it must be proved that the other party had unreasonably favorable contract terms; in essence, the lender swindled the borrower out of their money, and the borrower did not understand the proceedings.

How do I use it?

Because a mortgage is a signed contract, and there are so many regulations in place that deal with all aspects of the origination of loans, the courts do not entertain claims of unconscionability lightly. Unlike breach of contract, this is not a defense to be added along with others in the hopes of a good outcome. This defense should only be implemented when certain provable factors are involved.

One type of unconscionability, referred to as "procedural unconscionability," results in "unfair surprise" for the consumer. Some of the factors that constitute an unfair surprise are:

- The borrower's age, experience, and ability to reason.
- The borrower's ability to understand or read the contract.
- The language of the sale in relation to the contract — for example, the real estate agent spoke Spanish with his client, but the mortgage is written in English.
- The settlement being conducted without the assistance of a translator when necessary.

Other factors under this heading include the terms of the contract and whether they contained fine print clauses, a manipulation of rules, and even whether the seller intentionally took advantage of the borrower's deficiency for his own good. These factors also encompass predatory lending practices such as deceptive payment schedules, false "teaser" rates, last-minute rate hikes, and oppressive terms.

Unconscionability factors of another type are substantive and focus on how the contract is biased in favor of one party — in this case, the lender. These factors involve the integrity of the lender and mortgage broker and focus on whether the broker did any of the following:

- Pushed the consumer into an unnecessary refinance, which does not benefit the consumer at all.

- Used a "stated" income product or a "no income, no asset" product, rather than helping a qualified consumer into a more stable and probably lower payment through a traditional loan.

- Filled out the application for the borrower — often demonstrated by major discrepancies between the application and other documents.

- Employed negative amortization.

The courts will also compare the loan in question with other loans available at the time to determine whether there is a great disparity in interest rates or payments.

If unconscionability can be proved, the loan may be deemed invalid. The court decides whether the loan should be rescinded and whether damages will be awarded. The borrower needs to prove that both parts of this defense exist — that he or she was unable for some reason to understand the terms of the loan, and that the loan is unfavorable for the borrower. In the case, for example, of an elderly person who refinanced a home, both factors would need to be proved. If the person did not understand the loan but could afford the payments and is in default for some other reason, the defense will not work. The defense will work if the terms of the loan show negligence or predatory practices.

Defense #11: Failure to state a claim upon which relief can be granted

This defense is similar to the breach-of-contract defense in that it can be coupled with just about any other legal defense against foreclosure.

What is it?

This defense makes the claim that the lender's lawsuit is essentially flawed because of omission or negligence. If the lender forgets something as simple as stating that the loan is in default in the paperwork it filed in the foreclosure suit against you, the claim can be made that the plaintiff does not have a claim upon which relief can be granted. It is a "technicality" defense, but it is associated with other defenses because its interpretation can be so broad.

How do I use it?

Failure to state a claim can also be used as a kind of back-up defense with the standing defense discussed previously in defense No. 9 because if the plaintiff does not actually own the loan, they do not have standing and failed to state a claim. This defense often cannot stand alone, but adds an additional level to another type of defense. It can be helpful in halting or delaying foreclosure and in getting a lender to negotiate a loan modification.

Defense #12: Failure to establish conditions precedent

The "failure to establish conditions precedent" is similar to other defenses of omission. In this case, the condition precedent refers to something that is triggered once the default has occurred, rather than a part of the mortgage or settlement papers.

What is it?

Within the language of your mortgage, there is probably a covenant stating the procedure that will be followed to foreclose on the property. Often a notice of acceleration must be mailed to the borrower before the foreclosure begins, followed by a waiting period during which the borrower can make good on the mortgage commitment and stave off foreclosure proceedings.

How do I use it?

If your lender has proceeded with a foreclosure without sending a notice of acceleration (check your mortgage to be sure this is required), you can defend yourself with the "failure to establish conditions precedent" and have the foreclosure dismissed. Of course, if you do not reconcile the default with your lender, it can send the notice of acceleration out and begin the foreclosure proceedings again. If your lender did not wait the 30 days — or the time period stated in the mortgage — before beginning the foreclosure, you could also mount this defense. This defense tends to result in dismissal of the proceedings and buys the borrower more time to find a means of paying the delinquent amount. If the lender files twice and the claim is dismissed twice under this defense, the property reverts to the borrower with no mortgage or lien.

Defense #13: Failure to comply with FHA pre-foreclosure requirements

If you purchased your home using a FHA loan, then you know that your home and your loan were subject to more stringent rules than with a conventional loan. The special terms and lower interest rates provided through the FHA require a little more work for the buyer at the outset.

What is it?

Similarly, if you find yourself facing foreclosure on a loan insured by HUD, your lender will have to complete additional steps before pursuing foreclosure on your property. The lender is required to mail a publication named *How to Avoid Foreclosure* and often will arrange a face-to-face meeting with you.

How do I use it?

Failure to comply with the additional regulations in the case of an FHA loan foreclosure is equal to the failure to meet a condition precedent as outlined in the last section. If you are successful, this defense may set the clock back on foreclosure, but your lender has the opportunity to comply with the regulations and re-file the foreclosure suit.

Defense #14: Mortgage or note not attached to complaint

Like the last few defenses, this defense can buy time for you and hold off foreclosure proceedings until the lender has time to reorganize and refile. It does not win damages for the borrower and will probably not be a permanent solution to the default on the loan, but it can give the borrower more time to get his or her affairs in order and get back on track financially.

What is it?

In most states, the plaintiff is required to produce an actual copy of the mortgage or note on the property and attach it to the complaint that they file in court. In addition, a sworn affidavit should accompany the mortgage, stating that the documents are accurate and true. As the defendant, you have the right to demand that the lender produce the actual signed copies of your mortgage, rather than an electronic version.

How do I use it?

As with the two previous defenses, this one will result in a dismissal of the complaint, but your lender will have the option to refile. If you have requested that the originals of the mortgage be included, and they cannot be located and produced, the entire foreclosure may be defeated.

Defense #15: Insufficiency of process

Another defense that can buy you some time to get your financial affairs in order is the simple insufficiency of process.

What is it?

This defense states that the lender, the plaintiff in foreclosure cases, did not serve the defendant with a copy of the lawsuit. Laws governing process serving vary from state to state, so consult your state and local laws regarding service of process where you live.

How do I use it?

If the lender did not provide you with a copy of the lawsuit in accordance with state and local laws regarding service of process, you can challenge the foreclosure suit. This defense is likely to result in a motion to dismiss the lawsuit, but the lender is free to refile and correct their mistake.

Defense #16: National Flood Insurance Act

You might be able to use this defense if you have stopped paying your mortgage because your home is damaged due to flooding.

What is it?

If your home is situated in a flood area or was found to be in a flood area after purchase, you are required to hold property insurance in an amount at least equal to the outstanding amount on your mortgage.

How do I use it?

If your lender did not require insurance on the property initially or did not force-place insurance — buy insurance and require the borrower to pay for it — then once the hazard was determined, your lender is liable under federal law — not to the homeowner, but to the government. This defense is only applicable if your home was damaged due to a flood and you were not properly insured due to lender negligence. In that case, you could apply for specific flood relief assistance from the government. The court will decide whether to dismiss the foreclosure proceedings and what action to take against the lender.

Defense #17: Bankruptcy

Filing for bankruptcy protection is a way to halt the foreclosure proceedings, just as it stops collections of other debts included in the bankruptcy.

What is it?

Filing for bankruptcy is a legal process that seeks forgiveness for unmanageable debt, including delinquent mortgage payments.

How do I use it?

Bankruptcy is a complicated process and should not be used as a quick fix. Losing your home to a foreclosure is hard enough; seeking a bankruptcy filing can add to your distress or can be a relief, depending on your individual circumstances.

Because bankruptcy trumps foreclosure, it can bring proceedings to an immediate halt. It puts the sale or loss of your home into the hands of the bankruptcy court, which will determine whether you can afford to repay the loan. If the court determines that you are unable to fulfill your commitment to the mortgage, the foreclosure will begin again, and you will have to vacate your property.

If the bankruptcy court determines that you are able to fulfill your commitment to your mortgage, it has the authority to modify the terms of your loan and the schedule of your payments so that you can make the mortgage payments, and it will work with your lender to create a payment plan. With your unsecured debt wiped out, you will be in a better position to make your mortgage payments after a bankruptcy.

Filing a bankruptcy in response to a foreclosure suit has a negative effect on your credit; it will remain on your credit report for ten years. Also, filing for bankruptcy will not automatically allow you to stay in your home. Consult an attorney and weigh your options carefully. Remember that a foreclosure is also detrimental to your credit, and that losing your home while you are still drowning in credit card debt will not help you rebuild your future.

Defense #18: MERS

Mortgage Electronic Registration Systems, Inc. (MERS) is a component of two of the defenses discussed previously: standing and failure to state a claim. MERS is a private company that serves as an electronic register for mortgage transfers.

What is it?

Your county has a recorder of deeds office, where your original mortgage was probably recorded and a copy still resides. In the past, if your mortgage was sold to another lender, an "assignment of mortgage" with the name of the new owner was filed with the recorder of deeds to document the change of ownership. In recent decades, as Wall Street began to "securitize" mortgage loans, bundling them into collateralized debt obligations (CDOs) and selling them repeatedly — often to hedge funds, pension funds, and overseas investors — MERS became an electronic clearinghouse and filing system for mortgages. Lenders use MERS to facilitate and record the transfer of loans as they change hands. MERS acts as the mortgagee of the loan while other transfers are being made, even though it rejects the concept that it holds ownership of the loan at any time. Rather, MERS maintains that it is simply the "nominee" for the lender and does not hold claim for securing the loan. It does, however, often serve as the party of interest when foreclosures are on the table. An estimated 60 million mortgages, or half of all new U.S. mortgages, are held by MERS.

How do I use it?

If your loan has been sold, and sometimes even if it has not, do some research to find out where MERS has been involved. The first place to look is your county recorder of deeds office. A MERS case is based on exposing flaws in the chain of ownership and contesting who is the party of interest in your foreclosure proceeding. MERS typifies the messy, questionable practices prevalent in the inflated mortgage industry. By providing electronic registrations of loan sales or even just "holding" the loan while transfers are being made, MERS breaks down the concept of party of interest while working for the lender to make sales, transfers, and even foreclosures quick and efficient. MERS also shields the real owners of the mortgages from claims of predatory lending practices.

Individual states are still working out the purpose and scope of MERS in foreclosure cases, but finding out how your loan was involved can be a crucial part of your defense. A groundbreaking case in the Nebraska Supreme Court found that MERS was unable to secure loans because it neither provided credit nor served as the entity that would receive payment for the loans. This ruling, at least in Nebraska, proved that the place of MERS is simply as recorder of the deeds and disallowed it from pursuing foreclosure actions against homeowners in its own right. In Landmark National Bank v. Kesler, 2009 Kan. LEXIS 834, the Kansas Supreme Court held that MERS has no right or standing to bring an action for foreclosure, stating that the role of MERS "is more akin to that of a straw man than to a party possessing all the rights given a buyer." A MERS defense can challenge a foreclosure in two ways: MERS does not have standing to pursue a foreclosure, and the parties who purchased the mortgage from the original lender do not have standing because they were not signatories to the original contract.

Defense #19: Predatory lending

The term "predatory lending" is often given as an excuse when someone has taken on a loan he or she cannot afford, or even to explain a case of unconscionability. Unlike most of the defenses we have explored in this section, a predatory lending defense is not based on a single item or issue; rather, it is necessary to prove a pattern of abuse by a lender or mortgage broker.

What is it?

There has been much discussion in the media about questionable lending practices and brokers who promise to get a loan for anyone, regardless of his or her financial circumstances. Marketing campaigns promise to refinance at lower rates and to obtain mortgages for buyers with bad credit. What makes this bad practice, and when does it become predatory lending? The Office of the Comptroller of the Currency (OCC) watches the mortgage market and, in 2003, described predatory lending as "a disregard of the basic principles of loan underwriting."

Some of the practices recognized as predatory lending are:

- Loan flipping and refinancing that favors the lender or broker, with negligible benefit to the borrower.

- Refinancing loans that had benefits — such as an FHA — into products that remove that benefit to the homeowner.

- Piling excessive fees and charges onto the balance of a refinance.

- Implementing negative amortization — where the balance gets larger, rather than smaller.

- Offering teaser payments in the beginning that make the homeowner feel they can afford more than they can, while a balloon payment looms in the future.

- Seeking out clients who are elderly or otherwise unable to fully understand the products they are being offered and putting them in a disadvantageous financial position.

- Failing to adequately disclose fees and the true cost of the credit being provided.

How do I use it?

You will need the help of an attorney to demonstrate that you are the victim of predatory lending practices and are unable to pay your mortgage as a result. A predatory lending defense exposes the questionable activities of your lender, rather than providing legal details that will help you defend against foreclosure. Proving that your lender has used predatory practices is a good defense because it allows the court to decide how to remedy the situation if it rules in your favor. The court might require the lender to return all the money you have paid on the loan (and take the property), or it might work out a better payment plan for you. Either way, you will avoid foreclosure.

High-rate, high-fee loans (HOEPA/Section 32 mortgages)

Excerpt from the Federal Trade Commission

www.ftc.gov/bcp/edu/pubs/consumer/homes/rea19.shtm

If you are refinancing your mortgage or applying for a home equity installment loan, you should know about the Home Ownership and Equity Protection Act of 1994 (HOEPA). The law addresses certain deceptive and unfair practices in home equity lending. It amends the Truth in Lending Act (TILA) and establishes requirements for certain loans with high rates and/or high fees.

The rules for these loans are contained in Section 32 of Regulation Z, which implements the TILA, so the loans also are called "Section 32 Mortgages." Here is what loans are covered, the law's disclosure requirements, prohibited features, and actions you can take against a lender who is violating the law.

WHAT LOANS ARE COVERED?

A loan is covered by the law if it meets the following tests:

- For a first-lien loan — that is, the original mortgage on the property — the annual percentage rate (APR) exceeds by more than 8 percentage points the rates on Treasury securities of comparable maturity;

- For a second-lien loan — that is, a second mortgage — the APR exceeds by more than 10 percentage points the rates in Treasury securities of comparable maturity; or

- The total fees and points payable by the consumer at or before closing exceed the larger of $583, or 8 percent of the total loan amount. (The $583 figure is for 2009. This amount is adjusted annually by the Federal Reserve Board, based on changes in the Consumer Price Index.) Credit insurance premiums for insurance written in connection with the credit transaction are counted as fees.

The rules primarily affect refinancing and home equity installment loans that also meet the definition of a high-rate or high-fee loan. The rules do not cover loans to buy or build your home, reverse mortgages, or home equity lines of credit (similar to revolving credit accounts).

WHAT DISCLOSURES ARE REQUIRED?

If your loan meets the above tests, you must receive several disclosures at least three business days before the loan is finalized:

- The lender must give you a written notice stating that the loan need not be completed, even though you have signed the loan application and received the required disclosures. You have three business days to decide whether to sign the loan agreement after you receive the special Section 32 disclosures.

- The notice must warn you that, because the lender will have a mortgage on your home, you could lose the residence and any money put into it, if you fail to make payments.

- The lender must disclose the APR, the regular payment amount (including any balloon payment where the law permits balloon payments, discussed in the next section), and the loan amount (plus, where the amount borrowed includes credit insurance premiums, that fact must be stated). For variable rate loans, the lender must disclose that the rate and monthly payment may increase and state the amount of the maximum monthly payment.

These disclosures are in addition to the other TILA disclosures that you must receive no later than the closing of the loan.

WHAT PRACTICES ARE PROHIBITED?

The following features are banned from high-rate, high-fee loans:

- All balloon payments — where the regular payments do not fully pay off the principal balance and a lump sum payment of more than twice the amount of the regular payments is required — for loans with less than five-year terms. There is an exception for bridge loans of less than one year used by consumers to buy or build a home; in that situation, balloon payments are not prohibited.

- Negative amortization that involves smaller monthly payments that do not fully pay off the loan and causes an increase in your total principal debt.

- Default interest rates higher than pre-default rates.

- Rebates of interest upon default calculated by any method less favorable than the actuarial method.

- A repayment schedule that consolidates more than two periodic payments that are to be paid in advance from the proceeds of the loan.

- Most prepayment penalties, including refunds of unearned interest calculated by any method less favorable than the actuarial method. The exception is if:

  o The lender verifies that your total monthly debt (including the mortgage) is 50 percent or less of your monthly gross income;

  o You get the money to prepay the loan from a source other than the lender or an affiliate lender; and

  o The lender exercises the penalty clause during the first five years following execution of the mortgage.

- A due-on-demand clause. The exceptions are if:

  o There is fraud or material misrepresentation by the consumer in connection with the loan;

  o The consumer fails to meet the repayment terms of the agreement; or o   There is any action by the consumer that adversely affects the creditor's security.

Creditors also may not:

- Make loans based on the collateral value of your property without regard to your ability to repay the loan. In addition, proceeds for home improvement loans must be disbursed directly to you, jointly to you and the home improvement contractor or, in some instances, to the escrow agent.

- Refinance a HOEPA loan into another HOEPA loan within the first 12 months of origination, unless the new loan is in the borrower's best interest. The prohibition also applies to assignees holding or servicing the loan.

- Wrongfully document a closed-end, high-cost loan as an open-end loan. For example, a high-cost mortgage may not be structured as a home equity line of credit if there is no reasonable expectation that repeat transactions will occur.

How are compliance violations handled?

You may have the right to sue a lender for violations of these requirements. In a successful suit, you may be able to recover statutory and actual damages, court costs, and attorney's fees. In addition, a violation of the high-rate, high-fee requirements of the TILA may enable you to rescind (or cancel) the loan for up to three years.

Defense #20: Failure to verify income or assets

Some loans are given without checking the borrower's income or assets. Stated-income, stated-asset (SISA) loans and no-income, no-asset (NINA) loans were originally used by people who were self-employed or whose income came from tips or large bonuses. These people had difficulty securing conventional loans because of the nature of their income. SISA or NINA loans typically required a substantial down payment and carried a higher interest rate than traditional mortgages.

What is it?

Beginning around 2000, these loans were increasingly used by borrowers to secure mortgages on properties they could not afford. Many people agreed to these types of loans as speculative investments: Home prices were going up so quickly that they were confident they could soon refinance and get out of the loans. When the housing bubble began to burst late in 2007, many people were left with these high-interest, high-risk loans and were now unable to afford their mortgage payments. Requirements for loans have become stricter, and even if these borrowers still have equity in their homes, they cannot refinance because their incomes are not high enough to qualify for a mortgage of that size.

In response to SISA and NINA loans, the government passed an addendum to TILA covering loans that exceed the prime rate by more than 1.5 percent and requiring that all loans must verify the borrower's income and assets.

You should already know if you took out one of these loans, but you can verify it by looking at your stated income on your loan documents. This number is rarely a round figure like $3,000 a month — it is calculated by dividing your annual salary by 12. If that area of the document is blank, you have a NINA loan.

How do I use it?

Verify that all the facts related to your income and assets are correct. Any discrepancy between what you provided to your lender and what is in your documents is cause for alarm. Your length of employment, job title, and income amounts should be correct. Double-check all numbers and information about your assets.

SISA and NINA loans are not illegal, and many people knowingly took out these loans in an attempt to capitalize on a changing, volatile market. If you are using SISA or NINA as a defense to foreclosure, it will be as part of a larger defense, such as predatory lending or negligence. Additionally, if you have been making payments for a year or more, your ability to claim this defense is greatly diminished because you are alleging negligence; the fact that you have been paying the mortgage implies that you were able to afford it when it was written for you.

Defense #21: Defective mortgage or note

Another technicality defense, a defective mortgage or note could result in the voiding of the entire contract or could just buy you a few extra weeks or months to hold off the foreclosure.

What is it?

The many details on your loan document must all be correct for the mortgage to be valid. This defense requires careful investigation on your part. Take your mortgage documents and go through them, line by line. From the terms to the signatures, ensure that everything in the document is correct. Here is what to look for:

- Do all terms match?
- Are the terms even possible?
- Are there are any blank spaces?
- Were the notary stamps current and not expired at the time of the loan origination?
- Are all signatures included and in the correct spaces?
- Are all copies available and complete?

How do I use it?

If you find a miscalculation or discrepancy in your loan documents, the loan could be defended using a TILA violation defense, which is a strong defense. You might also uncover chain of title or standing issues when you inspect your mortgage documents. Errors in mortgage documents can be used in court to halt the foreclosure, at least until the lender has made corrections and a new court date has been set.

Defense #22: Equal Credit Opportunity Act

If you believe you were discriminated against in your mortgage terms on the basis of race, color, religion, national origin, gender, or marital status, you may have a claim under the Equal Credit Opportunity Act (ECOA).

What is it?

The act requires lenders not to discriminate against any borrower for any reason, including race, religion, gender, or disability. The Federal Financial Institutions Examination Council (FFIEC) (**www.ffiec.gov/hmda**) provides information on the Home Mortgage Disclosure Act (HMDA) and reports data illustrating national patterns of lending to minorities. Disparities among lending practices seem to exist even within areas with minorities. Reports from the FFIEC can give you an idea of the lending practices in your area so you can evaluate whether you have been the victim of discriminatory practices.

How do I use it?

You will need the assistance of a lawyer specializing in discrimination cases to pursue this defense, because it may be difficult to prove that you have been the victim of discriminatory lending. A decision in your favor can result in punitive damages of up to $10,000 in addition to actual damages and lawyer's fees. This defense can delay foreclosure and, if successful, provide funds that could be used to make up delinquent payments. If you have had difficulty making monthly payments that were higher than they should have been because of discriminatory lending, you might succeed in lowering your interest rate and monthly payments.

Defense #23: Servicing abuse

Many of the defenses we have discussed have centered on the construction of loan documents and applications and the process of the foreclosure. This final defense is based on the actual servicing of your loan — that is, the way the payments are accepted and how fees are assessed during the repayment process.

What is it?

In a case of servicing abuse, the courts evaluate how late fees were applied, whether payments were recorded on time, and whether the lender force-placed insurance on the loan after its inception.

Prior to revisions to TILA in 2008, lenders could continue to assess fees on a single late payment, causing the borrower to end up in default even after the delinquency had been resolved. The loan's default status resulted in an increasing number of fees charged to the homeowner for items such as appraisals or inspections, in preparation for a foreclosure that the lender had set into motion with the late fees.

Force-placed insurance benefits the lender rather than the borrower. In essence, the lender is insuring itself against a possible default, similar to what PMI borrowers must carry when they hold less than 20 percent equity in their homes. Unlike homeowner's insurance, force-placed insurance and PMI are only protecting the bank against the loss of its investment. When a lender tries to force a homeowner to buy additional insurance on a property, that insurance is typically more expensive than the available alternatives that the homeowner could find on the market. The bank is making money by forcing the borrower to pay for the insurance, and it is receiving the protection from that insurance policy.

How do I use it?

A defense of servicing abuse can be used to reduce the expenses, such as late fees, penalties, interest, and other costs, that you may be facing in a foreclosure suit. In some cases, if the infraction was a blatant violation of the terms of the mortgage contract, it may be an entire defense against foreclosure, as part of a breach-of-contract defense.

Legal defenses against foreclosure and legal strategies to delay foreclosure proceedings, bring about rescission (cancellation of the loan transaction), or collect penalties and damages from the lender are based on the mortgage contract, promissory note, and accompanying disclosures and notifications. If, after reviewing your mortgage documents, you believe you have grounds for a legal defense against foreclosure, consult an experienced real estate attorney who is familiar with similar cases and knows how to construct a solid case against your lender. If you feel you are the victim of predatory lending or false advertising, you can seek assistance from the Federal Trade Commission Bureau of Consumer Protection (**www.ftc.gov/bcp/menus/ consumer/credit/mortgage.shtm**) and from your state and local consumer protection agencies. A legal defense may not keep you in your home if you are not able to manage your monthly payment, but it can help you achieve an equitable solution to your problem and avoid having a foreclosure on your credit report. It can also buy extra weeks and months in which you can seek to arrange your finances and make up delinquent payments, renegotiate the terms of your loan, or sell your house on the market.

Tactics to Delay Your Foreclosure

Avoiding foreclosure is a race against time. Once the process has begun, you have only a few weeks or months to develop a plan to either prevent or stop your foreclosure and to get your finances back on track. The following tactics can delay foreclosure just a little longer while you come up with a more permanent solution to your financial problems.

Forbearance

Most people use forbearance — or a type of mortgage payback — as a way to avoid foreclosure altogether, but it can also be a good way to delay it. When you enter into a forbearance contract with the bank, you agree to make up delinquent payments in monthly installments. As long as you can manage to make these payments for a few months, this tactic can be used to delay foreclosure while you figure out a better solution.

Question the sheriff's appraisal

In most states, a foreclosure auction can be delayed if you argue that the sheriff's appraisal is incorrect and insist on having a new one done. Depending on your county appraiser, a second appraisal can take anywhere from a few weeks to a few months.

Demand a sale delay

In many jurisdictions, the court can force a delay of a sheriff's sale if you show intent to find a better solution than foreclosure. This delay is usually granted for six to 12 months. One warning: When a delay like this has been granted, most lenders seek a deficiency judgment to ensure that they get the entire amount due if the house eventually sells for less than the mortgage payoff amount.

Ask for as many court delays as possible

The court system can move quite slowly, especially when you ask for repeated delays and contingencies. Every time you are forced to stand before a judge, ask for a continuance. A continuance means that you are asking the court to set a later date for the foreclosure hearing, typically 30 to 90 days later. You can ask the court to postpone your hearing so that you can consult a lawyer, or for time to file "appearance" and "answer" forms indicating that you intend to represent yourself and believe you have a legal defense against foreclosure. A hearing can also be delayed if there are errors in the mortgage documents, or if you can demonstrate that some kind of temporary hardship, such as an illness or injury, makes it difficult for you to respond immediately. These delays are time you can use in your favor. Consult with a foreclosure lawyer to see what types of court delays you can reasonably request.

File for bankruptcy

Some people have filed for bankruptcy with no intention of going through with it, but rather to only delay their foreclosure proceedings. Once you file for bankruptcy, your foreclosure must be stopped until your formal bankruptcy hearing. Although pulling out of a bankruptcy is not illegal, the court may question your actions if it appears that you only initiated the bankruptcy as a way to stave off a foreclosure. Consult a qualified legal professional for advice in this matter before moving forward.

Challenge your lender in court

Your lender must follow strict legal regulations when foreclosing on your home. Should the lender miss any step along the way, the entire process can be delayed for 30 to 90 days. Be sure to track every letter and notice you receive, and double-check to make sure all legal requirements, schedules, and notice verifications have been met. If your lender failed to follow any of the steps exactly as required by law, you can ask for a halt — or at least a delay — in your foreclosure by making a formal request to the court.

Negotiate extra time to clear out

In some cases, you can ask your lender to give you a few extra days or weeks to move out of your home once it has been sold at auction. This is done either through a certified letter of request or during one of your many court hearings. This extra time is not always granted, but there is certainly no harm in asking.

CHAPTER 8

Selling Your House

After you have calculated your monthly expenditures, seen your credit score, and determined the amount of equity you hold in your home, you might decide that holding onto your property is not in your best interest financially. Selling your house might be the most effective route to keeping foreclosure off your credit report. Though leaving a home you love is painful, selling it and moving to a more affordable accommodation can help get your finances back on track and let you make a new start. If your equity has increased since you purchased the home, you will recover extra funds to pay off debt or make a deposit on another property. You will not have a foreclosure on your credit report. If you can repair your credit and bring your credit score up, you have a significantly better chance of securing a new loan at a lower interest rate.

Whether you sell your home yourself, find someone to assume the mortgage, or use the services of a real estate agent, selling before you go to foreclosure can save your credit and set you up for a positive future. The earlier you make the decision to sell your home, the more time you will have to prepare the house, find a buyer, and negotiate for a reasonable price. After your lender begins foreclosure proceedings, you still have the authority to sell your home right up to the day of the foreclosure auction, but you will be working under a very tight timeframe. The closing must be completed before the auction date.

Preparing Yourself to Sell

Selling your home takes much more effort than simply sticking a "for sale" sign in the lawn. If you are selling to avoid foreclosure, you have many decisions to make in a very short time. You must decide whether to hire an agent or sell the property yourself. You will need to stage your home to show it to potential buyers in its best light. You will also have to decide whether to make repairs before you show the house or whether to deduct the cost of repairs from the selling price. If the foreclosure notice has already arrived, you have only a few months to accomplish these tasks and find a buyer, so time is working against you.

Tip : How long will it take to sell your house?

The amount of time it will take to sell your house depends on the area where you live and the price you are asking. In early 2010, real estate agents in many American cities reported that the average time for selling a home was three to four months. If you live in an economically depressed area, or one where an excessive number of homes are for sale, it could take much longer. You may owe more on your mortgage than the current selling price for a house like yours, in which case you will have to ask your lender to approve a short sale. You can look up home prices and average time on the market for your area at HouseHunt.com (**www. househunt.com/realestate-markettrends**).

Getting in the Selling Mindset

No one likes being forced to sell a home, but it might be an unpleasant necessity if you are facing foreclosure. Adjust your attitude to accept that this is the best route for you to recover your losses and move on with your life. No matter how you feel about leaving your home, if you have done all that you possibly can up to this point to keep the property, embrace your predicament. To achieve the best results, you must motivate yourself to be proactive and stay positive during the selling process. Separate yourself emotionally from the property and regard it as the object that it is, so you can remain objective and make sound decisions.

Spend some time making peace with your decision to sell. Though you may have been forced to this point by circumstances beyond your control, it is still possible to make the experience a positive and productive one. Anger and resentment will not change the situation change and will only do you harm. You have done all that was in your power — now it is time to recover as much of your equity as possible and look ahead to the next stage of your life.

Deciding Who Will Sell the Home

There are two ways to sell a home — do it yourself or hire an agent. The benefit of selling a home yourself is that you save on the commission fee charged by a real estate agent. The average commission for an agent is 6 to 7 percent, so on a home that sells for $250,000, you would save $15,000 to $17,000. That is a considerable sum, especially if you are selling because of financial hardship. By not paying an agent's commission, you might be able to price your home more aggressively, which will make your home more attractive in a competitive market. Without the involvement of a third party, negotiations between you and a buyer can be dealt with quickly. Selling your home on your own is not a complicated process, but time is of the essence when you are approaching foreclosure. This is not the best time to venture into unfamiliar territory.

A real estate agent will do much of the work involved with selling your home for you. The agent will show the home, market it to potential buyers, and help with the endless stream of paperwork. A good agent works hard to sell your home quickly. If you are already in the process of foreclosure and have only a few weeks or months to sell your house, it is advisable to hire an agent. A local real estate agent understands what your property is likely to sell for in the current market, how long it will take, and who is most likely to purchase it. The agent can help you decide what repairs or improvements should be made to help sell the property. Considerable time and energy is required to sell a house; someone needs to be available to show the home at various times of the day, answer phone calls, handle advertisements, and manage the paperwork. The agent's contacts could prove invaluable when that foreclosure time clock is ticking. A real estate agent can also help potential buyers secure funds from a lender.

Try to find a real estate agent who has experience selling homes facing foreclosure. This type of agent will already have a strategy for selling homes quickly and will know how to move the negotiations along in a timely manner. This is not the time to take a chance on a novice or someone inexperienced in foreclosure sales. Increase you chances of selling by giving the job to the best agent you can find. A good agent might also be able to negotiate a "short sale," an agreement by the lender to accept a price lower than the amount owed on the mortgage as satisfaction of the debt, if the pending sale is scheduled to close around the date of the auction. *See the following section on short sales and foreclosure for more information.* When looking for an agent, ask friends and family for references, then carefully interview prospective agents. Ask these questions when interviewing agents:

- How many foreclosing homes have you handled?

- What is your success rate?

- How do you plan to market my property? What is your detailed plan of action?

- Can you give me references from past clients who have gone through similar experiences?

Contact references and talk to them to find out what the agent was like. How creative is the agent likely to be? Ask for specific details, such as how close the closing price was to the asking price, whether the amount covered the loan that was due, and how quickly their homes sold.

Ask whether the agent plans to list your property in a multiple listing service (MLS). The MLS is a resource used by agents both selling homes and looking for homes on the market for clients. It is updated on a daily basis and provides real estate agents in your area with information on particular properties that are for sale. This is the best way of making sure anyone looking for property like yours will be aware that it is up for sale. Do not rely on newspaper listings to sell your home — get the word out in as many ways as possible, and to the right people. Put pictures of the home on notice boards at work and at local churches. Tell your friends, relatives, and neighbors that you are selling.

Before deciding on a real estate agent, be sure to work out the figures. How much does the agent realistically think you can get for your home? How does this figure compare to the figures you gathered in your research for refinancing? Does it seem like a reasonable estimate? Ask what commission will be charged. As mentioned before, most agents will charge around 6 percent — which they may or may not split with the buyer's agent.

Listing Agreements

After finding a real estate agent, you will need to enter into a listing agreement. There are three general forms: an exclusive listing, an exclusive agency, or an open listing agreement. Each offers various benefits and drawbacks. Listing agreements are often negotiable, so do not hesitate to ask for changes before you sign the paperwork.

Exclusive listing agreements are fairly straightforward. You agree to pay the agent a commission if your property is sold within a given time period. For conventional sales, this period could be up to six or seven months. The terms may be shorter, however, if you are already in the foreclosure process. The drawback for you as a homeowner is that, if you enter into this type of agreement, the commission must be paid regardless of who finds the buyer. If your cousin decides to purchase your property to help you out, the agent still gets the commission.

Exclusive agency agreements work similarly, but the agent only receives a commission if *he or she* finds the buyer. This is helpful if you are both working actively to sell the property — a probable situation in foreclosure. Confusion could arise over who actually found the buyer. If you enter into this form of agreement, be certain that you both keep your paperwork clear and straight. If you show the home and manage the contacts with someone who eventually makes an offer, be certain that you can prove your active role.

Open listing agreements are better in theory than practice — though you may consider it as a viable option. Like an exclusive agency agreement, the commission goes to whoever sells the property. The advantage of this agreement is that you can have multiple agents working to sell your home at the same time. The disadvantage is that agents may not be motivated to compete against one another if the potential commission is not large enough. Because time is of the essence, you want to have agents actively working to sell your home, so try not to create unnecessary obstacles. If you find a capable agent who specializes in properties in foreclosure, give them the benefit of the doubt and let them make selling your home a priority.

The listing agreement is similar to other real estate contracts, containing stipulations and clauses that you need to be aware of. Listing agreements contain standard clauses, but a few changes might need to be made when you are trying to keep your home out of foreclosure.

Time limitations are of the utmost importance in your agreement. While most agents expect to be working to sell your property over a four- to six-month period, when you are facing foreclosure, even four months is too long. Ask that the term of agreement be limited to 60 days. If your home has not sold within two months, it is unlikely that selling will prevent foreclosure. An agent who understands that time is extremely limited will be more proactive in finding you a buyer.

The next item to alter is the conditions upon which the agent earns his or her commission. Most of the time, the agent will have earned his or her commission when he or she has presented a buyer who is "ready, willing, and able" to purchase. Unfortunately, this means that if the closing does not occur in time to save your property from the foreclosure auction block, you will still be obligated to pay the commission. Cross out the "ready, willing, and able" aspect of the clause and replace it with new wording so that it stipulates that the agent earns the commission when the property closes. It can be as simple as "when the closing has completed and papers are passed." Be sure that the agent signifies acceptance by initialing next to the changes.

There might be other conditions you would like to include in the agreement, depending on your needs. If you require additional services from your agent, such as wanting them to work with you on all aspects of the selling and closing, include that information specifically. Make the detailed marketing plan you asked for when you were interviewing the agent part of the agreement, too. That way, should your agent not do what was promised, you have a means of ending the contract.

A termination agreement is the most important amendment you can make to the contract. Your agent may explain all the different actions he or she will take to sell your property quickly, but fall far short of his or her promises. Include in your contract a few sentences that say you have the right to end the agreement at any point in time should the agent not handle the selling process appropriately. This will protect you from losing valuable time and money — and potentially your home — if an agent's work is unsatisfactory.

Finding a Real Estate Lawyer

Though it is an additional expense, if you decide to sell the property yourself, it is wise to hire a real estate lawyer to help you with the negotiations and contracts. In addition to helping you navigate the paperwork, he or she can act as a legal entity to hold any deposits, as well as make sure you are meeting all your mortgage commitments before closing takes place. It is reassuring to have a professional third party draw up the legal documents that determine the conditions the sale.

Ask friends and relatives to recommend a good lawyer, and get references from potential lawyers. If you have worked with a broker to consider refinancing, ask him or her to refer a lawyer. Find out how long the lawyer has been in the business, whether he or she has experience with "for sale by owner" properties, and what fees he or she will charge.

Find out whether your state legally requires a lawyer to be involved in a sale of real estate. In many states, only a certified real estate attorney is allowed to draw up the contract, hire title searches, and handle the closing.

Disclosures

A real estate agent or lawyer can assist you in the preparation of disclosures. When you put your home on the market, you are legally required to disclose certain information to potential buyers. This information includes:

- **Real estate disclosure transfer statements**
  These disclosures provide information about your property's condition. When you have an inspection or valuation of your

property, you receive a report listing all of its defects. "Defects" can be anything from cracked roof tiles and mold in the basement to disruptive neighbors and the crime rate of the neighborhood. This information is provided to all potential buyers so that they can make an informed decision about buying your home. It also protects you from being sued by a buyer in the future for home repairs necessitated by damage that occurred while you owned the home.

- **Flood and seismic disclosures**
  Flood and seismic disclosures are required if your property is located in an area that could potentially flood or suffer from earthquakes. Look at your mortgage agreement. If your lender required you to purchase flood or earthquake insurance, then you must make this information readily available to potential buyers.

- **Fire hazards**
  Finally, you must inform potential buyers if your home is located within a state-mandated fire hazard area. Some regions of Florida and California, for example, are prone to wildfires that would put homes in the region in danger. If your home is in such an area, be certain to disclose this in writing.

Preparing Your Home

There is more to making your home ready for potential buyers than simply putting the laundry away and vacuuming the carpets. By making your home look like someplace special to live, you will have a much greater chance of selling before the foreclosure auction date arrives.

Making necessary repairs

You may not feel inspired to put money into a home that you are trying to sell, but it is a necessary expense. Look at the appraiser's report, if you had one done, to see what brought down the value of your property. If you have not had an appraisal done, spend a day going over the entire house with a notebook. Make a list of everything that needs fixing in the house, from loose doorknobs to roof repairs. Your transfer disclosure statement could be helpful in identifying repairs to be made. Your real estate agent can also suggest minor repairs and improvements that would make the house more attractive to buyers.

Be certain that you know everything that is affecting the value of the property. An interested buyer may have a survey done before making an offer to confirm that the property description in the title deed is accurate. Every factor that affects the value of your property should be taken into account when you determine the selling price.

If you are selling your property to try to stop a foreclosure already underway, you probably do not have the time to make major improvements before putting the house on the market. Do all the fast, easy repairs that you can, though, so you do not give your viewers a reason not to buy.

Staging to shine

Contemplate your home's best features and remember what you loved about it when you viewed it the first time. Ask yourself who is most likely to purchase a home like yours — is it a family, a young couple, or a young professional? Unless you have a clear idea of the type of person or family that might buy your home, you will have a hard time selling it. Presenting your home in a way that appeals to your ideal buyer is crucial to getting the most money for your property. When you decide to sell your home, it essentially becomes the home of whomever you are targeting as a buyer. The space should be presented as it *could* be, not necessarily as you have kept it, which might require reorganizing furniture and getting rid of personal items and clutter. The following are some tips for staging your home:

- **Rearrange rooms into their original purposes.**

  Begin by going through each room in your home and making a
  note of what its purpose is. Though many rooms can have dual
  purposes — a third bedroom acts as a study, for example — you
  will want to show off your home as it was intended to be. If it
  is a three-bedroom home, make sure each bedroom is made up
  as a bedroom. If you are currently using your dining room as a
  sitting room, return it to its original purpose. Though it may
  be an inconvenience to move rooms around, this is among the
  most important preparations for showing your home. Potential buyers make up their minds quickly. When they walk into
  a home, they see it as it is, not as it could be. Potential buyers
  who are able to imagine a space arranged differently from how
  it currently looks are rare.

- **Remove all clutter.**

  The first step in preparing your home is getting rid of clutter.
  Consider this an opportunity to get rid of items you no longer
  use in order to make your eventual move easier. Are boxes in the
  closet filled with random papers? Sort them out and recycle what
  is not needed. Have the bicycles in the garage gone rusty? Donate
  them to someone who can refurbish them. Hold a yard sale for
  items that are usable but no longer needed by your family.

- **Remove personal items and anything you do not want to sell
  with the house.**

  Once the clutter is gone, go through the house and remove
  anything that you do not want to sell with the home. If your
  expensive appliances will be going with you, put a sticker on each
  to let potential buyers know that they are not part of the deal.
  Sometimes a potential buyer loves furniture or accessories that
  you have in the home (expensive curtains, for example) and asks
  that they be left behind. You do not want to risk losing a buyer

because they want to get your antique grandfather clock with the house. Buyers will not covet what they do not see, so remove anything that could potentially become a deal breaker.

- **Clean from floor to ceiling, including windows and closets.**
  Many sellers do not realize that cleaning is more than sweeping the floors and wiping down counters. Pull out the rubber gloves and bleach. Wash all the moldings and radiators, scour the windows inside and out, be certain your closets are sparkling, and get rid of any pet odors that might linger. If you do have pets, now is a good time for them to go live with a relative or friend until the house is sold.

- **Apply fresh paint and remove outdated wallpaper and carpet.**
  Now is also the time to give the rooms a fresh coat of paint and remove any outdated decorations. If you have put off stripping the 1950s wallpaper in the dining room, get out the scraper and steamer. You do not need to make drastic changes — just try to modernize your home. A fresh coat of neutral paint can make a big difference.

- **Bring in furniture if you have already moved out.**
  If you are moving out of your home prior to its sale, do not remove all the furniture. Remember that buyers will want to see a home as a home — which means having a sense of how much space is left after a double bed is put in the bedroom or what the dining room looks like with a table for six.

- **Set up props to suit the ideal buyer.**
  Leave some personal touches around to suggest that people live there, but not so many that buyers feel as though they are intruding on your life. One of the best touches to brighten any home and make visitors feel welcome is having a vase of fresh flowers on

hand at all times. Especially in the winter and early spring, this touch of life, and color will go a long way.

- **Improve curb appeal.**
  Do not neglect the outside of your home. Make sure that the lawn is mowed, the leaves are raked up, and the garden areas are maintained. If you have pets, be sure that their waste is not in any space where a viewer may wander. Pick up children's toys and sweep dirt from steps and walkways. If you are selling in winter, ice and snow could pose potential safety hazards, so keep walkways clear and safe.

Your home is on show, and you want to show it to its best advantage. Bring out all the charm and beauty of your house so that buyers will feel they are getting a beautiful home for a reasonable price.

Finding a Buyer

Your real estate agent should have provided you with a marketing scheme to let you know how he or she plans to find you a buyer. If you are selling your home yourself, you will need to come up with a plan of your own and invest considerable time, energy, and diligence. Be certain you can devote the time and energy necessary to find a new owner for your property.

If you are not using an agent, you will not be able to list in the traditional way, which means making fliers to post in public areas, putting up signs in front of the property, and spreading the news by word of mouth. Advertise in community magazines and newspapers. Call your local title company to see whether they offer a free direct-mail list. Consider sending a color brochure or postcard to those on the list, announcing an open house and pricing arrangements.

You will need to arrange frequent open houses for potential viewers. An open house is a certain day and time when potential buyers can view the property and ask questions. Mark out the property clearly by placing helium balloons in visible areas, posting "for sale" signs with phone numbers, and turning on all the lights to welcome visitors.

During each open house, have the following information available as photocopies:

- All disclosures (can be printed on one page)
- Asking price and provisions
- Dimensions of each room, with a description of the property and photos
- Offer closing date (if applicable)

Consider having bottled water or soft drinks and snacks available to make viewers feel welcome.

In conventional sales, homeowners welcome offers on a rolling basis and take the home off the market when an acceptable one comes along. Selling in foreclosure might require different measures. If you are unsure whether selling will save you from foreclosure, and you want to have time to exercise other options, consider setting an offer closing date. This is simply a date by which all offers on the property should be made in writing. On the day after this assigned date, go through each with your real estate agent or attorney and decide whether any are acceptable.

An effective marketing scheme does not sell your home directly, but it generates interest in the property. The real selling begins when interested parties come to your home. That is when you seal the deal — or send viewers away dissatisfied.

Selling in Foreclosure

The biggest obstacle you face in selling your home while in the foreclosure process is the time barrier. You will need to sell the home and receive the funds before the auction date in order to stop the foreclosure. This could be a timeframe of 30 to 60 days. Unfortunately, this is not the only factor you will need to keep in mind.

You might struggle with getting an offer that is to your liking simply due to the risks involved. Many buyers will not be comfortable with making a deposit on property and investing time in closing costs unless they are certain that the sale will be finalized. If the auction date is rapidly approaching, many buyers will walk away.

Obviously, accepting an offer that does not cover the cost of the loan outstanding is not going to help you stay out of foreclosure. Neither is accepting an offer from someone who does not have the funds available — as in someone who needs to sell their own home first, or someone who has not been preapproved for a mortgage with a lender. These are some of the issues you may have to confront when selling your property while in the process of foreclosure.

Short Sales and Foreclosure

A short sale is one in which the lender is willing to accept less than what is owed on the property in order to avoid a costly and time-consuming foreclosure process. When foreclosure threatens, you may think only of your own hardship, but the lender also faces a substantial loss when it takes back your home. Lenders are in business to extend credit to homebuyers and collect interest, not to own and manage real estate. Your mortgage holder does not want to own your home or go through the lengthy process of taking you to court, taking possession of the property, and then selling it.

Before the current foreclosure crisis and the collapse of the housing bubble in 2008 and 2009, a short sale was rarely, if ever, considered by a lender. Lenders were not motivated to accept a short sale offer in a good market because they could quickly sell a property after taking possession through a foreclosure, often for a profit. Now, in the nearly stagnant housing market, taking back ownership of a home is hardly worth the expense and effort. Lenders are finding it difficult to sell repossessed properties and often have to accept less than they are worth and write off their losses. Banks are unwilling to pay the costs of landscaping, maintaining, and cleaning repossessed homes while they stay vacant month after month. Lenders suffer a double loss: the expense and inconvenience of the foreclosure process and the sale of the property for less than its original market price.

You might have had your home on the market for several months without attracting much interest from buyers. Home sales, in many areas of the United States, are flatter than they have been in decades. People in a position to buy a home are looking for the bargain of a lifetime, and you may get offers that are well below your asking price. You might feel insulted by low offers because you paid much more for your home or refinanced at the height of the market, but it is important to treat the sale of your home as a business transaction. Before you reject any offers, talk with your lender to see whether it will accept a short sale. If an offer is close enough to the amount owed on the loan, your lender might be willing to accept net sale proceeds as payment in full.

It is vital to have a reputable and experienced real estate agent who understands the complexities of this type of transaction working with you on a short sale. The details of a short sale need to be worked out with your lender prior to the sale of the home. As a seller, you cannot simply accept a low offer without approval from your lender; you will be liable for the difference between the sale price and the amount you owe on your mortgage, and you could entangle the buyer of your home in legal difficulties. A short sale generates a number of legal documents. Throughout the process, you will need to get details of the agreement in writing from your lender. A real estate agent or real estate lawyer can assist you in putting together the necessary documents.

To initiate a short sale, contact your lender's loss mitigation department. Part of the process is the writing of a hardship letter explaining your current situation in detail and why it will not improve in the near future. The lender will also require an account of all your household income and expenses. If the lender approves, the short sale will satisfy your entire debt. Make sure this approval is spelled out in a written agreement.

Advantages and disadvantages of using a short sale to avoid foreclosure

A short sale might be to your advantage for several reasons. A short sale can often be completed more quickly than a foreclosure proceeding, reducing the financial and emotional toll on the homeowner. A short sale feels more like selling a home than losing a home, and the timeline can be tailored to the needs of the seller.

Short sales are not court proceedings. The transaction is negotiated between the borrower and the lender, and the buyer assumes ownership at a conventional closing. The bank simply agrees to accept the offer as full or partial payment of the amount owed by the seller. An agreement from the lender to consider a short sale will halt foreclosure proceedings while a prospective buyer's offer is under consideration, giving the homeowner time to make arrangements for moving into new accommodations after the sale.

Your bank does not have to accept a short sale offer. At some point, depending on how delinquent your payments are, the bank might decide to go ahead with a foreclosure and reject any requests for short sales. A short sale has a significant negative effect on your credit score in nearly the same way as a foreclosure. In some cases, a lender can still sue for the difference between the sale price and the loan balance after a short sale. This is known as a deficiency judgment. It rarely occurs after an agreement has been reached, but it is still within the lender's rights.

Tip : A short sale can incur tax liabilities.

The capital gains tax that you pay when you sell a property for more than you paid for it will be based on the total outstanding debt owed rather than the price for which you actually sold your home in a short sale. Also, when you sell the property in a short sale for less than you owe, and the bank accepts the proceeds of that sale as full payment of your debt, the amount that has been forgiven (known as the "deficiency") is treated as taxable income by the IRS. The lender sends the IRS a Form 1099C, reporting the forgiven debt as income to you.

The Mortgage Forgiveness Debt Relief Act of 2007 (H.R. 3648) established a tax exemption for up to $2 million of forgiven debt during the 2007, 2008, and 2009 tax years only. The deficiency must stem from the sale of your primary residence (the home that you live in), and the loan must have been used to buy or improve the house. A loan used to purchase a vacation home or investment property, or a home equity loan used to pay for other expenses such as a child's education, is not eligible for the exemption. If you do not qualify for the exemption under the Mortgage Forgiveness Debt Relief Act, you might still qualify for tax relief if you can prove to the IRS you were legally insolvent at the time of the short sale (your total debts were greater than the value of your total assets).

Factors to consider in a short sale

Consider the real estate market in your area when thinking about pursuing a short sale agreement with your lender. If houses are not selling in your area, it is unlikely that you will get an acceptable offer on your home. If houses are selling, but the prices are slightly depressed, you might be able to put together an attractive offer for your lender.

Another factor to consider is the amount you owe on the loan compared to the average price of homes in your area. If you are one of the unfortunate homeowners who bought at the height of the market and then took out home equity loans or second mortgages to pay off other debt, you may find that you are not a good candidate for this method of avoiding foreclosure. Some homeowners owe as much as $100,000 more than their home may be worth in the current market — a loss the lender is unlikely to absorb.

Making Homes Affordable Foreclosure Alternatives Program

Making Homes Affordable offers a Foreclosure Alternatives program that simplifies and standardizes the short sale and deed-in-lieu processes and provides incentives to borrowers, servicers, and investors to pursue short sales and deeds in lieu instead of foreclosure. Lenders participating in the program must evaluate each borrower before proceeding to foreclosure to see if a short sale is appropriate. The lender provides guidance to the borrower and allows a period of 90 days to one year for the borrower to market the home and find a buyer. After the short sale, the borrower is entitled to receive $1,500 to assist with moving expenses. The lender may, at its discretion, include a condition in the short sale agreement that the borrower will deed the property to the lender in exchange for a release from the debt if the property does not sell within the time specified for the short sale. You can find more information about this program on the Making Home Affordable Web site (**http://makinghomeaffordable. gov/pr_051409.html**).

CHAPTER 9

Deed in Lieu

A deed in lieu, in which you give your property back to the mortgage holder, is best used when you have zero or negative equity in the property. If you have reached the point where you know you cannot sell your house to satisfy the loan(s), and you no longer want to keep the property, speak to your lender about arranging a deed in lieu.

In a deed-in-lieu arrangement, you are signing over ownership of the property directly to the lender. By voluntarily giving up the property, you are relinquishing all rights and giving the lender the opportunity to sell it and recover its money.

How a Deed in Lieu Benefits You

Even if you could produce the funds to halt a foreclosure, you might not want to keep the property if the monthly mortgage payments are beyond your means. If you have put considerable time and energy into trying to sell the property and have not found a buyer, a deed in lieu could allow you to walk away from the home and still keep foreclosure off your credit record. When you have owned a house for only a short time, or you purchased it with a no-down-payment mortgage, you have very little equity in it. You may even have negative equity if home prices have fallen so that the house is now worth less than you paid for it. If you are not going to recover any equity by selling your house, there is no point in trying to sell.

When you agree to and sign a deed-in-lieu arrangement with your lender, the foreclosure process stops immediately. There are no exceptions — whatever process was started by the lender ends the moment they agree to accept the property in lieu of payment on the loan. This prevents any further damage to your credit report. Your credit score will be lower because of the missed mortgage payments and the initiation of foreclosure, but it will not be nearly as low as it would have been had the foreclosure process continued.

When you sign a deed in lieu, your lender cannot ask for a deficiency judgment against you if it is unable to find a buyer for the property. If you sold the property yourself for less than the loan amount, you might still be liable for the balance owed. If your property went into foreclosure and the amount received at auction did not cover the outstanding debts, you would be responsible for the balance. If the lender accepts a deed in lieu of payment, they *cannot* get any more money from you.

How a Deed in Lieu Benefits Your Lender

Lenders are first and foremost investors who want to protect their investment. By accepting a deed in lieu, a lender is avoiding all the fees and expenses associated with processing a foreclosure. The lender ends up with exactly what it would have gotten through the courts, without the cost.

Accepting a deed in lieu is also considerably faster than the foreclosure process. Rather than waiting a minimum of three months to get the property, the lender owns it the minute you both sign the agreement. The property can be on the market the next day, if the lender chooses. The lender will be able to market the property through a real estate agent rather than selling at auction, which could potentially yield much more money.

When you sign a deed in lieu, the lender knows right from the outset that you no longer want the property and are happy to walk away. It does not have to be concerned that you will take legal measures to stop the foreclosure; there will be no enjoining, bankruptcy filings, or other maneuvers.

Complications

When your property goes to auction in a foreclosure, the proceeds pay off any outstanding loans in the order of the date they were recorded. Whatever is not paid off when the proceeds are exhausted is your responsibility. With deed-in-lieu arrangements, any liens against the property remain. The lender must then pay for the other outstanding debts *in addition* to covering your loan. For this reason, if you have other liens against your property, there is a good chance your lender will not accept a deed in lieu.

Another risk a lender faces with a deed in lieu is that you could potentially try to set it aside later and reclaim ownership of the property. Though this happens rarely, there have been individuals who had second thoughts and claimed that they were coerced into signing over the deed. If a lender believes there is any chance you might try to reclaim the property in the future, it could reject a deed-in-lieu offer. Most lenders will not proceed with a deed in lieu until they receive a written statement from you confirming that you are entering into the agreement voluntarily.

If the property has any structural flaws or liability issues, your lender will be reluctant to take on your deed. This includes homes that have been condemned for a variety of reasons. If the home is not resalable, there is little motivation for the lender to agree to a deed in lieu. Consider your property and your situation carefully when deciding whether offering a deed in lieu makes sense.

$T\!ip$: There are special foreclosure provisions for FHA- and VA-insured loans.

FHA- and VA-insured loans have special provisions to deed-in-lieu offers that will either encourage or dissuade your lender from accepting one. For both types, you will need to prove at the outset that you have defaulted due to circumstances beyond your control (such as unemployment), that you are unlikely to be able to make the debt current and keep up with future payments, and that there are no secondary (junior) liens on the property. VA-insured loans also require you to demonstrate that you have tried but failed to sell your property on the open market and that the value of the property is equal to or less than the balance owed, and to agree to be liable should the VA suffer monetary loss in the reselling.

Arranging a Deed in Lieu

Call your lender — and the FHA or VHA, if applicable — to ask whether they will consider a deed in lieu. Follow this phone call up with a letter asking your lender to accept a deed in lieu in place of foreclosure. Direct both the phone call and the letter to the individual with whom you spoke earlier when trying to make alternative arrangements. Include any information you feel is pertinent to your plea in this letter, such as your financial situation, lack of liens on the property, the balance owed on the loan, and the condition and fair market value of the property.

Once the lender has agreed to accept this arrangement, a date and time must be set for exchanging documents, and a representative who is legally able to accept the deed on behalf of the lender must be identified. An unbiased witness should be present so that if any questions arise in the future, there is evidence of equal and willing compliance.

In the exchange of documents, you will hand over both a signed deed in lieu and all keys to the property. Special arrangements might be made with the lender to allow you to remain on the property for a short period of time if you are unable to move right away. In return for these items, the lender should return the original loan document with a signature acknowledging cancellation of the debt on the back.

You might also ask your lender to contact the three main credit reporting agencies in the United State — TransUnion, Experian, and Equifax — to remove all traces of the foreclosure, including the notice of default and notice of sale. The lender is not required to do this, but it will not hurt to ask. Do not end the process if the lender refuses — you can still bring your credit score back up quickly in spite of these marks by paying down other debts and paying your bills on time.

Negotiate for a waiver of deficiency in which the lender releases you from any financial liability with regard to the property, including attorneys' fees and foreclosure costs. One reason why a deed in lieu is preferable to foreclosure is that it eliminates the potential for deficiency judgments if the property sells for a price that is not to the lender's satisfaction. Have your lender put this agreement in writing, preferably attached to the cancellation of the loan.

In all correspondence, from the initial query to the final agreement, make sure everything is documented and signed by all interested parties. When you write your letter to the lender, leave space at the bottom for an "agreed and accepted by" section, with a signature line for the authorized bank officer.

Once the lender has agreed to accept the deed in lieu, it will either draw up the agreement or ask you to have one created. Be certain that any document you create or any document that the lender asks you to sign contains the words "deed in lieu of foreclosure" at the top of the page. Some lenders will use a quitclaim deed instead, which serves the same purpose. Check that "deed in lieu of foreclosure" is still typed above the words "quitclaim deed."

Elements of a Deed in Lieu of Foreclosure

A deed-in-lieu agreement is fairly straightforward and clear, though careful attention should be given to completing it because any mistake can nullify the contract. Make a special effort to get the correct mailing addresses and telephone numbers of all parties involved in the agreement before even touching a pen or keyboard. This information must be entered correctly on the deed-in-lieu contract.

When reviewing the document, be sure the location of the property is correctly stated, all owners listed on the original deed of trust or mortgage are listed correctly, and that there is a statement noting that the transfer is exempt from tax. Unlike the sale of your home, arranging a deed in lieu of foreclosure exempts you from having to pay capital gains tax.

When the form has been filled out correctly, all listed owners must sign the document in front of a notary. Once notarized, the deed in lieu is returned to the lender in exchange for cancellation of the debt. Find out when the deed is recorded with the registry, and get a copy for yourself. This helps to confirm that you no longer hold any interest or liability in the property.

Many homeowners who purchased their homes after 2004 now find that they have no equity in their homes because home prices have dropped. "Negative equity" means that you owe more on the mortgage than your home is now worth. A deed in lieu is an appropriate solution for homeowners who have no equity or negative equity. In May 2009, the U.S. government announced a Foreclosure Alternatives program as part of the Making Homes Affordable initiative that provides incentives to borrowers, servicers, and investors to pursue deed-in-lieu agreements instead of foreclosure. It offers standardized documents and procedures and sets a minimum timeframe for a deed in lieu. Though a deed in lieu appears on your credit report, it does not have the same negative effect as a foreclosure. You will have to give up your home, but you will be able to make a new start without the heavy burden of mortgage debt.

Chapter 10

Filing for Bankruptcy

Though bankruptcy should be an absolute last resort, in some cases it is the best option for halting foreclosure and simultaneously dealing with other debts. This Chapter will help you decide whether your financial situation warrants bankruptcy. Both bankruptcy and foreclosure can seriously affect your life for many years afterward, so it is not a decision to be taken lightly.

The first thing you should be aware of when considering bankruptcy is that it is going to be a separate process from your foreclosure. Many people do not realize that bankruptcy will be a court process requiring legal assistance from a specialized attorney or aide. Individuals who file for bankruptcy rarely have to appear before a judge in court. The majority of the process is carried out administratively by filing various documents with the trustee appointed to the case. Filing is done on the federal, not the state, level. The U.S. Court System has allocated 94 bankruptcy courts throughout the country to specifically handle bankruptcy claims. To find the court nearest you, visit the U.S. Court System Web site at **www.uscourts.gov**.

Bankruptcy laws were made stricter at the end of 2005, particularly regarding Chapter 7 bankruptcy, which liquidates the debtor's property to pay creditors instead of imposing a repayment plan. The Bankruptcy Abuse Prevention and Consumer Protection Act of 2005 (BAPCPA) was signed into law by President George W. Bush to reduce the number of filings by individuals who could solve their debt problems in other ways. A result of this change is that average fees for bankruptcy lawyers have increased due to the extra work required, and filers are required to prove that there is no other solution to their financial troubles other than bankruptcy. Debtors who file for bankruptcy must now undergo mandatory credit counseling with an approved agency. If you have not yet consulted a professional about your situation, you can find a list of approved credit counseling agencies by state on **www.uscourts.gov**.

An individual or organization who files for bankruptcy is seeking a discharge of debt. A discharge is a court order that permanently relieves the debtor from paying back certain debts to creditors. The order prohibits any creditor from seeking repayment from the debtor at any time, through any means. Creditors are not allowed to contact the debtor in any way, nor are they allowed to garnish wages or seek a legal judgment. The debt essentially disappears.

Certain debts cannot be erased by bankruptcy; debts secured by your property (secured liens), for example, remain. Tax debts, school loans, alimony, child support, and any debt not listed on the schedules and forms filed by the debtor will still require repayment in full after the bankruptcy has been declared. The U.S. Bankruptcy Code lists 19 non-dischargeable debts, depending on your filing status. There is a difference between what is dischargeable under each type of bankruptcy, so read closely within each section in this chapter to learn more.

When you file your forms with the court, you will be asked to separate your debts into three separate categories, depending on to whom the debt is owed, whether a lien on your assets secures the debt, and whether the debt is dischargeable through foreclosure. These three types of debts are referred to as priority, secured, and unsecured.

Priority debts are those that must be paid first. The major priority debts for homeowners include debts owed to the government (such as taxes), alimony and child support, any wages owed to independent contractors, and money owed to anyone who deposited funds for purchasing or renting property for their personal use. This means that if you had work done on your property shortly before filing for bankruptcy, or if you tried to sell the property and accepted a deposit, those funds must be paid or repaid first out of the liquidated assets.

Secured debts are those that involve written documents that state the creditor has the right to sell your property to satisfy the debt, such as a mortgage or deed of trust. This also includes liens related to taxes, construction (mechanic's liens), or legal judgments. If the lien is recorded properly, it is considered a secured debt.

Unsecured debts do not have collateral, such as a home or car, to satisfy the debt if it goes into default. Unsecured debts include credit cards, medical bills, student loans, and utility bills. Unsecured creditors are paid last in bankruptcy — provided they are dischargeable. Note that though student loans are unsecured, they are exempt from discharge and must be paid in full.

Though most discharges are granted when a thorough and honest filing of bankruptcy takes place, the court has an option to refuse the request, and creditors have a right to officially object. There is a long list of reasons for which the court might deny a discharge, including missing documents or the omission of property in the listing of assets.

Courts may also revoke the bankruptcy granted if it can be shown that fraud was committed or, in some cases, that the debtor has come to possess assets that could be used to clear the debts owed. Again, this depends on the type of bankruptcy filed and the time at which a complaint is made in relation to the original hearing.

Types of Bankruptcy

In 1934, the Supreme Court stated that bankruptcy "gives to the honest but unfortunate debtor...a new opportunity in life and a clear field for future effort, unhampered by the pressure and discouragement of pre-existing debt" (Local Loan Co. v. Hunt, 292 U.S. 234, 244. 1934). Today, this sentiment is echoed in the phrase "fresh start," which many use to refer to personal bankruptcy.

In effect, the purpose of bankruptcy is to wipe the slate clean so that those who are actively trying to be contributing members of a consumer society can do so without previous creditors seeking retribution.

Many different types of bankruptcy options are available. Each accomplishes the clearing of debt, but each has different requirements and consequences. Unless your home is part of a business or farm, there are only two options to homeowners: Chapter 7 and Chapter 13. The types of bankruptcy are named for the Chapters in which they are described in the U.S. Bankruptcy Code.

Chapter 7

Chapter 7 is a form of bankruptcy involving court-ordered liquidation. A trustee is appointed to liquidate, or sell, all a debtor's non-exempt property and distribute the funds to creditors. Chapter 7 is often filed by individuals who have little or no assets to liquidate. If you own a home, it is very likely that it will be sold to satisfy your debts.

If you are in a situation where the amount of money owed on your home is more than the home is worth, or you feel that continuing to own the home is not in your best interest but have been unable to sell it yourself, then Chapter 7 might be a good option. You will lose the property, but all dischargeable debts will be cleared.

BAPCPA changes now require debtors to prove that their income is less than the average income of individuals in the state and that they are unable to pay 25 percent of the debt owed to creditors. If the debtor's income is greater than the average income of individuals in that state, or they are able to pay 25 percent or more of the debt, they will be ineligible to file Chapter 7 bankruptcy.

The following items are non-dischargeable under Chapter 7 bankruptcy:

- Alimony
- Child support
- Taxes
- Student loans
- Court-ordered restitution
- Fines due to criminal actions
- Dues owed to condominiums or cooperative associations
- Personal injury or death damages owed as a result of driving under the influence of alcohol
- Debts due to fraud
- Debts related to theft or embezzlement
- Marital settlement agreements other than alimony and child support
- Debts due to malicious injury to another
- Any debts owed to a creditor for luxury items and cash advances in excess of $1,000 (made within 60 days of filing bankruptcy)

Chapter 13

Chapter 13 of the bankruptcy code is entitled Adjustment of Debts of an Individual with Regular Income and is probably the form you will be required, or will choose, to file. Unlike Chapter 7, this form of bankruptcy allows the debtor to retain certain assets, such as a home. Debtors are required to come up with a plan to repay creditors, which is then approved or declined at a confirmation hearing. Under this agreement, payment plans reflect the debtor's income and ability to pay, rather than what is actually owed.

Though Chapter 13 does not allow for an immediate discharge of the debts, like Chapter 7, it does protect the debtor from any action being taken against him or her by creditors. As long as the debtor is making payments according to the court-approved plan, creditors cannot file lawsuits or garnish wages. At the end of the payment plan, outstanding debts are discharged.

Like Chapter 7, certain debts have to be repaid regardless of being granted Chapter 13 bankruptcy. These are the same as Chapter 7, with the exception that if any of the following debts are unsecured, they are discharged after the payment term is complete:

- Debts due to fraud
- Debts related to theft or embezzlement
- Marital settlement agreements other than alimony and child support
- Debts due to malicious injury to another
- Any debts owed to a creditor for luxury items and cash advances in excess of $1,000 (made within 60 days of filing bankruptcy)

If you want to file for bankruptcy, but have a regular income and want to keep your home, then Chapter 13 is the best option for you. Your payment plan should involve monthly payments high enough to cover 100 percent of your priority debts — such as mortgage, taxes, and alimony — 100 percent of the overdue payments and interest on your secured debts (missed mortgage payments, for example), and a percentage of your disposable income for the payment of unsecured debts. This last aspect may or may not be enforced by the court and can possibly equal the value of your non-exempt property. The court wants to be certain that you are making an appropriate effort to pay back a portion of the unsecured debt.

Unfortunately, in approximately half of all approved Chapter 13 bankruptcies, the filer is unable to follow their payment plan and ends up losing everything. If you are seriously considering this option as a means of saving your home, it is crucial that you construct a payment plan that you know you will be able to follow for the next seven years. If you have any doubt, find an alternative solution.

Is Bankruptcy Right for You?

Bankruptcy does not come without its share of difficulties — including the stress and stigma associated with being unable to pay back your debts. Depending on the type of bankruptcy you file, the effects and commitments can stay with you for quite some time.

When you file Chapter 7 bankruptcy, you will lose some of your assets, including your home, your car, and anything else of value that can be sold to clear the debt. Certain types of property are exempt; exemptions vary from state to state. Your home might be exempt if you have a specific amount of equity. You can look up the Chapter 7 exemptions for your state on the Filing-Bankruptcy-Form.com Web site (**www.filing-bankruptcy-form. com/bankruptcy-exemptions.html**). Chapter 7 bankruptcy does not cancel a foreclosure because it only cancels personal liabilities. Though your promissory note is a personal liability, the mortgage contract that places a lien on the property is not. You might be able to continue living in the house for several weeks or months without paying because the foreclosure is temporarily halted during the bankruptcy proceedings. Unless you find another solution for your mortgage debt during that time, your lender will continue with foreclosure proceedings when the bankruptcy is complete.

If you want to keep your home, you can file for Chapter 13 bankruptcy, in which the court arranges a long-term repayment plan that includes mortgage payments and delinquent amounts. The court may renegotiate the terms of your mortgage to make the payments more affordable. If you fail to keep up these payments according to the repayment plan, however, your lender can once again initiate foreclosure proceedings.

During bankruptcy proceedings, considerable time is devoted to negotiating with your creditors in person. You will be required to attend a "341" meeting where each debt and its repayment is discussed ("341" refers to the section of the U.S. Bankruptcy Code that covers this aspect). These meetings can be emotionally draining and require you to thoroughly defend your inability to pay the debts.

A bankruptcy filing will have lingering effects on your credit. Obtaining unsecured credit, such as credit cards, may be difficult; a foreclosure will remain on your credit report for seven years, but bankruptcy stays for ten. It will be easier to improve your credit score after a bankruptcy because your other debts have mostly been discharged and your finances are more stable than after a foreclosure, when you are still saddled with fees, costs, credit card debt, and other financial obligations. This increases the income-to-debt ratio that influences your credit score.

With regard to foreclosure, filing bankruptcy avoids any chances of deficiency judgments if the property does not cover the debt owed when it is sold (in the case of Chapter 7) and allows for the possibility of keeping your home (for Chapter 13 filings). Bankruptcy will stop the action of foreclosure even after a judgment has been ordered, allowing homeowners to protect their assets.

It is up to you to decide whether the benefits of bankruptcy outweigh the consequences. If you do choose bankruptcy, be sure that you can organize a way to get your financial situation back on track. If unmanageable debt is not the reason your home is being foreclosed on, filing bankruptcy is not the best option for you.

Proving You Are Eligible

To prove to the courts that you should be granted either Chapter 7 or Chapter 13 bankruptcy, you will need to show an itemized list of your income and every expense you have during the course of a month, as well as write a hardship letter with details about your situation. If you have already listed your income and expenses in preparation for fighting foreclosure, this process will be easier. When you create this itemized list for the courts, organize all your debts into three categories: priority, secured, and unsecured.

Here is an example of a situation where bankruptcy is a viable option:

Mr. and Mrs. Merchant are a middle-income couple living in rural America. Mrs. Merchant works for a telecom company, while Mr. Merchant worked, until recently, in the automotive industry. If we were to read the Merchants' hardship letter, we would learn that much of their financial problems are due to Mr. Merchant's current unemployment because of a workplace accident. If their income had remained what it previously was, they would have been able to work out a plan to pay off their debt without bankruptcy.

As it stands, though, Mr. Merchant has little chance of getting back to work in the next year or two. Because his injury was the result of his own actions on the job, he has been denied unemployment. This means that Mrs. Merchant is now, and will continue to be for some time, the sole breadwinner in the household.

When Mr. Merchant's accident occurred, the couple drastically reduced their expenses. They canceled memberships to clubs and changed their lifestyle considerably. Unfortunately, this has still not been enough to enable them to meet their obligations with only Mrs. Merchant's income. The couple has decided that they will try to file Chapter 13 bankruptcy in order to save their home, as they have already missed one payment, and they may be late on the next. Mrs. Merchant is forward-thinking and knows what their future holds if she does not act quickly.

Below is a sample of Mrs. Merchant's itemization after she canceled and reduced items of luxury:

Income on a monthly basis:

Work salary (gross):	$4,100
Taxes at 20 percent:	$820
Monthly salary (net):	$3,280

General expenses on a monthly basis:

House/car insurance:	$350
Utilities:	$200
Cell phone:	$75
Groceries:	$400
Transportation	$300

Priority debt:

Back taxes (2 years)	$2,300

Secured debt:

Mortgage payment:	$1,500/month, 18 years left
Home equity loan	$708.56/month, 5 years left
School loans:	$670/month, 3 years left
Car payment	$250/month, 3 years left

Unsecured debt:

Acme MasterCard	$5,304.32 at 15 percent interest
Storyland Visa	$4,786.93 at 14.5 percent interest
Mrs. Boots' Daycare	$1,465.87
Peapod's Grocery	$546.98
Anytown Savings	$3,208.56
Merrytown Hospital	$16,987.34

By looking at these numbers, we can see that the Merchants are in serious financial trouble. They have a monthly income of $3,280, but an outflow of $4,453.56, which means that the couple is spending $1,173.56 more each month than is being brought in. In addition the couple owes two years' worth of back income taxes to the government, hospital expenses due to Mr. Merchant's injury, and debts on credit cards.

If the Merchants are able to file Chapter 13 bankruptcy, $32,300 worth of unsecured debts could be potentially wiped away. The school loans and taxes would not be cleared, but by arranging alternative payments on the other debts for three to five years, the couple has a far greater chance of getting back on their feet so that their debts can be paid off in time.

When writing their hardship letter, Mrs. Merchant includes not only the explanation of how she and Mr. Merchant got into difficulties, but what she expects the future will entail. She includes all the hardships that have worked against them, but she also includes a strategic plan to pay off the debt over time.

In her letter, Mrs. Merchant notes that she has already arranged forbearance on her son's school loans, which she has been paying since his death, and has identified a scheme for making up the taxes owed. She plans on taking a second job in the evenings until Mr. Merchant can get back on his feet, and they are pursuing a claim against Mr. Merchant's employer for denying benefits. In the meantime, they are also waiting to find out how much they will receive for his social security disability payments.

By explaining her situation clearly, and showing that she is thinking about how to pay her debts, Mrs. Merchant is proving to the courts that she and her husband are deserving of a fresh start — the exact reason for which bankruptcy was created in the first place.

CHAPTER 11

Where to Go for Help

When you are facing foreclosure, you might feel isolated and think that you have to deal with the situation alone. This is not the truth. Plenty of people want you to stay in your home, including your lender, your neighbors, your family, your friends, your church, advocacy groups, financial advisors, mortgage counselors, consumer associations, and even your local, state, and federal governments. Help is available if you know where to look for it.

The kind of help you need depends largely on your situation. Is foreclosure imminent, or are you just on the threshold? Do you need help gaining control over your spending, or is bankruptcy your only way out? Would one-time monetary help stop your foreclosure — or only delay it? The answers to these questions will determine where you should turn for assistance. This chapter covers some of the many resources available to homeowners threatened by foreclosure.

Your Family and Friends

Feelings of pride and shame may make it difficult for you to approach family and friends and ask for help. If you find yourself in the midst of foreclosure due to a misfortune such as an illness or job loss, your family may be more sympathetic than you realize. If a one-time monetary gift or loan can help get you out of this mess, then by all means, ask. Financial assistance can take the form of a loan, with a written formal agreement to pay the money back at a later date.

Another Lender

If your current financial situation is temporary or could be improved by consolidating some of your debt, a consolidation loan or mortgage refinance with another lender may be the solution.

Credit Counseling

Sometimes foreclosure can be avoided simply by learning how to manage money. A credit counselor can help you evaluate your finances, prepare a budget, and consolidate credit card debt with a lower interest rate and monthly payment. Be wary, though, when signing on for this type of service. Many non-profit organizations offer genuine assistance to people who are struggling with debt, but there are also commercial credit card services that prey on debtors by charging large commissions and sometimes failing to deliver the promised results. You can find a list of government-approved credit counseling agencies on the Web site of the U.S. Trustee Program (**www.justice.gov/ust/eo/bapcpa/ccde/cc_approved.htm**). The publication *Fiscal Fitness: Choosing a Credit Counselor* on the Federal Trade Commission Web site (**www.ftc.gov/bcp/edu/pubs/consumer/credit/cre26. shtm**) also gives helpful suggestions for finding a reputable and affordable credit counseling organization.

Real Estate Lawyers

Real estate lawyers are well-versed in foreclosure law and procedure and are experienced at helping people avoid foreclosure. They can offer legal advice, help you prepare your defense, and even represent you in court. You can find a real estate lawyer in your community by searching the directory on Lawyers.com (**www.lawyers.com/Real-Estate/browse-by-location. html**), Findlaw.com (**http://lawyers.findlaw.com/lawyer/practice/Real-Estate-Law**), or AttorneyPages.com (**http://attorneypages.com/580**) and by contacting a local real estate agents' association or state bar association, or by asking friends or local real estate agents for a recommendation. Interview prospective lawyers to see how well they understand your situation, and compare their fees. If you cannot afford to hire a lawyer, pay an hourly fee to get legal advice, or seek free legal aid in your community.

Foreclosure Consultants

Foreclosure consultants typically work with lenders to renegotiate loan terms or refinance a property. Although there are many qualified and capable foreclosure consultants, there are also commercial self-described foreclosure consultants who offer little real help.

A qualified consultant can:

- Offer credit counseling advice
- Negotiate with your lender
- Arrange loan extensions
- Provide general foreclosure advice
- Help you find a company willing to refinance your mortgage
- Offer bankruptcy assistance
- Work as your advocate with your lender

Tip : Watch out for unscrupulous mortgage consultants.

An unqualified consultant will make grandiose promises but offer little if any help in planning a strategy for stopping your foreclosure. Be wary of consultants who tell you they can stop your foreclosure without an in-depth look at your financial situation and mortgage documents. Until they know the whole story, they have no idea how to proceed.

Fannie Mae offers a "Find A Counselor" search on its Web site (**www.fanniemae.com/findCounselorApplication/fanniemae/findCounselor.jsp**)   and makes the following recommendations:

"Carefully investigate firms (including those who provide counseling exclusively online) that promise 'easy' debt consolidation programs or that offer to 'repair' your credit report for a fee. Unfortunately, if you face serious credit problems, there may be no 'easy' answers. Also, in October 2003, the Federal Trade Commission, the Internal Revenue Service, and state regulators issued a consumer alert for those seeking assistance from tax-exempt credit counseling organizations. This consumer alert recommends that consumers check the following Web sites for further information:

- **www.ftc.gov** (to become familiar with the latest scam alerts)
- **www.irs.gov/charities** (to determine whether the organization is tax-exempt and what an organization must do to maintain that status)
- **www.nasconet.org** (to obtain a list of state charity official offices)
- **www.treas.gov/financialeducation** (to find more information on federal financial education programs and resources)"

Your Lender

One of your best resources for help in preventing foreclosure can be your lender's loss mitigation department. Your lender is the only one who can give you a loan modification, forbearance, or payment plan to rehabilitate your mortgage. Poor communication between loan servicers and distressed mortgage holders frequently results in unnecessary foreclosures. Consult your lender to see what options may be able before expending time, energy, and money seeking outside help.

Chase, which services about 10.3 million loans, has opened 51 Chase Homeownership Centers in 14 states and Washington, D.C., to help homeowners complete applications for refinancing or loan modification. For more information, go to **www.chase.com/myhome** or call (866) 550-5705.

The Federal Government

The Federal Housing Administration makes refinancing available to qualified homeowners who are having difficulty making their mortgage payments.

On July 30, 2008, Congress passed the Economic and Housing Recovery Act, amending TILA to protect lenders from increasingly prevalent predatory lending practices, including inflated interest rates and loans written without income verification. Millions of homeowners had already fallen behind on loans they had taken out in the early part of the decade. When housing values began to decline and unemployment escalated, foreclosure rates increased dramatically. The Economic and Housing Recovery Act also authorized the HOPE for Homeowners program (**www.hud.gov/hope-forhomeowners**) to refinance mortgages for borrowers who can afford a new loan insured by HUD's FHA. In many cases, HOPE for Homeowners requires banks to write down existing mortgages to 90 percent of the new appraised value of the homes.

In March 2009, the Obama administration announced a $75 billion "Making Home Affordable" plan, expected to assist between 3 and 4 million distressed homeowners whose loans are secured by Fannie Mae or Freddie Mac with Home Affordable Refinance Program (HARP) loans or Home Affordable Modification Program (HAMP) loan modifications. Information is available on the Making Home Affordable Web site (**http://makinghomeaffordable.gov**). By the end of 2009, mortgage companies had modified 759,000 loans on a trial basis, typically lasting three to five months, but only about 31,000 homeowners had received permanent loan modifications, which lower payments for five years. In January 2010, the U.S. Treasury said it would speed up the loan modification process by making documentation requirements less stringent. In January 2010, Freddie Mac began opening a series of new Borrower Help Centers in Chicago, Illinois; Phoenix, Arizona; Maryland; and California to guide borrowers with Freddie Mac loans through the loan modification process and provide financial and credit counseling to help them make their monthly payments. Freddie Mac also launched a separate Borrower Help Network where participating non-profit organizations will provide similar free financial counseling by phone.

HARP and HAMP

You might qualify for HARP if:

- The home you want to refinance is your primary residence.

- The loan on your home is controlled by Fannie Mae or Freddie Mac (it must be a conforming loan — you can call Fannie at 1-800-7FANNIE and Freddie at 1-800-FREDDIE to learn more).

- You have not been more than 30 days late on your mortgage payment in the last 12 months.

- You have enough income to support a new mortgage.

You might qualify for HAMP if:

- Your monthly mortgage payments exceed 38 percent of your monthly income.

- Your loan does not exceed conforming loan limits.

- The home is your primary residence.

- Your mortgage debt exceeds the market value of your home.

Find out if you qualify by using the questionnaire at **http://makinghomeaffordable.gov/eligibility.html**.

On March 26, 2010, as part of its ongoing commitment to continuously improve housing relief efforts, the Obama Administration announced adjustments to the HAMP and FHA programs. These adjustments will better assist responsible homeowners who have been affected by the economic crisis through no fault of their own. The program modifications will expand flexibility for mortgage servicers and originators to assist more unemployed homeowners and to help people who owe more on their mortgage than their home is worth because their local markets saw large declines in home values. These changes will help the administration meet its goal of stabilizing housing markets by offering a second chance for 3 to 4 million struggling homeowners through the end of 2012. Costs will be shared between the private sector and the federal government; the federal cost of these changes will be funded through the $50 billion allocation for housing programs under the Troubled Asset Relief Program (TARP).

Unemployed borrowers meeting eligibility criteria will have an opportunity to have their mortgage payments temporarily reduced to an affordable level for a minimum of three months — and up to six months, for some borrowers — while they look for a new job. If homeowners do not find a job before the temporary assistance period is over, or if they find a job with a reduced income, they will be evaluated for a permanent HAMP modification or may be eligible for HAMP's Foreclosure Alternatives Program.

To expand the use of principal write-downs, servicers will be required to consider an alternative modification approach that emphasizes principal relief. This approach will include incentive payments for each dollar of principal write-down by servicers and investors. The principal reduction and the incentives will be earned by the borrower and lender based on a pay-for-success structure.

Other program enhancements are designed to help more borrowers complete a HAMP modification. Borrower outreach and communications rules will be clarified and strengthened to protect responsible borrowers from unnecessary and costly foreclosure actions and to expand modification opportunities for borrowers in bankruptcy. Servicers will receive increased incentives, allowing them to expand borrower outreach and counseling efforts. With the introduction of FHA-HAMP, the HAMP pay-for-success incentives will be expanded to include borrowers with FHA loans.

For borrowers who continue to struggle and are unable to complete a modification, these program enhancements will help homeowners move to more affordable housing. Relocation assistance payments to borrowers who use the foreclosure alternatives program will be doubled, and incentives will be increased for servicers and lenders to raise participation.

Local and State Governments

In the second half of 2008, state governments began responding to mushrooming foreclosure rates by initiating foreclosure mediation programs. By September 2009, there were 25 loan mediation programs underway in 14 states. Several states with high foreclosure rates, including Florida, Michigan, California, Nevada, and Ohio, now require mediations before foreclosure sales. For example, an order in December 2009 by the Florida Supreme Court mandated a meeting between the lender and homeowner to discuss a loan modification or short sale before any foreclosure hearing in which the home is a primary residence. The lender is required to pay the cost, up to $750, of the mediation. It is hoped that such mediation will bring down the number of foreclosure hearings flooding the court system.

One obstacle encountered by many homeowners is that their loans have been "securitized" — packaged with other loans and sold by the original lender to an investment company. Most loans are owned by investors, and the banks who collect the payments simply serve as "servicers." In some cases, the loan has been repackaged and resold multiple times, and the homeowner cannot locate the owner who has authority to renegotiate the terms of a loan. State mediation programs can help to locate the owner of a loan in cases where the bank is reluctant or unable to do so.

In addition to mediation, some states offer grants or short-term loans through mortgage assistance programs to help homeowners experiencing temporary financial setbacks to make up delinquent loan payments. Go to your official state Web site or call your state information number to find out what programs are available in your state. A list of state foreclosure assistance programs can be found on the Realtor.org Web site (**www.realtor.org/ home_buyers_and_sellers/foreclosure_assistance_programs_by_state**).

State Foreclosure Working Group

The State Foreclosure Working Group, made up of representatives of the attorneys general of 11 states (Arizona, California, Colorado, Iowa, Illinois, Massachusetts, Michigan, New York, North Carolina, Ohio, and Texas), two state banking departments (New York and North Carolina), and the Conference of State Bank Supervisors, was formed in summer 2007 to work with servicers of subprime mortgage loans to identify ways to work together to prevent unnecessary foreclosures. This group makes regular reports and recommendations to policy-makers in the U.S. government. In January 2010, it warned that six out of ten seriously delinquent homeowners are not involved in any kind of loss mitigation process, and that courts and foreclosure counseling services are heavily backlogged. It strongly recommends that HAMP make the reduction of loan principal a priority in areas where a majority of homeowners are "underwater." It also recommends that states expand homeowner counseling and foreclosure mediation programs.

Beware of Scams

Just as predatory lenders and unscrupulous mortgage brokers take advantage of ingenuous homebuyers, unscrupulous scammers attempt to profit from the foreclosure crisis by preying on distressed and fearful homeowners. If your bank has begun foreclosure proceedings against you, it is a matter of public record, and your personal information is available to anyone who wants it — especially if your state laws require that the information be put in the newspaper.

Tip: Do not fall for these ads.

Excerpt from the Foreclosure Rescue Scams: Another Potential Stress for Homeowners in Distress

U.S. Federal Trade Commission

www.ftc.gov/bcp/edu/pubs/consumer/credit/cre42.shtm

Foreclosure rescue firms use a variety of tactics to find homeowners in distress: Some sift through public foreclosure notices in newspapers and on the Internet or through public files at local government offices, and then send personalized letters to homeowners. Others take a broader approach through ads on the Internet, on television, or in the newspaper, posters on telephone poles, median strips, and at bus stops, or fliers or business cards at your front door. The scam artists use simple and straight-forward messages, like:

"Stop Foreclosure Now!"

"We guarantee to stop your foreclosure."

"Keep your home. We know your home is scheduled to be sold. No problem!"

"We have special relationships within many banks that can speed up case approvals."

"We Can Save Your Home. Guaranteed. Free Consultation"

"We stop foreclosures every day. Our team of professionals can stop yours this week!""

Some of these foreclosure scams are very elaborate and present themselves as legitimate foreclosure assistance programs with professional-looking Web sites and marketing brochures. The scams may present themselves differently from one area of the country to another, but the methods they use are similar. Common foreclosure scams are discussed in the following sections.

Credit counseling agencies

Credit counseling agencies promise to help you "wipe the slate clean" or negotiate lower payments with your creditors. Some ask you for a fixed monthly payment, which they then distribute to your creditors. There are legitimate government-approved credit counseling services for consumers who need them, and a number of churches, charities, and nonprofit organizations that offer genuine assistance, often at no cost to you. Commercial credit counselors take commissions from your payments and sometimes require a hefty "down payment" that does not go toward your debt at all. In the worst cases, these "agencies" take your monthly payment and never pay your creditors, and you end up in default.

Consultations with credit counselors require your time and energy and may take an emotional toll on you; select a credit counselor carefully so you do not have to go through the process more than once. Check the organization's background with your local chamber of commerce, the Better Business Bureau, and lists of government-approved credit counseling agencies. Ask for references. Question any fees or commissions, and find out exactly how the credit counselor proposes to help you.

Tip: **You can never free yourself from debt without consequences of some kind.**

Whatever route you take to manage your debt and halt foreclosure, there will always be consequences, such as a negative effect on your credit or the necessity of sticking to a very tight budget for several years. Be skeptical of anyone who makes unrealistic promises.

"Save your house by selling it to me"

A group of investors may approach you and offer to buy your home from you for the amount owed on your mortgage, rent it back to you until you get back on your feet, then resell it to you for a small profit. They may tell you that they can obtain new financing for your mortgage because they have a better credit rating. Once the deed to your house is transferred into their names, they become the legal owners of your home and any equity you have in it. The terms of these arrangements are often so burdensome that it becomes impossible for you to buy back your home. Sometimes, they default on the new loan and your home is foreclosed on anyway, or the monthly "rent" is gradually increased until it is unmanageable. When you miss a few payments, you are evicted from your home. In a similar scheme, a scammer offers to find a buyer for your house and give you a portion of the profit from the sale, but only if you sign over the title deed and move out of the home. Once this is accomplished, the scammer rents out the house and pockets the rent, leaving you responsible for your mortgage while your lender continues with the foreclosure.

Payoff scam

In a similar scam, an "foreclosure relief agency" charges a hefty fee to pay off a homeowner's mortgage and become the new lender. During closing, the homeowner inadvertently signs over the deed to the home. With no intention of requiring the homeowner to make mortgage payments, the new owners sell the house right out from underneath them. The homeowner not only loses the home, but also the thousands of dollars paid to the agency. Never sign the deed to your home over to anyone without consulting an lawyer who is independent of the transaction.

Tip : These pointers will help you avoid foreclosure scams.

- Be suspicious of all mortgage consultants or foreclosure services that approach you.
- Find your own help; do not hire anyone who solicits business through the mail or door-to-door.
- Never sign anything that is too complicated to understand.
- Do not let anyone rush you into making a quick decision. Legitimate companies give you the time you need to make an informed decision — scammers do not.
- Be wary of anyone who offers to pay off your house and then lease or sell it back to you in the future for virtually no profit.
- Do not sign the deed of your house over to anyone.
- Do not make mortgage payments to anyone but your lender without consulting your lender first.

Where to Look for Help and Information

Consumer associations, lenders, and local, state, and federal agencies offer a wealth of information on mortgages and the foreclosure process, as well as free counseling services. Begin your search using following resources:

- The Department of Housing and Urban Development (HUD) offers information on avoiding foreclosure online at **http://portal.hud.gov/portal/page/portal/HUD/topics/avoiding_foreclosure**. For free foreclosure-avoidance counseling, call HUD at (800) 569-4287 or (877) 483-1515.

- HOPE NOW, sponsored by the Department of the Treasury and HUD, is an alliance of counselors, mortgage companies, investors, and other mortgage professionals. It is committed to helping homeowners in distress stay in their homes. The HOPE NOW Alliance includes a number of counseling organizations that provide in-depth debt management, credit counseling, and foreclosure counseling. Call (888) 995-HOPE or go to **www.hopenow.com** for assistance.

- Making Home Affordable provides information on HARP and HAMP at **www.makinghomeaffordable.gov**, along with self-assessment tools and calculators to help borrowers determine whether they might be eligible; free counseling resources; notices about homeowner events in your communities; and a checklist of key documents and materials to have on hand when negotiating with your loan servicer.

- The Federal Trade Commission offers education about mortgages, foreclosure, and refinancing at **www.ftc.gov/bcp/edu/pubs/consumer/homes/rea04.shtm**.

- The Federal Reserve Banks have established regional Foreclosure Resource Centers to help small municipalities, housing counselors, and consumer and community groups. The Federal Reserve Board also provides information and links to agencies and organizations that may be able to help you at **www.federalreserve.gov/ consumerinfo/foreclosure.htm**.

- Federal Deposit Insurance Corporation (FDIC) offers foreclosure prevention education and resources at **www.fdic.gov/consumers/ loans/prevention**.

- Federal Financial Institutions Examination Council (FFIEC) provides information on the Home Mortgage Disclosure Act at **www.ffiec.gov/hmda**.

- NeighborWorks America, a national nonprofit organization created by Congress to provide financial support, technical assistance, and training for community-based revitalization efforts, offers foreclosure assistance at **www.nwconsumer.org/foreclo- sure_help.html**.

- Office of the Comptroller of the Currency (OCC) offers a number of resources to help consumers, community groups, and bankers preserve their home ownership, avoid foreclosure, and protect themselves against foreclosure and debt elimination scams. Go to **www.occ.gov/consumernews_foreclosure.htm** or **www.helpwithmybank.gov**.

- The Survivors Club offers information and advice on its Fore- closure Support Center at **www.thesurvivorsclub.org/support- center/money/foreclosure/foreclosure.html**.

You are not alone when facing foreclosure; there are many people you can turn to for help and guidance. Keep asking questions until you are sure you understand your options. If you do not get a helpful response from your lender, persevere until you find someone who is willing to listen and work with you. You might need the assistance of a professional such as a financial advisor, credit counselor, or real estate lawyer. Many foreclosures can be avoided if prompt action is taken.

CHAPTER 12

After Foreclosure

$\mathcal{E}$arlier chapters have covered a number of possible solutions to imminent foreclosure:

- Forestalling foreclosure by finding a solution to your financial crisis
- Halting foreclosure and rehabilitating your mortgage
- Halting foreclosure with a legal defense
- Refinancing
- Selling your home
- Arranging a deed in lieu
- Declaring bankruptcy
- Letting the foreclosure process take its course

Whatever direction you take, your problems are not over when the foreclosure proceedings stop. You have confronted foreclosure and come to terms with your lender, but you are still on shaky ground financially. There may be debts for legal expenses, or a deficiency judgment from the sale of the home. Your savings might be depleted, and you may not have an adequate "safety net" to protect you in an emergency. You might be faced with paying off high-interest credit card debt or school loans. The events that led up to foreclosure have probably taken a heavy toll on your finances and your family, and you will need time to recover.

You did not arrive in this situation overnight, and it will not be resolved overnight. This is an opportunity for you to reevaluate what is important in your life — what matters most to you and your family. The lessons you learned, both personal and financial, while fighting foreclosure will continue to help you as you reestablish yourself.

Rebuilding Your Finances

What is going to prevent you from finding yourself in the same predicament a year or two from now? Formulate a clear plan for meeting your financial obligations. The plan should include putting aside some savings in an emergency fund. If you have filed for bankruptcy, make sure you do not default on the agreement you made with the court. Create a budget and stick to it.

Prioritize your debts by making a chart of what is due each month, with the most important items at the top. Pay the mortgage and homeowners' insurance first, then your car payment and automobile insurance. Work your way down the list. As long as your home is paid for and the agreement kept, you will never have to think about foreclosure again.

Tip: Prioritize your bills.

Here is a simple order for prioritizing your bills:

1. **Family necessities.** Think about what is necessary for your family's well-being: food, shelter, and essential medicines.

2. **Mortgage payment or rent.** If you do not keep up monthly payments, you will face foreclosure again and may lose your home.

3. **Homeowner's insurance and property taxes.** Many mortgages include homeowner's insurance in your monthly payments; others require it as a condition of the loan. Failure to keep up homeowner's insurance could be a reason for the lender to foreclose. Do not forget that homeowner's insurance is a safeguard to make sure you still have a home in case of a fire, flood, tornado, or other catastrophe. Failure to pay property taxes will result in a lien being placed on your home.

4. **Utilities.** It will be difficult to live in your home without water and electricity, and failure to pay for sewer or other services could result in a lien being placed on your home. If money is tight, you can call your utility provider to arrange for a late payment or a payment plan. Some local governments and utility companies have programs to assist customers having financial difficulties. Cancel nonessential services such as cable TV and high speed Internet until you can pay for them.

5. **Car payments and car insurance.** If you need your car for transportation to your job, keep up with your car payments. It is illegal to drive without car insurance, and even a minor accident could cost you thousands of dollars.

6. **Child support.** Child support is legal obligation. Failure to keep up with payments could have serious consequences, including prison time.

7. **Income taxes.** You must file your tax return even if you cannot afford to pay income taxes right away. Arrange a payment plan. If you are self-employed, remember to make quarterly payments of your estimated taxes.

8. **Cell phone.** Do you need your cell phone for work or for contacting prospective employers? Look for an inexpensive pay-by-the-month plan or prepaid cell phone. Cancel unnecessary extra lines and avoid extra charges.

9. **Student loans.** Defaulting on a student loan can have consequences such as the seizure of your tax refunds, garnishing of wages, and denial of future student loans. If you are having difficulty making payments, contact your lender to discuss an income-based repayment plan or forbearance, but do not ignore your payments.

10. **Unsecured debt.** Credit card debt, retail and gas accounts, medical bills, and other debts should be paid off, but not at the expense of your mortgage or other high-priority debts. Do not be intimidated by threats from debt collectors. Your creditors regularly report your debt status to credit bureaus, regardless of what a debt collector does or says. Contact creditors to make payment arrangements, and seek credit counseling if you need help.

11. **Cosigned debt.** If you have cosigned a loan for someone else and put your home or car up as collateral, you could lose your property if they default. Make arrangements to have these debt payments made regularly.

Stay away from unsecured debt, such as credit cards. For the first year after foreclosure, try living only on cash. If you do not have the cash to pay for something, go without. Live within your means. If you have credit cards, put them away and use them only for real emergencies. Look for inexpensive ways to do the things you enjoy.

If you have credit cards that need to be paid off, prioritize these, too. The card with the highest interest rate has top priority, regardless of how much is owed. Pay the minimum payment on each card every month, and use any extra money to pay down the card with the highest interest. When that card has been completely paid off, start on the card with the next-highest interest rate. Work your way down until all your debt has been paid off.

Rebuilding Your Credit Score

No one who has been threatened with foreclosure walks away with a clean credit report. You will have to repair the damage by being particularly conscious of your spending habits and how they affect your credit:

- Always pay your bills on time. Do not rely on grace periods to gather the needed funds; try to plan ahead and have enough money on hand for bills before they are due.

- Use credit cards for necessities and emergencies only — and pay off those balances every month.

- Use cash.

- Monitor your credit report. Check it at least once a year for mistakes, and contact the reporting agency about fixing those questionable items.

Living in Your Home Free During Redemption

Depending on where you live, your state's timeline for foreclosure, and the backlog of foreclosures in the courts, you may be able to live in your house for months — or even years — without paying a penny in rent. This is money that you can save and use to start over once the foreclosure on your home is complete.

If you live in a state with a lengthy redemption period — during which you have the right to buy back your home — or your mortgage requires a court hearing in order to list your home for sale at auction, there may be a long period between the time you miss your first payment and when your eviction notice arrives.

With so many foreclosures clogging the court system during the current crisis, some jurisdictions have found they have a backlog of up to three years. During this time, you can legally remain in your home, paying nothing in either mortgage or rent. If you have been unable to afford your entire mortgage payment but could have afforded part of it, take that portion and put it in a savings account. If it takes your bank 36 months to foreclose on your home and sell it at auction, and you save $1,000 per month, you could save $36,000 by the time you have to leave your home. If you know foreclosure is inevitable, stop making payments. Partial payments will not stop your foreclosure or even slow the process, so you may as well keep that money. However, this is not a strategy to implement if you want to keep your home.

$\mathcal{Tip}$: Do not stop paying your property taxes.

If your taxes and homeowner's insurance are tied to your mortgage, those bills are not being paid when you stop making mortgage payments. The local tax collector can foreclose on your home faster for tax delinquencies than the bank can for a delinquent mortgage account.

CONCLUSION

Moving On

Whether you have managed to keep your home or have been forced to give it up, the experience of facing foreclosure can be overwhelming. In addition to adjusting to harsh economic realities and seeing the effects of these changes on your family, you might have feelings of failure, guilt, shame, and embarrassment. But financial hardships are not a reflection on you as a person. At least some of the circumstances leading up to the foreclosure were beyond your control. It is time to start rebuilding your psychological well-being as well as your finances.

Congratulate yourself for managing to accomplish what you have. Even if you were unable to keep your home, navigating the foreclosure process and bringing it to closure is a major achievement. Try not dwell on what could have been, and focus on the future.

Keep a journal of everything you have learned from the process. What has it taught you about practical finances and about yourself? Have you learned anything about your habits and practices that you need or want to change? Have you acquired knowledge that will make a difference to you in the future?

Let go of anger, resentment, and blame. Your value is not determined by the size of your home or bank account. Learn to trust yourself again, as going through significant financial hardship can cause you to doubt yourself. Resolving a foreclosure situation successfully is a testament to your ability to make sound financial decisions — especially now that you are more educated.

Think in terms of the future. You have made a difficult and complicated financial decision in choosing the best route out of foreclosure. Now that it is behind you, determine your financial, social, and spiritual needs, and set your priorities for the future. The economic hardship you are experiencing is not yours alone — millions like yourself are encountering similar heartbreaks, obstacles, and frustrations. You have the power to make the most of your circumstances and to gain something from your setbacks, as well as your successes.

APPENDIX A

Sample Letters

In this appendix, you will find sample letters that may be of use to you in various stages of preventing your home's foreclosure. Pay attention to the details included in each so that you can provide your lender and the courts with all the information needed to act on your requests.

Letter to Lender Explaining Hardship

This type of letter should be used early in the process, before you have missed payments or shortly after the first missed payment. It is asking your lender to meet with you so that you can make alternative arrangements to your loan agreement, even if only temporary. Make sure you contact the correct person from the start — remember that credit collectors and bank tellers are of no use to you in this situation.

January 1, 2010

Mrs. Judith Macrae
Anytown Savings and Loan

300 Banker Street
Boston, MA 02125

RE: 199 Main Street, Anytown, MA
Loan Number: 22332

Dear Mrs. Macrae,

This letter is in regard to the property listed above, owned by my husband, Roger, and myself. Though we have not missed any payments on
this loan as of yet, we are very concerned that the recent changes in our
financial situation could cause us to do so in the near future. I am writing
today to request a meeting with a qualified loan officer to discuss options
that Anytown Savings and Loan might be able to offer us during this time
to prevent our home from going into foreclosure.

Roger and I both feel very certain that our financial situation will resolve
itself in the near future. Due to an on-the-job injury, Roger is out of work
until June, at which point he will return to work. We are hoping that your
bank will be able to help us by allowing for interest-only payments until
July 25, 2010.

Please contact me at your earliest convenience. We are both eager to
establish an agreement to keep our home from the risk of foreclosure.
Thank you for your time and consideration.

Sincerely,

Mary. S. Merchant
cc: Margaret Stone, Bank President

Letter to Lender Contesting a Default

When your loan has gone into default, whether because of missed payments or for other reasons, it is important that you respond to your lender
immediately. This is most important if the reason for the default is inac-

curate in any way. Though the following letter is to contest a missed payment, the template can work just as well for any other type of default.

January 1, 2010

Mrs. Judith Macrae
Anytown Savings and Loan
300 Banker Street
Boston, MA 02125

RE: 199 Main Street, Anytown, MA
Loan Number: 22332

Dear Mrs. Macrae,

This letter is in response to a notice of missed payment I received from your bank on December 27, 2009.

In the letter sent, it is noted that the mortgage payment of $1,230.45 due on December 1, 2009 was not made. Attached you will find a photocopy of the check received and cashed by your bank on the 28th of November for this exact amount.

I am requesting that you check your records carefully and credit my loan immediately. Additionally, I would like for you to be certain that the missed payment is not recorded on any of the three credit reporting agency reports as a mark against my credit.

Thank you for your time and consideration. Should you have any further questions or concerns about this request, do not hesitate to contact me. I look forward to your prompt response.

Sincerely,

Mary. S. Merchant
cc: Margaret Stone, Bank President

Letter to Request a "Short Sale" with Lender

Before you can sell a home for less than the amount owed on the mortgage (a short sale), you need to get formal permission from the lender. The fastest way to arrange this is to send them a certified letter explaining the situation in detail and what you desire.

January 1, 2010

Mrs. Judith Macrae
Anytown Savings and Loan
300 Banker Street
Boston, MA 02125

RE: 199 Main Street, Anytown, MA
Loan Number: 22332

Dear Mrs. Macrae,

I am the sole owner of the property listed above. On October 30, your bank began foreclosure proceedings against me with regard to this debt. As I had explained in great detail in June, the loss of my husband Roger has left me in serious financial difficulty, which resulted in my default of the loan.

I am writing today to request that you accept a "short sale" agreement on this property. I have been trying to sell it since November so as to cure the debt, but have been unsuccessful with offers. Yesterday, I was given an offer that I feel is reasonable and fair.

As my beneficiary statement shows, the outstanding debt on this property equals $95,000. The fees and additional charges associated with the foreclosure proceedings and selling of the home have, as of today, amounted to $3,000.

The offer made on the property is for cash and in the amount of $94,000. Though it is less than the amount outstanding, I am hoping that, given the situation, your bank will accept the net proceeds of this sale ($91,000) as payment in full on the loan.

I believe that this offer is very fair, considering the condition of the housing market at this time. My real estate agent and I have worked diligently to sell this property as high as we could, but this is the best offer we have received. I do not believe that, should the property go to auction, your bank will do any better than this.

Attached to this letter are copies of the written offer, as well as details about my personal income and expenses so that you can see what my financial situation currently is.

Please contact me as soon as possible to discuss this arrangement in greater detail. The potential buyer is willing to close within the week so as to make the funds available to you before the auction date. Thank you for your time and consideration.

Sincerely,

Mary. S. Merchant
cc: Margaret Stone, Bank President

Letter to Request a Deed-in-lieu Arrangement

If you have reached the point where you cannot sell and no longer want your home but want to avoid foreclosure, you will need to compose a letter to your lender requesting that they accept a deed in lieu of foreclosure. Below is a sample letter:

January 1, 2010

Mrs. Judith Macrae
Anytown Savings and Loan
300 Banker Street
Boston, MA 02125

RE: 199 Main Street, Anytown, MA
Loan Number: 22332

Dear Mrs. Macrae,

At the present time, Anytown Savings and Loan holds the first and only mortgage in the amount of $95,000 on the property listed above. On October 30, 2009, I received a notice of complaint from your bank notifying me of foreclosure proceedings being initiated. The notice of sale I received yesterday states that the sheriff's sale will take place on March 21, 2010.

This letter today confirms that we have mutually agreed to organize a deed in lieu of foreclosure on this property. In addition to accepting the deed in lieu of foreclosure, Anytown Savings and Loan will also:

- Prepare the deed in lieu of foreclosure documents for my signature on January 15, 2010;

- Advise the Sheriff to halt the foreclosure process as soon as I have signed the deed in lieu of foreclosure; and

- Immediately make the three credit reporting agencies, Experian, TransUnion, and Equifax, aware that all marks against my credit relating to this foreclosure should be removed, including the notice of complaint and notice of sale.

In addition, I agree to vacate the premises and turn over all keys on the date of the signing.

Please sign in the space below to acknowledge that these terms accurately reflect the agreement between Anytown Savings and Loan and myself. Afterward, please return a copy to me for my records.

Sincerely yours,

Mary S. Merchant

AGREED AND ACCEPTED BY:

_____

Authorized Officer, Anytown Savings and Loan

Letter to Lender Requesting Reduction in Interest Rate

Under the Servicemembers Civil Relief Act, formerly called the Soldiers' and Sailors' Civil Relief Act, anyone who is on active military duty has a right to have the interest on their mortgage loan reduced to 6 percent for the duration of their duty. You will need to notify your lender about your duty status; otherwise, it will have no other way of knowing that it should make the reduction.

January 1, 2010

Mrs. Judith Macrae
Anytown Savings and Loan
300 Banker Street
Boston, MA 02125

RE: 199 Main Street, Anytown, MA
Loan Number: 22332

Dear Mrs. Macrae,

At the present time, Anytown Savings and Loan holds a promissory note secured by the property listed above. The interest rate agreed to in this note is an adjustable rate, currently at 9.8 percent and an outstanding balance of $95,000. I am writing today to notify you that my husband, Roger, on whom I depend to pay this debt, has been called into active service with the U.S. Marine Corps.

On December 1, 2009, Roger was placed on active duty and has since shipped out to serve in Iraq. Because of this, he has lost his civilian employment with Acme Automotive, which has reduced our household income considerably. My employment at the Sunnyside Diner allows for some income, but Roger's duty has caused us to be materially affected. The military estimates that Roger will remain on active duty until August 2011. We will provide notice as soon as he has been discharged.

Roger's military supervisor has informed us that, under the Servicemembers Civil Relief Act, we are allowed a reduction in the interest rate we pay on our current mortgage while Roger remains on active duty. According to the act, this includes any service charges, carrying charges, renewal charges, and fees attached to our loan.

When you have received this notification (sent by certified mail), please alter our account to reflect the statutory 6 percent interest rate and notify me of the revised payment schedule. Thank you for your time and consideration. I look forward to speaking with you soon.

Sincerely,

Mary. S. Merchant
cc: Margaret Stone, Bank President

APPENDIX B

Sample Foreclosure Documents

On the following pages, you will find sample copies of the different foreclosure documents you are likely to see during the process. These forms are not meant to be used during your foreclosure process and may vary from state to state. You should always have a qualified attorney review any document before you sign or respond to it.

Sample Notice of Complaint, or *Lis Pendens*

Just like the notice of default, the complaint, or *lis pendens*, lets a homeowner know that the lender has begun foreclosure proceedings. The complaint, however, is used only in judicial proceedings and is filed with the circuit court in the county where the property is located.

LAW OFFICES OF HOWE AND NOT
5544 Beacon Hill
Boston, Massachusetts 02020
781-777-8846

Attorney for Plaintiff
Anytown Savings and Loan

COURT OF THE STATE OF MASSACHUSETTS
COUNTY OF SUFFOLK

ANYTOWN SAVINGS AND LOAN: SUPERIOR COURT
Plaintiff,
VS: JUDICIAL DISTRICT OF BOSTON

ROGER ALLAN MERCHANT: October 30, 2009
AND
MARY SAMANTHA MERCHANT
Defendants

COMPLAINT FOR JUDICIAL FORECLOSURE

Plaintiff, Anytown Savings and Loan ("Lender") complains and alleges as follows:

VENUE

1. Venue in the Court of the County of Suffolk is proper under the laws of the State of Massachusetts because the property subject to this action is located within Suffolk County.

THE PARTIES

2. Bank is, and at all times mentioned herein was, a Massachusetts bank, chartered by the Federal Deposit Insurance Corporation, and doing business in the State of Massachusetts.

3. Bank is informed and believes, and thereon alleges that Defendants Roger Allan Merchant and Mary Samantha Merchant ("Borrowers" or "Defendants") are, and at all relevant times herein were, individuals residing in the State of Massachusetts.

THE LOAN DOCUMENTATION

4. On July 20, 1987, the defendants, Roger Allan Merchant and Mary Samantha Merchant, owed the Plaintiff two hundred thousand ($200,000) dollars as evidenced by his note dated on said date and payable to the order of the Plaintiff, together with an interest at the rate of six (6) percent per annum until July 20, 1992, being variable thereafter, and together with all costs of collection, including reasonable attorney's fees, in the event of foreclosure of the mortgage securing the note. Under the terms of the Note, Borrower agreed to make monthly payments of $1,020.00, comprised of principal and interest. The interest was calculated at a fixed rate of eight (8) percent per year, payable on the last day of each month. The Note provided upon default the holder could declare all monies payable thereunder immediately due, owing and payable. The Note also provided for a default interest rate of three (3) percent plus the contracted rate.

5. On said date, by deed of that date, the defendants, Roger Allan Merchant and Mary Samantha Merchant, to secure said note, mortgages to the plaintiff the real estate described in Exhibit "A" attached hereto and made a part hereof. Said deed is conditioned upon the payment of said note according to its tenor and was recorded on 10 September 2009 in Volume 24, Page 204 of the Boston Registry of Deeds.

6. Said note and mortgage are still owned by the plaintiff, and the debt is due and partially unpaid.

7. Bank complied with all of its contractual obligations under the Note by disbursing monies as required.

LOAN DEFAULTS

8. The defendants, Roger Allan Merchant and Mary Samantha Merchant, have defaulted under the terms of the mortgage note and deed.

9. Although the note is in default and demand was made upon the defendant, said defendant has neglected and refused to make payment.

WHEREFORE, THE PLAINTIFF CLAIMS:

1. Monetary damages and that the amount, legal interest or property in demand is greater than $95,000.00 exclusive of interest and costs.

2. Strict foreclosure of said mortgage, but in the event that the United States of America is a part defendant at the time of judgment, then a foreclosure by sale.

3. Possession of mortgaged premises.

4. A deficiency judgment.

5. Such other equitable relief as the court may deem necessary.

6. Reasonable attorneys' fees as called for in the note.

Dated at Boston, Massachusetts, this 30th of October, 2009.

NOTICE

NOTICE: A person who is unemployed or underemployed and who (for a continuous period of at least two years to the commencement of this foreclosure action) owned and occupied the property being foreclosed as such person's principal residence may be entitled to contain relief provisions under Massachusetts General Statute 32-67W, as amended. You should consult an attorney to determine your rights under this law.

THE PLAINTIFF

BY: _____

Judith Macrae for
Anytown Savings and Loan

Sample Notice of Default for Non-Judicial Filings

DOC # 2007-0698543
10/30/2007 09:00A Fee: 14.00
page 1 of 2
Recorded in the Official Records
County of Suffolk
James. B. Jones
Assessor, Country Clerk and Recorder

RECORDING REQUESTED BY
ANYTOWN SAVINGS AND LOAN

and when recorded mail to

ANYTOWN SAVINGS AND LOAN
300 BANKER STREET
BOSTON, MASSACHUSETTS 02125

NOTICE OF DEFAULT AND ELECTION TO SELL UNDER DEED
OF TRUST

"IMPORTANT NOTICE"

T.S. No, F3395032 MA   Unit Code: B   Loan No: 22332
AP #2: 064-431-329-0
Property Address: 199 Main Street, Anytown, MA

If your property is in foreclosure because you have fallen behind in your payments, it may be sold without any court action., and you may have the legal right to bring your account in good standing by paying all of your past due payments plus permitted costs and expenses within the time permitted by law for reinstatement of your account, which is normally five business days prior to the date set for the sale of your property. No sale date may be set until three months from the date this notice of default may be recorded (which date of recordation appears on this notice).

This amount is $96,045.45 as of 30 October 2009 and will increase until your account becomes current.

While your property is in foreclosure, you still must pay other obligations (such as insurance and taxes) required by your note and deed of trust or mortgage. If you fail to make future payments on the loan, pay taxes on the property, provide insurance on the property, or pay other obligations as required in the note and deed of trust or mortgage, the beneficiary or mortgagee may insist that you do so in order to reinstate your account in good standing. In addition, the beneficiary or mortgagee may require as a condition of reinstatement that you provide reliable written evidence that you paid all senior liens, property taxes, and hazard insurance provisions.

Upon your written request, the beneficiary or mortgagee will give you a written itemization of the entire amount you must pay. You may not have to pay the entire unpaid portion of your account, even though full payment was demanded, but you must pay all amounts in default at the time payment is made. However, you and your beneficiary or mortgagee may mutually agree in writing prior to the time the notice of sale is posted (which may or may not be earlier than the end of the three-month period stated above) to, among other things, (1) provide additional time in which to cure the default by transfer of the property or otherwise; or (2) establish a schedule of payments in order to cure the default; or both (1) and (2).

Sample Answer to Notice of Complaint

When your lender begins judicial foreclosure proceedings, it will file a notice of complaint with the circuit court in your county. You will probably have 30 days to respond to this complaint before the judge will make a summary judgment of foreclosure in the lender's favor. While it is advisable that you hire an attorney to file your answer, it is not necessary. Below is a sample answer that can be filed in response to the notice. Pay attention to the way each point brought up in the complaint is addressed.

LAW OFFICES OF TRY AND MIGHT
200 Boylston Street
Boston, Massachusetts 02015
781-777-4546

Attorney for Defendants
Roger A. and Mary S. Merchant

COURT OF THE STATE OF MASSACHUSETTS
COUNTY OF SUFFOLK

ANYTOWN SAVINGS AND LOAN: SUPERIOR COURT
Plaintiff,

VS: JUDICIAL DISTRICT OF BOSTON

ROGER ALLAN MERCHANT   : November 10, 2009
AND
MARY SAMANTHA MERCHANT
Defendants

COMPLAINT FOR JUDICIAL FORECLOSURE

Defendants, Roger Allan Merchant and Mary Samantha Merchant ("Borrowers") complain and allege as follows:

VENUE

1. It is agreed that the venue in the Court of the County of Suffolk is proper under the laws of the State of Massachusetts because the property subject to this action is located within Suffolk County.

THE PARTIES

2. It is agreed that the Bank is, and at all times mentioned herein was, a Massachusetts bank, chartered by the Federal Deposit Insurance Corporation, and doing business in the State of Massachusetts.

3. It is agreed that Defendants Roger Allan Merchant and Mary Samantha Merchant ("Borrowers" or "Defendants") are, and at all relevant times herein were, individuals residing in the State of Massachusetts.

THE LOAN DOCUMENTATION

4. It is agreed that on July 20, 1987, the defendants, Roger Allan Merchant and Mary Samantha Merchant, owed the Plaintiff two hundred thousand ($200,000) dollars as evidenced by this note dated on said date and payable to the order of the Plaintiff, together with an interest at the rate of six (6) percent per annum until July 20, 1992, being variable thereafter, and together with all costs of collection, including reasonable attorney's fees, in the event of foreclosure of the mortgage securing the note. Under the terms of the Note, Borrower agreed to make monthly payments of $1,020.00, comprised of principal and interest. The interest was calculated at a fixed rate of eight (8) percent per year, payable on the last day of each month. The Note provided upon default the holder could declare all monies payable thereunder immediately due, owing and payable. The Note also provided for a default interest rate of three (3) percent plus the contracted rate.

5. It is agreed that on said date, by deed of that date, the defendants, Roger Allan Merchant and Mary Samantha Merchant, to secure said note, mortgages to the plaintiff the real estate described in Exhibit "A" attached hereto and made a part hereof. Said deed is conditioned upon the payment of said note according to its tenor and was recorded on 10 September 2009 in Volume 24, Page 204 of the Boston Registry of Deeds.

6. It is agreed that said note and mortgage are still owned by the plaintiff, and the debt is due and partially unpaid.

7. It is CONTESTED that Bank complied with all of its contractual obligations under the Note by disbursing monies as required.

LOAN DEFAULTS

8. It is CONTESTED that the defendants, Roger Allan Merchant and Mary Samantha Merchant, have defaulted under the terms of the mortgage note and deed.

9. It is CONTESTED that although the note is in default and demand was made upon the defendant, said defendant has neglected and refused to make payment.

WHEREFORE, THE DEFENDANT CLAIMS:

1. An enjoinment is made on this case brought before the court, until such time that:
2. An audit of the account in question can be made by the defendants' accountant.
3. Such other equitable relief as the court may deem necessary.
4. Reasonable attorneys' fees as a result of unlawful action.

Dated at Boston, Massachusetts, this 10th of November, 2009

<u>NOTICE</u>

NOTICE: A person who is unemployed or underemployed and who (for a continuous period of at least two years to the commencement of this foreclosure action) owned and occupied the property being foreclosed as such person's principal residence, may be entitled to contain relief provisions under Massachusetts General Statute 32-67W, as amended. You should consult an attorney to determine your rights under this law.

THE DEFENDANTS

BY: _____
Roger Allan Merchant and

_____
Mary Samantha Merchant

Sample Tax Lien

As you are sorting through your documents, it is important to find and identify any liens you may have against the property. Liens can come from the Internal Revenue Service, from mechanics and contractors who worked on your property under your request, or anyone to whom you owe a substantial amount of money.

In order for a lien to be viable, it must be recorded with the county record office. The following is a sample of a tax lien. Other liens will look very similar.

Recording requested by Internal Revenue Service. When recorded, mail to: INTERNAL REVENUE SERVICE PO BOX 54365 STOP 4563H ANYTOWN, MASSACHUSETTS 01101	DOC # 2009-0698543 10/30/2009 09:00A Fee: 14.00 page 1 of 2 Recorded in the Official Records County of Suffolk James. B. Jones Assessor, Country Clerk & Recorder
Form 668 (Y)(c) (Rev. February 2007)	1872 Department of the Treasury — Internal revenue Service Notice of Federal Tax Lien
Area: SMALL BUSINESS/SELF-EMPLOYED AREA #7 LIEN UNIT PHONE: (800) 777-6565	Serial Number 96758930222

As provided by section 6321, 6322, and 6323 of the Internal Revenue Code, we are giving notice that taxes (including interest and penalties) have been assessed against the following-named taxpayer. We have made a demand for payment of this liability, but it remains unpaid. Therefore, there is a lien in favor of the United States on all property and rights to property belonging to this taxpayer for the amount of these taxes, and additional penalties, interest, and costs that may accrue.

Name of Taxpayer ROGER ALLAN MERCHANT

Residence   199 MAIN STREET
               ANYTOWN, MASSACHUSETTS

IMPORTANT RELEASE INFORMATION: For each assessment listed below, unless notice of the lien is refiled by the date given in column (e), this notice shall, on the day following such date, operate as a certificate of release as defined in IRC6325(a).

Kind of Tax (a)	Tax Period Ending (b)	Identifying Number (c)	Date of Assessment (d)	Last Day for Refiling (e)	Unpaid Balance of Assessment (f)
1040	12/31/2005	XXX-XX-4352	12/30/2007	01/29/2016	4532.97
1040	12/31/2006	XXX-XX-4352	12/30/2008	01/29/2017	15437.99
1040	12/31/2007	XXX-XX-4352	12/30/2009	01/29/2018	17655.43

Place of Filing COUNTY RECORDER SUFFOLK COUNTY Total BOSTON, MA 02125	37626.39

This notice was prepared and signed at Boston, Massachusetts, on this, the 30th day of September, 2009.

Signature: _____

Sample Grant Deed

Like a warranty deed, a grant deed transfers property to another individual with the assumption that there are no outstanding claims against the property. A full title search of the property should be performed, though, to prove this.

Recording requested by ANYTOWN SAVINGS AND LOAN When recorded, mail to: ANYTOWN SAVINGS AND LOAN 300 BANKER STREET BOSTON, MASSACHUSETTS 02125	DOC # 2009-0698543 10/30/2009 09:00A Fee: 14.00 page 1 of 2 Recorded in the Official Records County of Suffolk James. B. Jones Assessor, Country Clerk and Recorder

Massachusetts Grant Deed

[ ] This transfer is exempt from the documentary transfer tax.

[X] This documentary transfer tax is $__30,000____ and is computed on:

    [ ] the full value of the interest in the property conveyed

    [X] the full value less the value of any encumbrances and liens on the property at the time of sale

The property is located in an [ ] unincorporated area. [X] the city of Anytown.

For a valuable consideration, the receipt of which is hereby acknowledged,

ROGER ALLAN MERCHANT AND MARY SAMANTHA MERCHANT

Hereby grant(s) to

ANYTOWN SAVINGS AND LOAN

The following real property in the City of _Anytown_, County of _Suffolk_, State of _Massachusetts_.

Date _____   _____

Date _____   _____

State of (Massachusetts)
County of (Suffolk)

On _____, 20__, before me, _____, a notary public in and for said state personally appeared _____
_____, personally known to me (or proved to me based on satisfactory evidence) to be the person(s) whose name(s) is/are subscribed to within instrument and acknowledged that he/she/they executed the same in his/her/their signature on the instrument the person(s) or entity on behalf of which they acted, executed the instrument.

_____
Signature of Notary

Sample Quitclaim Deed

A quitclaim deed transfers ownership in a property to another, without any guarantees on the status of the property. When arranging a deed in lieu of foreclosure, your lender may draft a quitclaim deed to transfer the property from your name into their own. Be certain that you clearly write "Deed in Lieu of Foreclosure" next to the words "Quitclaim Deed" to signify that the deed is being signed to remove your future liability. Consult a real estate attorney for assistance with a deed in lieu.

Recording requested by ANYTOWN SAVINGS AND LOAN When recorded, mail to: ANYTOWN SAVINGS AND LOAN 300 BANKER STREET BOSTON, MASSACHUSETTS 02125	DOC # 2009-0698543 10/30/2009 09:00A Fee: 14.00 page 1 of 2 Recorded in the Official Records County of Suffolk James. B. Jones Assessor, Country Clerk and Recorder

QUITCLAIM DEED

THE UNDERSIGNED GRANTOR(S) DECLARE(S):

DOCUMENTARY TRANSFER TAX IS: $_____   CITY TAX IS: $_____

       ☐ computed on the full value of the property conveyed, or

       ☐ computed on the full value less and liens or encumbrances remain at the time of sale,

       ☐ Realty not sold

       ☐Unincorporated area   ☐ City of Anytown, and

For valuable consideration, receipt of which is hereby acknowledged, _ROGER ALLAN MERCHANT AND MARY SAMANTHA MERCHANT__ hereby deed to __ANYTOWN SAVINGS AND LOAN__ in lieu of foreclosure, the following real property in the City of Anytown, County of Suffolk, State of Massachusetts, commonly known as 199 Main Street, Anytown, MA.

Date: _____, 2009 _____

Date: _____, 2009 _____

Date: _____, 2009 _____

ACKNOWLEDGEMENT

State of (Massachusetts)
County of (Suffolk)

On _____, 20__, before me, _____, a notary public in and for said state personally appeared _____ _____, personally known to me (or proved to me based on satisfactory evidence) to be the person(s) whose name(s) is/are subscribed to within instrument and acknowledged that he/she/they executed the same in his/her/their signature on the instrument the person(s) or entity on behalf of which they acted, executed the instrument.

_____
Signature of Notary

Sample Deed in Lieu of Foreclosure

Just as with a quitclaim deed, the deed in lieu of foreclosure transfers all interest you have in the property to another — in this case, the lender.

Recording requested by ANYTOWN SAVINGS AND LOAN When recorded, mail to: ANYTOWN SAVINGS AND LOAN 300 BANKER STREET BOSTON, MASSACHUSETTS 02125	DOC # 2009-0698543 10/30/2009 09:00A Fee: 14.00 page 1 of 2 Recorded in the Official Records County of Suffolk James. B. Jones Assessor, Country Clerk and Recorder

DEED IN LIEU OF FORECLOSURE

    1. This transfer is exempt from the documentary transfer tax.

    2. This property is located in ____Suffolk_____,

        [ ] an unincorporated area.

        [ ] the city of ___Anytown__.

    3. For valuable consideration, receipt of which is hereby acknowledged, _ROGER ALLAN MERCHANT AND MARY SAMANTHA MERCHANT__ hereby deed to __ANYTOWN SAVINGS AND LOAN__ in lieu of foreclosure, the following real property in the City of Anytown, County of Suffolk, State of Massachusetts, commonly known as 199 Main Street, Anytown, MA.

Date: _____, 2009 _____

Date: _____, 2009 _____

Date: _____, 2009 _____

ACKNOWLEDGEMENT

State of (Massachusetts)
County of (Suffolk)

On _____, 20__, before me, _____, a notary public in and for said state personally appeared _____

_____, personally known to me (or proved to me based on satisfactory evidence) to be the person(s) whose name(s) is/are subscribed to within instrument and acknowledged that he/she/they executed the same in his/her/their signature on the instrument the person(s) or entity on behalf of which they acted, executed the instrument.

_____

Signature of Notary

APPENDIX C

Foreclosure Laws by State

Foreclosure can look quite different from state to state. It is important to understand the regulations in the area in which you live. Below is a brief description of the foreclosure process in each of the 50 states. Many states institute both judicial and non-judicial methods; where this is the case, the preference is listed, along with any caveats. See the state Web sites listed for specifics about the foreclosure process and legalities in a particular state.

Alabama: Both judicial and non-judicial procedures are allowed in Alabama, with the preference for non-judicial. Deficiency judgments may be requested before or after the sale of the property. Homeowners have one year to redeem the property for the price paid at auction, taxes, insurance, improvements, and 10 percent interest. For more information, visit **www. legislature.state.al.us**.

Alaska: The preferred manner of foreclosure in Alaska is through non-judicial means, though judicial procedures are also possible. If the foreclosure is non-judicial, deficiency judgments cannot be requested. The non-judicial process also allows the homeowner the ability to halt the sale and foreclosure by making up the total missed payments plus attorney's fees. The lender cannot demand the full sum of the outstanding loan. See **www. legis.state.ak.us** to learn more.

Arizona: Both judicial and non-judicial procedures are followed. There is no redemption period in Arizona, and deficiency judgments are not allowed if the property was 2.5 acres or less and contained a one- or two-bedroom family dwelling. Deficiency suits are allowed in other types of property, but only for the difference between the fair market value of the property and what is owed. This suit must be filed within 90 days of the power of sale foreclosure. Go to **www.azleg.gov** to find out more about Arizona's processes.

Arkansas: Arkansas law allows for both methods of foreclosure, depending on the type of security document signed. The borrower has one year to redeem the property in foreclosure, provided they did not waive that right in the original agreement. A deficiency judgment can be sought for either the balance on the loan after the sale of the property at auction or the balance due minus the fair market value. The judgment will be for whichever sum is less. See **www.arkleg.state.ar.us** for additional information.

California: California has what is referred to as a "one-act rule." A lender can either foreclose through non-judicial means, in which case it must settle for whatever it can sell the property for at auction, or it can pursue a judicial foreclosure. The second allows the lender to foreclose and sue for deficiencies should the sale be lower than the amount owed. The non-judicial route is by far the most prevalent. Lien holders other than lenders, though, can reclaim other property of the homeowner to satisfy debts owed. Redemption is only permitted after judicial foreclosure. Go to **www. leginfo.ca.gov** to learn more.

Colorado: Again, both types of foreclosure are allowed under Colorado state law. Borrowers have a "right-to-cure," which means that they can give notice up to seven days before the sale of the property that they will make up the missing payments, plus accrued fees. They must pay the amount due by noon on the day preceding the sale of the property, or it will go to auction. Delinquency judgments for any outstanding balance may be sued for by the lender. The homeowner has a redemption period of 75 days. Visit **www.state.co.us** for more information on Colorado's laws.

Connecticut: Though both types of foreclosure are available, Connecticut has a high preference for judicial foreclosure through both the strict method and decree of sale. Lenders on property in Connecticut can get a court order showing the borrower to be in default, at which point in time the lender receives title on the property. A decree of sale puts the selling and disbursement of funds into the hands of the court. There are special protections under Connecticut law, particularly if you are unemployed. See **www.cga.ct.gov** for more information.

Delaware: Delaware allows only for judicial foreclosures. No redemption is allowed. Delaware does allow for *scire facias,* which is a procedure requiring the homeowner to show there is no just cause for the foreclosure. A separate lawsuit may be initiated to recover deficiencies between the amount owed and the sale price of the property. See **http://legis.delaware.gov** to find out more about Delaware's laws regarding foreclosure.

Florida: Florida allows for judicial foreclosures only. Unfortunately, there are few options available to a borrower when a lender decides to foreclose. The court can order the property sold at a low price, and a deficiency suit can be brought against the borrower up to four years afterward. Visit **www.flsenate.gov/statutes** for additional information on Florida's foreclosure process.

Georgia: Both types of foreclosure are available via Georgia's state law, though the preference is toward non-judicial. Deficiency judgments can only be requested if the lender pursues a judicial foreclosure process. One plus for homeowners here is that the court must approve the sale as meeting the fair market value of the property, which in all likelihood will cover the cost of the outstanding debt. See **www.legis.state.ga.us** to learn more.

Hawaii: Judicial foreclosure is the primary mode of foreclosure. Non-judicial procedures are possible, but rare. There are no redemption rights. See **www.capitol.hawaii.gov** for additional information.

Idaho: Non-judicial procedure is the standard in Idaho. The borrower is allowed to pay the amount owing on the debt within 15 days of notice — and before newspaper publication — to halt the foreclosure process. Deficiency suits can be filed within three months following the sale of the property for outstanding debt owed. The redemption period is six months for property 20 acres or less, and one year for property over 20 acres. Visit **www.legislature.idaho.gov** to find out more.

Illinois: Foreclosure will take a judicial route in Illinois, with strict foreclosure and entry and possession an option. Redemption rights by the borrower can be waived only if the lender waives the right to a deficiency suit. If this does not take place, the borrower has the right to redeem the property within seven months of the foreclosure filing, or three months after the judgment was entered. There is the option to halt the proceedings by clearing the debt of missed payments within 90 days of being served with the notice. In Illinois, possession of the property can take place prior to the final judgment and sale of the property, with forced eviction of the homeowner. If the property is in rental, the lender can take possession of the rents paid. To learn more about Illinois foreclosure law, go to **www.ilga.gov**.

Indiana: Indiana is fairly simple and straightforward: judicial foreclosure, with no right to redemption after the sale. See **www.in.gov/core/index.htm** for additional information.

Iowa: Both methods are possible for foreclosure on non-agricultural property in Iowa. Interestingly, the state has the right to prevent the filing of foreclosures during times of economic difficulty — which is wonderful for homeowners during national economic slumps. Non-judicial foreclosures often include the borrower signing over the title in return for the lender relinquishing their right to sue for deficiency. Judicial foreclosure takes the normal process route, with rights to redemption at the discretion of the lender. Visit **www.legis.state.ia.us** to find out more.

Kansas: Judicial foreclosure is the only method used in Kansas. Redemption is allowed up to 12 months after the sale, and deficiency judgments can be sought. Go to **www.kslegislature.org** to learn more about Kansas foreclosure law.

Kentucky: Kentucky requires all foreclosures to be judicial. Possession of the property can only be taken by the lender if the property has been abandoned or once the court judgment has been made in their favor. Redemption is available if the property has been sold at auction for less than two-thirds of its appraised value. If this is the case, the homeowner has one year after the sale to redeem it.

Deficiency judgments are possible if the borrower was personally served with the lawsuit. For more information on Kentucky's foreclosure procedures, go to **www.lrc.state.ky.us**.

Louisiana: Only judicial foreclosures are allowed in Louisiana. Visit **www.louisiana.gov** for more information.

Maine: Maine observes only judicial means of foreclosure, and it can be a strict foreclosure with or without possession of the property. Redemption periods vary depending on when the mortgage agreement was signed, and deficiency suits are possible only for the difference between the fair market value of the property when it was sold and the balance owed on the loan. Visit **www.maine.gov** to learn more.

Maryland: Maryland allows solely judicial foreclosures. There is an unspecified redemption period, and deficiency suits are allowed within three years of the foreclosure's completion. See **www.mlis.state.md.us** for additional information.

Massachusetts: Non-judicial foreclosure is typical in Massachusetts, with entry and possession a possibility. Right to redeem is rarely an option, and deficiency suits can be brought for the balance left on the loan after the property has been sold. See **www.mass.gov/legis** for more information.

Michigan: Judicial and non-judicial foreclosure is possible in Michigan, depending on whether a "power of sale" clause is in the mortgage agreement. Redemption periods vary depending on its size and length of ownership before default. Deficiency judgments can be filed separately but are complicated to do. See **www.legislature.mi.gov** for more information.

Minnesota: Both processes are possible in Minnesota. Deficiency charges are possible only by a lawsuit by the lender. The judgment for deficiency is decided on by a jury and limited to the difference between the fair market value and the amount owed on the mortgage. Redemption is rare and has caveats depending on the size of the property. Go to **www.leg.state.mn.us/ leg/statutes.asp** to find out more information.

Mississippi: The type of foreclosure in Mississippi depends on the security instrument signed. Both processes are possible. Borrowers may cure the debt any time prior to the sale with the amount past-due and associated fees. There is no right to redemption if the process is non-judicial. To learn more, go to **www.ls.state.ms.us**.

Missouri: Missouri allows judicial foreclosures only, but a "power of sale" clause in the mortgage permits special procedures. Redemption is only possible if the lender purchases the property at the auction, and then lasts for one year. For additional information, visit **www.moga.mo.gov**.

Montana: Depending on the type of property and document used to secure it, both processes are possible. The right to redeem has been eliminated in Montana, as has the ability to file deficiency judgments. Go to **http://leg.mt.gov/css/default.asp** to find out more about Montana's unique stipulations.

Nebraska: Judicial foreclosure is the only acceptable proceeding in Nebraska. The foreclosure can be stopped by making up past payments plus additional fees, prior to the judgment being issued by the court. Deficiency can only be sought as a continuation of the foreclosure suit after the sale, and then only for the difference between the unpaid balance on the mortgage and the fair market value at the time of sale. See **http://nebraskalegislature.gov/laws/laws.php** to learn more about Nebraska's foreclosure laws.

Nevada: Both routes to foreclosure are possible. The borrower can cure the debt and stop the foreclosure within the first 35 days after notice has been given. Redemption is possibly only with judicial foreclosure and lasts for one year after the sale. Deficiency can be sought by lawsuit during the first three months after the sale. Go to Nevada's state Web site to learn more about their processes: **www.leg.state.nv.us/nrs**.

New Hampshire: New Hampshire has strict foreclosure laws that allow "entry and possession" as a means to reclaiming the property. They are more likely, though, to follow a non-judicial route using a "power of sale" clause in the mortgage. The borrower can cure the debt in the time before the sale. Visit **www.state.nh.us** to find out more.

New Jersey: Judicial foreclosure only. Deficiency judgments are permitted within the first three months after the sale of the property. Redemption is possible in the ten days the borrower has to refute the initial judgment or foreclosure. If the borrower is sued for deficiency, it reopens their right to redeem the property in question. Go to **www.njleg.state. nj.us** to learn more.

New Mexico: In New Mexico, both procedures are possible, but non-judicial foreclosures are limited to commercial properties where the loan is for $500,000 or more. Otherwise, foreclosures follow a judicial route. Both a right to cure before the sale and redemption are possible. Redemption has a nine-month period after the auction. Deficiency judgments may be brought against the borrower to cover additional costs. Visit **www.legis. state.nm.us** for additional information.

New York: Both methods are possible, with the preference given to judicial foreclosure. Deficiency judgment can be sought for the balance owed after the sale only if an express covenant to pay is included in the security instrument, and only within the 90 days following the sale. There is no redemption period. See **www.assembly.state.ny.us** to get more information on New York law.

North Carolina: Both processes are possible, depending on the security instrument signed, with a preference for non-judicial foreclosures. Deficiency suits are possible, but the borrower has more rights than in other states to prove such a suit unnecessary. See **www.ncga.state.nc.us** to learn more about North Carolina's caveats.

North Dakota: The sole route to foreclosure in North Dakota is judicial. Redemption is possible, but differs according to the property size — most often lasting six months to one year. Interestingly, North Dakota has a moratorium option giving the courts the power to postpone judgment if the debt owed is less than fair market value of the property. Go to the state Web site to learn more: **www.nd.gov**.

Ohio: Only judicial foreclosure is available in Ohio. The property can be redeemed only before the sale of the property at auction, but not afterward. Deficiency judgments can be brought within the two-year period after the sale of the property. For more information, visit **www.legislature.state.oh.us**.

Oklahoma: Both options are available, depending on the type of security instrument used. There is no redemption period after the sale, though the debt can be cured beforehand in many instances. Deficiency judgments can be brought within the first 90 days after the auction. More information is available at **www.lsb.state.ok.us**.

Oregon: Both processes are possible, with a tendency toward non-judicial foreclosures. The redemption rights and ability to file deficiency lawsuits depend on a variety of circumstances. To find out the various caveats, visit the state Web site at **www.leg.state.or.us**.

Pennsylvania: Foreclosure laws in Pennsylvania favor the borrower more than the lender. They follow a judicial route, but require the lender to meet with the borrower before filing suit to resolve the issue. There is no right to redemption afterward. Deficiency judgments can be brought against the borrower. More information can be found at **www.pacode.com**.

Rhode Island: Both type of foreclosure are available, depending on whether a "power of sale" clause is included in the mortgage. Visit **www.rilin.state.ri.us** to get more information about foreclosure processes in Rhode Island.

South Carolina: Only judicial foreclosure is allowed in South Carolina. There is no power of redemption, and deficiency judgments can be sought for outstanding debt owed after the sale. More information can be found at **www.scstatehouse.net**.

South Dakota: Both types of foreclosure can be followed, depending on whether a "power of sale" clause is included in the mortgage. Deficiency is not possible if the loan in default was used to purchase the property. Redemption rights vary depending on property size and circumstances. To learn more, go to the state Web site at **www.legis.state.sd.us**.

Tennessee: Non-judicial foreclosure is the primary process in Tennessee, though judicial is possible, as well. Redemption can take place up to two years after the sale, unless the right was waived in the original deed of trust. Deficiency judgments are possible. Go to **www.legislature.state.tn.us** to learn more about Tennessee laws.

Texas: Either type of foreclosure is a possibility in Texas, depending on the security instrument and whether a "power of sale" clause is included. There is no right to redemption, but deficiency judgments are limited to the difference between the amount owed and the fair market value of the property. More information can be found at **www.capitol.state.tx.us**.

Utah: Both types of foreclosure are allowed in Utah, though non-judicial seems to be most common on family homes. Deficiency judgments are possible, as is redemption — though both are regulated by the court. To learn more, go to **www.le.state.ut.us**.

Vermont: Vermont follows a strict foreclosure law. Redemption is possible prior to the sale, and deficiency judgments are possible if the sale does not clear the debt. Go to **www.leg.state.vt.us** to discover more.

Virginia: Both types of foreclosure are possible in Virginia, depending on the document signed. For residences, the foreclosure process is most frequently non-judicial. Redemption is only possible in judicial processes, but deficiency judgments can be brought in with few restrictions. The state Web site offers additional information at: **http://legis.state.va.us**.

Washington: Both type of foreclosure are possible, depending on the document used to secure the property. A borrower can cure the debt up to 11 days before the auction. Deficiency can only be sought if the foreclosure is judicial, but not if the property was abandoned for six months or more prior to the foreclosure judgment. To discover more, visit **www.leg.wa.gov**.

Washington, D.C.: Though not a state, the District of Columbia has its own legislation that regulates property and follows a non-judicial route. The borrower has up to five days before the sale of the property to cure the debt. After that, there is no right to redemption. Deficiency judgments can be sought for any outstanding debt after the sale. Visit the Department of Housing and Urban Development Web site for more information at **www.hud.gov**, or download the Foreclosure Mitigation Kit published by the Department of Insurance, Securities, and Banking of the District of Columbia (**http://disb.dc.gov/disr/frames.asp?doc=/disr/lib/disr/pdf/ foreclosure_mitigation_kit_v9_2.pdf**).

West Virginia: Judicial foreclosures tend to be initiated by tax and mechanic liens, while lenders follow a non-judicial route primarily for home foreclosures. There is no right to redeem, and deficiency lawsuits can be filed after a non-judicial foreclosure has completed. Go to **www.legis.state. wv.us** to find out more.

Wisconsin: Both types of foreclosure are possible, depending on the document used to secure the loan. The primary form of foreclosure on residences, however, is judicial. Redemption hinges on whether the court has confirmed the sale of the property. If so, there is no redemption. Otherwise, the borrower has one year to redeem the property and may live in it during this time. Deficiency depends on the intentions stated by the lender in the original application to foreclose. If not articulated, they cannot sue. Go to **www.legis.state.wi.us** to find out more.

Wyoming: Both judicial and non-judicial foreclosures are possible. Most residential property, however, is non-judicially foreclosed. Deficiency can be sought in both circumstances. Borrowers have up to three months after the sale to redeem the property. To learn more, go to **http://legisweb. state.wy.us**.

APPENDIX D

Finances Worksheet

This worksheet will help you to evaluate your monthly income and expenses and get an accurate picture of your financial situation. Remember to include bills that are paid annually, such as insurance and property taxes, by dividing those amounts by 12. If your monthly expenses exceed your monthly income, it is a signal that you need to refinance or renegotiate the terms of your mortgage to lower your monthly payment. Reevaluate the items on this worksheet for accuracy, and identify nonessential expenses that could be reduced or eliminated.

CREDITS	AMOUNT	BALANCE
Monthly income (after taxes)		
Other monthly income		
TOTAL MONTHLY INCOME		
DEBITS		
Mortgage payment		
House insurance		
Property tax		
Gas		

Oil		
Electricity		
Telephone (house)		
Internet		
Garbage collection		
Cable/satellite dish		
Grocery bill		
Dining out		
Lunches (for children and/or adults)		
Laundry		
General entertainment		
Car payments		
Car insurance		
Car maintenance		
Gasoline		
Tolls		
Parking		
Doctor and hospital fees		
Health insurance		
Prescriptions		
Gym membership		
Clothing		
Hair stylist		
Manicures		
Beauty products		
Other hobbies		
School loans		
Private school tuition		
Credit cards (total)		
Other loans		
TOTAL EXPENSES		

GLOSSARY

A-credit — A rating given to an individual with excellent credit, who is therefore deserving of the lowest interest rates a lender is willing to offer.

Acceleration clause — The section in your mortgage or deed of trust that allows your lender to bring the loan forward, or call it in, at any time that you default on the loan.

Accrued interest — Interest that accumulates over time because it has been earned but remains unpaid.

Adjustable-rate mortgage — A mortgage agreement in which the interest rates over the term of your loan can adjust according to the market, but no more than 2 percent in a given year.

Adjustment date — The date(s) noted in the mortgage or deed of trust on which your interest rate changes.

Affidavit — A written or video statement, given under oath pertaining to a legal issue.

Agreement of sale — The legal contract signed between two parties that stipulates the conditions of a sale, including price, time for closing, and reasons for backing out of the deal.

Amortization — The term of the loan, or the time it will take to pay off the entire loan, including interest earned.

Amortization schedule — The schedule of monthly payments, with dates and specific amounts, that a borrower must subscribe to.

Annual percentage rate — The annual rate charged on a loan; is expressed as a percentage of the total loan.

Application — In real estate, this is the request for a loan that includes information about the borrower, such as income, expenses, and credit history.

Application fee — The cost associated with the processing of an application.

Appraisal — An assessment of a property determined by the recent sale of similar properties in the area.

Appraised value — The monetary amount determined in the appraisal.

Appraiser — An individual with a strong knowledge of the local market who has the ability to give a fair evaluation of the property.

Appreciation — An increase in value.

Assessed value — The monetary amount determined by an assessment.

Assessment — Like an appraisal, the determination of a property's value for use in taxation.

Asset — Something worth money, as in a second home or a retirement account.

Assumable mortgage — A mortgage that can be taken over by another individual without new terms being drawn up by the lender.

Assumption — The taking over of another's property and assuming the debt owed.

Back-end fee — A fee paid to a broker by a lender, most often after a successful application has been processed.

Bad-faith estimate — An estimate that is deliberately lower than actual settlement costs to make a home purchase seem more attractive to potential buyers.

Balloon mortgage — A mortgage that acts like a fixed-rate for a period of time, then becomes due in total.

Balloon payment — The amount of money that must be paid at once when the loan period on a balloon mortgage ends. This tends to be an extremely large sum that makes up for low payments during the amortization period.

Bankruptcy — The use of the court system to relieve certain debts and allow for payment plans to cover others.

Bill of sale — Legal document that notes what property was sold, on what date, to whom, by whom, and for how much.

Biweekly mortgage — A mortgage payment system that allows payments to be made every other week.

Bond — A sum set aside to cover an individual's or a company's liabilities if they do not fulfill the terms of a contract.

Bridge loan — A home equity loan that is used to solve short-term financial problems.

Broker — An individual who can arrange and assist in the organization of mortgage loans.

Buy-down — A payment system that allows a large amount of money to be paid up-front in return for lower interest rates.

Buy-up — A payment system that allows for higher interest rates in return for smaller up-front costs.

Carry-back loan — When a seller agrees to finance the buyer so that the property deal can go through.

Cash-out refinance — Refinancing a present mortgage for more than is currently owed so as to receive cash in hand.

Closing — The appointment in a property sale at which all papers are signed and keys exchanged.

Closing costs — The fees associated with the closing.

Co-borrower — An individual who signs a loan agreement with another person.

Cost of fund index (COFI) — The cost of fund index is one of many interest-rate indexes used to determine the interest on an adjustable-rate mortgage.

Collateral — Property that acts as replacement for the monetary loan should the borrower default.

Collateralized debt obligations (CDOs) — Packages of mortgages that have been bundled together and resold to investors.

Collection — The act of reclaiming something that is owed, such as a debt.

Commission — The money paid out to a broker or real estate agent for assisting in a property transaction, most often expressed as a percentage of the final loan or sale.

Comparable sales — Recent sales of similar property, in a similar area. Comparable sales are used by appraisers to determine the fair market values of a property.

Contingency — A stipulated condition that must be met before an agreement is legally binding. A refinance officer may grant a second mortgage, contingent on your being able to prove the value of certain assets.

Contract — A legally binding document between two or more people.

Conventional mortgage — Home loans that are not associated or insured with either the Veteran's or Federal Housing Administrations.

Conversion option — The option to turn an adjustable-rate mortgage into a fixed-rate mortgage after a certain amount of time.

Cost of savings index (OSI) — One of many interest rate indexes used to determine the interest on an adjustable-rate mortgage.

Credit — A loan of money with the understanding that the total plus interest will be paid back at a later date; a promise to pay.

Credit history — The history of purchasing and payments of an individual, from their first transaction onward.

Creditor — An individual, institution, or company that loans money to another.

Credit report — A document that itemizes all the relevant transactions of a given individual over the course of their adult life.

Cumulative interest — The total sum of all interest payments made over the course of the loan to date; how much interest has been actually paid.

Debt — Something owed to another, usually monetary.

Debt consolidation — Combining multiple debts, such as credit cards, into one lump sum. This can be done in a mortgage in refinancing, or with an outside agency.

Debt elimination — Scams that offer to pay off all your debt, often with the exchange of a deed.

Deed — A document that specifies who owns a given property.

Deed in lieu of foreclosure — An arrangement made with a lender to sign over the deed of the property in return (lieu) for the foreclosure being halted and credit repaired.

Default — Not making good on an agreement made; breaking a promise.

Deferred interest — See "negative amortization."

Deficiency judgment — A court order that requires an individual to make up a debt to another.

Delinquent/delinquency — Late or outstanding on an agreement.

Demand clause — A clause in a security instrument that allows the lender to demand payment in full at any time, for any reason.

Deposit — An amount of money paid up-front when a loan is made. The difference between the cost of the property and the amount of the loan.

Depreciation — A decrease in value.

Down payment — See "deposit."

Due-on-sale provision — A clause that states a given amount of money (or item) is due on the sale of another; usually a fee paid to a real estate agent when a property is sold.

Eminent domain — The government's right to take property if it deems it is for the public good, provided it pays fair market value for it.

Encumbrance — A lien or restriction against a property, including how the property may be used.

Equal Credit Opportunity Act (ECOA) — A law prohibiting credit discrimination on the basis of race, color, religion, national origin, sex, marital status, or age, or because you get public assistance.

Equity — The amount of money left over after any debts against the property have been cleared, including all loans, mortgages, and liens.

Equity grabbing — A term referring to predatory lenders that give loans with the understanding that a borrower is likely to default. The intention is to recover the equity a borrower has in the property. More frequent in refinancing than initial loans.

Escrow — A third party that holds and disburses funds when certain conditions have been met. When selling or buying a home, money is put into escrow to be released when all documents have been signed and the transaction closed.

Escrow account — The account into which funds for a transaction are placed.

Eviction — The lawful removal of an individual from real property. A tenant, for example, can be evicted by a landlord for not paying rent.

Exclusive listing — An agreement between a property owner and an estate agent giving the agent the sole right to sell the property.

Executor — An individual named in a will (including a living will) that is given the authority to make certain that wishes of another individual are carried out. This most often means that the executor ensures property disbursed in a will goes to the individual specified in the will.

Fair Credit Reporting Act — A federal law that ensures that all information is disclosed in a lending arrangement, including interest rates and fees.

Fair Debt Collection Practices Act (FDCPA) — Legislation establishing the rights of borrowers who are in default on their loans.

Fair market value — The value of real property on the open market, based on the value of other properties of similar physical condition and location that have sold in the recent past. It is also considered the highest value that a buyer will offer, and the lowest offer a seller is willing to accept.

Fannie Mae (FNMA) — Federal National Mortgage Association; the nation's largest provider of home loans.

Federal Housing Administration (FHA) — A part of the department of Urban Housing and Development; insures residential mortgages with private lenders.

FICO — The number given to reflect an individual's likeliness to pay back a debt. The score is affected by a variety of factors.

First mortgage — The mortgage that has the priority debt owed against a property; the first mortgage agreement made against a property.

Fixed-rate mortgage — An agreement for a loan where the interest rate charged over the term of the loan does not change.

Flip — To buy a property with the intention of reselling it quickly for a profit.

Float — An agreement to allow the interest rate to fluctuate with the market, with the option of "locking" it in at any given time.

Float-down — A float agreement, with the added bonus that a locked-in rate can be reduced if the market goes down.

Flood insurance — Insurance that covers property in the event of a flood.

Foreclosure — The legal act of reclaiming and selling property to recoup funds.

Forbearance agreement — An agreement made between a lender and a borrower that states that the lender will not foreclose as long as the borrower makes good on a plan to pay down an outstanding debt from missed payments and incurred fees/interest.

Front-end fee — A fee paid to the mortgage broker by the borrower.

Gift of equity — A sale price below the fair market value that results in the seller's giving his or her equity in the property to the buyer, such as in a "short sale."

Ginnie Mae (GNMA) — Government National Mortgage Association; a federal agency that secures FHA and VA loans.

Grace period — A specific amount of time after a payment date during which the borrower can make a late payment without accruing fees. Grace periods tend to last only a few days after the due date.

Grantee — An individual who accepts something from another, such as funds for a home.

Grantor — An individual or organization that offers funds to another.

HOEPA — Home Ownership and Equity Protection Act.

Hazard insurance — Insurance that covers the cost of property damage should a hazard occur. Typical hazards include hurricanes and fire.

Home equity — The amount of money an individual has invested in a piece of real property. Equity is calculated by subtracting all the debts owed against a property from its fair market value.

Home equity line of credit — Also known as a second mortgage, HELOCs act like a credit card secured by the property against which they are taken out. This line of credit has interest rates that vary like any typical mortgage.

Housing expense — The total of all expenses associated with the ownership of a home, including mortgage payments, insurances, taxes, and association fees.

Inception date — Date when the mortgage agreement goes into effect.

Interest rate — The percent charged to a borrower on the principal amount due. The interest rate is given for the year, and each month, the homeowner is charged one-twelfth of the interest rate on top of the principal payment.

Interest rate adjustment — An upward or downward alteration in the interest rate charged on a loan.

Interest rate ceiling — The highest amount of interest a lender can charge on a loan.

Interest rate floor — The lowest amount of interest a lender will allow on a loan.

Investor — An individual who purchases property as part of an investment, rather than to live in.

Judgment — A legal decision made by a court of law. If the judgment is for funds that have not been paid, the court may issue a lien against the property of the individual in order to secure it.

Judicial foreclosure — The process of foreclosing on property through legal actions.

Late charge — A fee charged when a payment is made late, such as on a credit card or mortgage.

Late payment — An additional payment on a debt that is made after the date specified, even if only the next day.

Lease — The loan of property for a given amount of time in exchange for funds.

Lease-to-own purchase — An agreement in which a property owner leases to another individual with the understanding that the monthly payments are going toward paying for the cost of the property. After a certain amount of time, the buyer must pay off the agreed-upon sale price in full to possess a clear title.

Legal description — In a mortgage or deed of trust, or on foreclosure documents, the description in words of the property in question. Includes the address and any names the property may be known as.

Lender — An individual, organization, or institution that lends funds to another.

Liabilities — An individual's financial obligations, including school loans, rent, and debts owed to others.

Liability insurance — An insurance policy that covers a homeowner in the event of an accident occurring on their property to another person.

Lien — A legal claim against property that ensures that the debt must be repaid when the property is sold. When a foreclosure occurs, any liens against the property must be paid in the order that they were recorded with the county clerk.

Liquid asset — Cash or any physical asset that can be quickly and easily converted to cash, such as savings accounts, bonds, retirement insurance, or cars.

Loan officer — An individual who works for a lender in the role of finding new borrowers and arranging loan agreements.

Loan origination — The process of obtaining a new loan from a lender.

Loan-to-value (LTV) — The ratio of the loan amount requested to the value of the property, most often expressed as a percentage — a loan for 80 percent of the property's value, for example.

Mandatory disclosure — The information a seller is required by law to tell any potential purchaser. These most often take written form and can include issues such as fire and flood hazards, among others.

Maturity date — The date at which a loan comes due; when the amortization period ends.

Maximum loan amount — The greatest amount of money a lender will offer an applicant based on the information that the borrower provides, such as employment status and income.

MERS — Mortgage Electronic Registration Systems, Inc.; the company that keeps electronic records and facilitates transactions when mortgages are packaged and resold to investors.

Mortgage — A legally binding document that secures a given property as collateral in a loan.

Mortgage payment — The specified amount of money a borrower pays a lender each month.

Mortgagee — The individual to whom a loan of money is made for the purpose of purchasing real estate.

Mortgage insurance — A policy that covers a lender in the event that a mortgagee is unable to make their monthly payments.

Mortgagor — The individual, organization, or institution that makes a loan of money to another in order to purchase property.

NINA loan — No-income, no-asset loan that is not based on income from regular employment, used by someone who is self-employed or compensated with tips or bonuses.

Negative amortization — The act of deferring payment of interest on a loan so that only the minimum balance is made on the principal loan amount. As the amortization period continues, the interest accumulates, causing the debtor to owe more than he or she originally did.

No-cash-out refinance — A refinance where the loan is calculated on what is currently owed on the original mortgage, without additional funds being required.

Note — Otherwise known as a promissory note. A legal agreement between two parties to pay a given amount on a loan over time, plus interest.

Notice of default — The notice that a lender is required to file when starting a non-judicial foreclosure.

Option fee — A fee paid up-front by a purchaser in a lease-to-own situation; most often 1 to 3 percent of the total amount owed for the property.

Original principal balance — The amount a loan was for originally.

Origination fee — The fees required to initiate a loan. Expressed as points: One point equals 1 percent of the loan amount. The number of points required will vary from loan to loan.

Owner financing — When an owner of property agrees to a rent-to-own arrangement. See "carry-back loan."

Partial payment — A payment of only a percentage of the amount due. Partial payments often occur because homeowners do not realize variable interest has increased their payment amount.

Payment change date — The date on which the monthly payment amount on a loan changes to another amount.

Personal property — Property that belongs to an individual.

Point — Equals 1 percent of the mortgage amount. Points are charged to organize a mortgage.

Power of attorney — Also known as "proxy," this legally allows another individual to act on your behalf in all matters, including legal.

Preapproval — Approval for a loan or credit account based on credit history and without necessarily applying for the loan or credit. Preapproved credit cards offer a given amount of money available at a particular interest rate.

Predatory lending — A series of practices by lenders that are geared toward setting a borrower up for default.

Prepayment — Paying down a loan with a large amount before it is due. Prepaying on certain loans allows for a reduced amount of monthly payments.

Prepayment penalty — A fee charged by a lender for paying down a mortgage before it is due.

Price gouging — The act of charging fees and interest rates that are disproportionate to the average fees and interest rates currently available.

Primary mortgage insurance (PMI) — Insurance that reimburses the lender if the borrower defaults, used with mortgages with less than a 20 percent down payment.

Prime rate — The interest rate offered by lenders to preferred customers — those with good credit histories and solid employment.

Principal — The amount left on a loan, or initially borrowed.

Principal balance — See "principal."

Private mortgage insurance — Insurance required on subprime loans or those made with more than an 80 percent loan-to-value ratio. Typically raises interest rates on a loan one-half to two-thirds of a percent.

Procedural unconscionability — An abuse of the process during which a borrower commits to a loan agreement.

Promissory note — A legally binding document that requires an individual to pay back a given amount of money, plus interest, in a specific amount of time.

Property flipping — The act of purchasing a property with the intention of reselling again quickly. Most flippers purchase property that needs renovation, then sell it for a higher cost than originally paid.

Public auction — An auction held that is open to the public, often selling real estate.

Purchase agreement — An agreement to purchase property or goods for a given amount of money.

Qualification — A lender's process of determining whether a loan applicant will be able to pay back a certain loan. Most qualifications work to decide how much the lender is willing to give you a loan for.

Qualified written request (QWR) — A formal letter informing the lender of an error in a borrower's account or requesting information about the account.

Qualifying ratios — The ratios of income to expenses used to decide whether an individual qualifies for a home loan.

Quiet title action — A lawsuit seeking a court order to prevent any further claims on the property by the lender.

Quitclaim deed — A legal document that transfers ownership of property from one individual to another.

Real estate owned (REO) — A property owned by the bank.

RESPA — Real Estate Settlement Procedures Act; enacted in 1974 to improve the disclosure of real estate transaction settlement costs to consumers and eliminate kickbacks.

Recorder — An individual in the court of clerks who records any legal documents filed. The recorder will make note of all liens, judgments, and legal actions taken against an individual.

Referral fees — A fee paid to an individual that refers borrowers to a particular lender. Beware of brokers who receive referral fees from certain lenders, as they are not impartial or working in your best interest.

Remaining balance — The amount left to pay on a debt at any given time.

Remaining term — The amount of time left to pay on a loan.

Repayment plan — The schedule and plan of how payments will be made back to a lender or individual owed money. A repayment plan is necessary in the filing of bankruptcy documents to show good faith in paying back the debt.

Rescission — The cancellation of a contract by mutual agreement.

Rider — A document attached to an original agreement and treated as part of that agreement.

SISA loan — Stated-income, stated-asset loan that is not based on income from regular employment; used by someone who is self-employed or compensated with tips or bonuses.

Second mortgage — A loan taken out against a property that already has an existing debt against it; also known as a home equity loan.

Secured loan — A loan that uses some type of property as collateral.

Security — Property that acts as collateral on a loan.

Sheriff's sale — A sale at auction of a foreclosed property.

Short sale — When a lender agrees to let a borrower sell a property for less than its fair market value and the balance of the loan, in return for all net proceeds from the sale. Some lenders will allow a short sale if they think that they will not get more money than is being offered should the property go to auction.

Subordinate financing — Any debt against a property that is of less value than the original loan.

Subprime borrower — An individual with poor or no credit history and/or few assets to use as collateral on a loan.

Subprime loan — A loan made to a subprime borrower; most often has high interest rates to compensate for the risk to the lender.

Title — A legal document stating who owns a given piece of property.

Title company — A company that examines titles to ensure that the titles do not have any encumbrances.

Title insurance — A policy that protects an individual from issues and disputes arising as a result of property transfer.

Transfer of ownership — The movement of property ownership from one individual to another.

Transfer tax — Tax paid to the IRS for selling (or transferring) property to another.

Truth-in-lending Act (TILA) — A government act that ensures borrowers receive all the information that they have a right to before signing legal documents.

Trustee — The individual who accepts a loan secured by a deed of trust.

Trustor — A lender that loans money to an individual secured by a deed of trust.

Underwater — A situation in which the borrower owes more than the property is worth on the market.

Upside-down mortgage — A situation in which the borrower owes more than the property is worth on the market.

Unsecured debt — Debt that does not have property as collateral, such as credit card debt.

VA mortgage — A loan insured by the Veteran's Association.

Veteran's Association — A government organization meant to help military veterans in a variety of ways, including receiving and insuring a mortgage.

Workout — The process of arranging a new payment plan between a lender and borrower so that foreclosure can be halted.

Yield-spread premium (YSP) — A bonus paid by the lender to the mortgage broker when he or she writes a loan that has an interest rate higher than the minimum approved by the lender.

BIBLIOGRAPHY

Barr, Alistair. "'Tsunami' of adjustable-rate mortgage resets coming." Market Watch. March 23, 2007. (**www.marketwatch.com/story/mortgage-reset-tsunami-could-end-up-an-economic-ripple**)

Bay, Carrie. "State Regulators Say Federal Foreclosure Prevention Program Falls Short." DSNews.com. January 22, 2010. (**http://www.dsnews.com/articles/state-regulators-say-federal-foreclosure-prevention-program-falls-short-2010-01-22**)

Beck, Rachel, AP Business Writer. "Double standard in mortgage walk-away." The-Dispatch.com. January 30, 2010. (**http://www.the-dispatch.com/article/20100130/APF/1001300510**)

Blodget, Henry. "Yes, It's Okay To Walk Away From Your Mortgage." Yahoo! Finance. January 14, 2010. (**http://finance.yahoo.com/tech-ticker/yes-it%27s-okay-to-walk-away-from-your-mortgage-403924.html**)

Bureau of Labor Statistics. Mass Layoffs Summary. U.S. Department of Labor. December 22, 2009. (**http://www.bls.gov/news.release/mmls.nr0.htm**)

Curnutte, Katie. "Making Home Affordable Plan Expected to Help 4-5 Million Homeowners Refinance." Zillow. March 4, 2009. (**www.zillow.com/blog/details-are-in-making-home-affordable-plan-expected-to-help-4-5-million-homeowners-refinance/2009/03/04/**)

Federal Trade Commission. "High-Rate, High-Fee Loans (HOEPA/Section 32 Mortgages)." Facts for Consumers. February 2009. (**www.ftc.gov/bcp/edu/pubs/consumer/homes/rea19.shtm**)

Fletcher, Michael A. and Renae Merle. "Obama Proposes Package To Stave Off Foreclosures - Multibillion-Dollar Plan Aims to Help Modify Mortgages." *The Washington Post.* February 19, 2009. (**http://www.washingtonpost.com/wp-dyn/content/story/2009/02/18/ST2009021801211.html**)

Foreclosure Pulse. "Record Foreclosure Activity in 2009 Could Have Been Worse." RealtyTrac® . January 16, 2010. (**http://www.foreclosure-pulse.com/blogs/mainblog/archive/2010/01/13/record-foreclosure-activity-in-2009-could-have-been-worse.aspx**)

Foreclosurefish.com. "Do you qualify for a Mortgage Forbearance Agreement?" 2006. (**www.foreclosurefish.com/repaymentplan.htm**)

Goodman, Peter S. "Treasury Weighs Fixes to Foreclosures Program." *The New York Times.* January 21, 2010. (**www.nytimes.com/2010/01/22/business/economy/22modify.html**)

Hoffman Brinker & Roberts. Credit Card Debt Statistics. November 2009. (**http://www.hoffmanbrinker.com/credit-card-debt-statistics. html**)

Housing Predictor. "Foreclosures Eclipse Record in 2009." HousingPredictor.com. January 14, 2010. (**http://www.housingpredictor.com/fore-closures_2009.html**)

JP Morgan Chase & Co. "Chase to Open 24 More Mortgage-Counseling Centers." Press Release. December 16, 2009. (**http://investor.shareholder.com/JPMorganChase/releasedetail.cfm?releaseid=430707**)

Kells, Tina. Layoffs List: Job Losses in 2008 and 2009. NowPublic.com. March 6, 2009. (**www.nowpublic.com/tech-biz/layoffs-list-job-losses-2008-and-2009-ongoing**)

Merle, Renae. "Foreclosure relief program is stuck in first - Just 4 Percent in Final Stage." *The Washington Post.* December 11, 2009. (**www.washingtonpost.com/wp-dyn/content/article/2009/12/10/AR2009121003834.html**)

Merle, Renae. "Lawmakers growing frustrated with mortgage-relief failures." *The Washington Post.* December 9, 2009." (**www.washingtonpost.com/wp-dyn/content/article/2009/12/08/AR2009120804194.html**)

Miller, Kimberly. "Florida Supreme Court orders mediators to be first step in foreclosure cases." *The Palm Beach Post.* December 28, 2009. (**www.palmbeachpost.com/money/real-estate/florida-supreme-court-orders-mediators-to-be-first-152911.html**)

Nolo.com. "Short Sales and Deeds in Lieu of Foreclosure." (**www.nolo.com/legal-encyclopedia/article-30016.html**)

RealtyTrac Staff. "REALTYTRAC® YEAR-END REPORT SHOWS RECORD 2.8 MILLION U.S. PROPERTIES WITH FORECLOSURE FILINGS IN 2009." RealtyTrac. January 14, 2010. (**http://www.realtytrac.com/contentmanagement/pressrelease.aspx?itemid=8333**)

Redding, Jillian L. "STATE AND FEDERAL MORTGAGE ASSISTANCE PROGRAMS." OLR Research Report. April 6, 2009. (**http://cga.ct.gov/2009/rpt/2009-R-0159.htm**)

U.S. Department of Housing and Urban Development. "BUSH ADMINISTRATION LAUNCHES "HOPE FOR HOMEOWNERS" PROGRAM TO HELP MORE STRUGGLING FAMILIES KEEP THEIR HOMES: Detailed Program Eligibility Requirements Announced." HUD No. 08-150. October 1, 2008. (**www.hud.gov/news/release.cfm?content=pr08-150.cfm**)

U.S. Department of Housing and Urban Development. "Questions & Answers for Reservists, Guardsmen and Other Military Personnel." December 17, 2009. (**www.hud.gov/offices/hsg/sfh/nsc/qasscra1.cfm**)

Walsh, Geoffrey. "State and Local Foreclosure Mediation Programs: Can They Save Homes?" National Consumer Law Center. September 2009. (**http://www.consumerlaw.org/issues/foreclosure_mediation/content/ReportS-Sept09.pdf**)

White, Brent T., The University of Arizona, James E. Rogers College of Law. "Underwater and Not Walking Away: Shame, Fear and the Social Management of the Housing Crisis." Arizona Legal Studies Discussion Paper No. 09-35. October 2009. (**http://www.brokerexecutives.com/walking_away_by_brent_white.pdf**)

AUTHOR BIOGRAPHIES

Martha Maeda is an economic historian who writes on politics, ethics, finance, and modern philosophy. After graduating from Northwestern University, she lived and worked in Australia, Japan, Latin America, and several African countries before settling in the United States. She has a particular interest in microeconomics and in the effects of globalization on the lives and businesses of people all over the world. Maeda is the author of several books, including *The Complete Guide to Investing in Exchange Traded Funds, The Complete Guide to Investing In Bonds and Bond Funds, How to Wipe Out Your Student Loans and Be Debt Free Fast, The Complete Guide to IRAs and IRA Investing, The Complete Guide to Spotting Accounting Fraud & Cover-Ups,* and *Retire Rich With Your Roth IRA, Roth 401k, and Roth 403b.*

Maurcia DeLean Houck is a nationally known writer and editor with more than 1,500 bylines in 250 such well-known publications as *First for Women*, *Family Life*, *Writer's Digest*, *Your Health*, *AAA Going Places*, and *Modern Woman*.

She began her writing career in 1991 while still serving as the executive editor of a mid-sized weekly newspaper in Philadelphia. She has also worked as a staff writer at several suburban newspapers in and around the Philadelphia area.

An established non-fiction author, Houck has had the following books published:

- *But I Don't Know How To Start A Publicity Ministry in My Church* (Warner Press 2001)
- *If These Walls Could Talk ... A Guide to Tracking the Genealogy of Your Historic Home* (Picton Press 1999)
- *The Grandparent's Answer Guide* (Chariot-Victor 2000 collaborator)
- *The Writer's Life* (The Writer, Inc. 1998 collaborator)
- *Family Travel Guides* (Carousel Press 1995)

In addition to her work as a writer, publicist, and fundraising professional, Houck periodically reviews and edits current titles for Augsburg Fortress Publishing House, as well as a variety of private authors.

Houck is a 1999-2000 and 2000-2001 Inductee in Who's Who in the East and a former member of the National Writer's Association (1994-1999).

INDEX